Fascinating Footnotes From History

Also by Giles Milton

Fascinating Footnotes
From History

GILES MILTON

JOHN MURRAY

This collected edition first published in Great Britain in 2015 by John Murray (Publishers)
An Hachette UK Company

First published in paperback in 2016

1

A CIP catalogue record for this title is available from the British Library

ISBN 978-1-473-62499-3
Ebook ISBN 978-1-473-60906-8

Typeset in Bembo by Palimpsest Book Production Ltd, Falkirk, Stirlingshire

Printed and bound by Clays Ltd, St Ives plc

John Murray policy is to use papers that are natural, renewable and recyclable products and made
from wood grown in sustainable forests. The logging and manufacturing processes are expected to
conform to the environmental regulations of the country of origin.

John Murray (Publishers)
Carmelite House
50 Victoria Embankment
London EC4Y ODZ

www.johnmurray.co.uk

For Joseph

Contents

CONTENTS

CONTENTS

Preface

In the summer of 2012 a cache of extraordinary medical documents came to light in America. They included the records of Dr Theodor Morell, personal physician to Adolf Hitler, and notes written by four other doctors who treated the Führer.

At first glance, the documents seemed little more than an historical footnote, one to be added to the mass of existing material about Hitler. But footnotes can often conceal nuggets of gold and this one opened a wholly unknown chapter of history. The cache revealed that the Führer was being prescribed a heady cocktail of drugs including cocaine, amphetamines and testosterone. Indeed he was taking up to 80 drugs a day, at the same time as masterminding his attempted conquest of the world.

Much of my working life is spent in the archives, delving through letters and personal papers like those written by Dr Morell. The huge collection housed in the National Archives is incompletely catalogued and you can never be entirely sure what you will find in any given box of documents. Days can pass without unearthing anything of interest: I liken it to those metal-detecting treasure-hunters on the Thames foreshore who scour the muddy banks at low tide in the hope of turning up a Jacobean shilling or signet ring.

Persistence often pays rich dividends and this book – an idiosyncratic collection of fascinating footnotes – is the result of my own metaphorical metal detecting. Amidst the flotsam and jetsam, I've found (I hope) some glittering gems. There's the lone Japanese soldier still fighting the Second World War in 1974; the British agent-cum-hitman who assassinated Rasputin (as with Dr Morell, this story has only recently come to light); and the tale of the shipwrecked Dutch mariners who ate the last dodo.

Some of the stories are truly eye-stretching. The testimony of Sun Yaoting, the last eunuch of China, is not only painful but extraordinarily poignant. It sheds light on the twilight years of imperial China, when centuries of tradition were swept away in the blink of an eye. Sun Yaoting, alas, was to find himself on the wrong side of history.

I've long believed that historical detail is vitally important when attempting to reconstruct the past. Detail can illuminate events in a way that the broad brushstroke cannot. The obsessive quest on the part of Soviet scientists to find the 'genius' inside Lenin's brain is a case in point. It reveals much about neurological science of the 1920s – then in its infancy – and even more about the Soviet Union's cult of personality, of which this was one of the earliest manifestations.

Many of the stories in this collection are about individuals, often unremarkable in themselves, who found themselves caught up in truly extraordinary situations. Some were swept through defining moments of history: Tsutomu Yamaguchi, who survived the atomic bombs at both Hiroshima and Nagasaki, is one of them. Others were unwilling partakers in catastrophe: men like Charles Joughin, who not only survived the *Titanic* disaster, but did so with an amazing story to tell.

Just occasionally, the stories reveal something about ourselves. I've often found myself musing on what *I* would have done if I'd found myself in situations similar to the men and women in this collection. Would I have been as cool under pressure as Walter Harris, the Moroccan correspondent for *The Times*, when captured by murderous Islamic extremists in 1903? I doubt it.

These days, we're unlikely to be exhibited as a human freak, as was Ota Benga, and equally unlikely to be buried alive, as was Augustine Courtauld. But anything can happen to anyone: who knows, you may yet get caught in an adventure that will one day be recognised as a highly-prized footnote from history.

Giles Milton
London, 2016

Part I

I Never Knew That About Hitler

Göring has only got one ball,
Hitler's are so very small,
Himmler's so very similar,
And Goebbels has no balls at all.

The original words to 'Hitler Has Only Got One Ball',
circa August 1939,
attributed to Toby O'Brien, publicist for the British Council

Hitler's English Girlfriend

Unity Mitford was a plain-looking woman with bad teeth and a plump belly. But she had never been troubled by her strange looks, aware that she was more likely to catch the man of her dreams by speaking her mind rather than flaunting her body.

In the summer of 1934, she travelled to Munich in the hope of meeting her idol, Adolf Hitler. Although he was Führer of Germany, it was relatively easy to see him in public since he spent a great deal of time in the city and ate at the same cafes and restaurants each day.

When Unity learned that he often had lunch at the Osteria Bavaria, she began eating there as well. She did everything she could to catch his attention. Yet ten months were to pass before Hitler finally invited the persistent English girl to his table. The two of them chatted for half an hour and quickly realized they were soulmates.

'It was the most wonderful and beautiful [day] of my life,' wrote Unity to her father. 'I am so happy that I wouldn't mind a bit, dying. I'd suppose I am the luckiest girl in the world. For me he is the greatest man of all time.'

Her feelings were reciprocated. Hitler was particularly intrigued by Unity's middle name, Valkyrie. And he was fascinated to learn that her grandfather had translated from German the anti-Semitic works of Houston Stewart Chamberlain, one of his favourite authors.

Hitler began to see more and more of his fair-haired English companion, much to the annoyance of his 'official' girlfriend, Eva Braun. 'She is known as the Valkyrie and looks the part, including her legs,' wrote Braun scornfully in her diary. 'I, the mistress of the greatest man in Germany and the whole world, I sit here waiting while the sun mocks me through the window panes.'

Unity was now introduced to members of Hitler's inner circle. She got along particularly well with the thuggish Julius Streicher, publisher of the vitriolic anti-Semitic newspaper *Der Stürmer*.

When Unity delivered a racist diatribe against the Jews, Streicher asked if he could print it in his paper. Unity was flattered. 'The English have no notion of the Jewish danger,' began her article. 'Our worst Jews work only behind the scenes. We think with joy of the day when we will be able to say England for the English! Out with the Jews! Heil Hitler!' She ended her text with the words: 'Please publish my name in full, I want everyone to know I am a Jew hater.'

Hitler was so pleased with what Unity had written that he awarded her a golden swastika badge as well as a private box at the 1936 Berlin Olympics.

She now became one of the Führer's intimates, visiting him on numerous occasions and constantly expressing her admiration for him. He was no less smitten with her: in 1938, he even offered her an apartment in Munich. Unity had high hopes of replacing Eva Braun in his affections.

By now, her behaviour had aroused the suspicions of the British Secret Service. The head of MI5, Guy Liddell, was particularly alarmed by her closeness to Hitler. He felt that her friendship with him warranted her being put on trial for high treason if she returned to Britain.

Unity refused to leave Germany, even after Britain's declaration of war on 3 September 1939. Yet she was deeply depressed by what had happened, not least because of the implications it had for her relationship with Hitler.

She took herself to the English Garden in Munich, held to her head the pearl-handled pistol that had been given to her by Hitler and pulled the trigger.

She was badly wounded but, amazingly, survived. Hospitalized in Munich (the bills were paid by Hitler), she was eventually moved to Switzerland. When she had partially recovered, her sister, Deborah, flew to Bern in order to take her home to England.

'We were not prepared for what we found: the person lying in bed was desperately ill. She had lost two stone (28 pounds), was all huge eyes and matted hair, untouched since the bullet went through her skull.'

What happened next remains shrouded in mystery. According to the official account, she was taken to the family home at Swinbrook, Oxfordshire. She learned to walk but never made a full recovery. She eventually died in 1948 as a result of meningitis caused by the bullet in her brain.

But there is also a more intriguing story about her return to England. There are rumours, never confirmed, that she was taken to a private maternity hospital in Oxford. Here, in absolute secrecy, she gave birth to Hitler's love child.

The woman who made the claim, Val Hann, is the niece of the hospital's former manager, Betty Norton. Betty had told the story to her sister, who in turn passed it on to Val.

If true, it would mean that Hitler's child is quite possibly still alive and living somewhere in England.

But the facts will never be known for certain: Betty Norton died long ago and the maternity hospital neglected to register the babies who were born during the war.

Hitler's American Nephew

He kept his identity a secret until his dying day. None of his neighbours in Patchogue, Long Island, had any idea that William Stuart Houston was actually born William Hitler. Nor did they know that his uncle had been the Führer of Nazi Germany.

It was not until long after William's death in 1987 that the truth about his identity was made public. But several unanswered questions remain, questions that his sons, three of whom are still alive and living in America, have been unable to answer.

William's story begins in Edwardian Liverpool. Adolf Hitler's half-brother, Alois, had moved to the city in 1911. He married his Irish-born lover, Bridgit Dowling, and before long she was pregnant. When baby William was born, the neighbours called him Paddy Hitler.

Alois abandoned his wife and son in 1914 and returned to Germany. An entire decade was to pass before he renewed contact with Bridgit. When he did so, he asked her to allow William to travel to Germany.

William made a brief trip to see his father in 1929 and then returned four years later for a much longer stay. By now, he was hoping to profit from his uncle's position as Chancellor of Germany.

Hitler initially got him a temporary job in a bank. Soon after, he procured him employment in an automobile factory, a job that William disliked intensely. He repeatedly begged his uncle for a better job, but Hitler refused to help his nephew any further. Indeed, William eventually found himself suspended from his work on Hitler's orders. He was accused of trying to sell cars for his own profit.

William continued to see Hitler occasionally, but Adolf was no longer the friendly uncle of old. 'I shall never forget the last time he sent for me,' wrote William. 'He was in a brutal temper when I arrived. Walking back and forth, brandishing his horsehide whip . . . he shouted insults at my head as if he were delivering a political oration. His vengeful brutality on that day made me fear for my physical safety.'

William realized it was time to leave Germany. In February 1939, he sailed for the United States.

At the outbreak of war William embarked on a lecture tour of the USA, denouncing his Führer-uncle for his extravagant lifestyle. 'Far from scorning lavish display,' he told his audiences, 'he has surrounded himself with luxury more extravagant than any Kaiser ever enjoyed. To decorate his new chancellery in Berlin, every museum in Germany was plundered for priceless carpets, tapestries, paintings.'

When America joined the war, William wrote to President Roosevelt asking for permission to join the US Army. The letter was sent to the FBI, who cleared him for service. According to one paper, his recruiting officer said: 'Glad to see you, Hitler. My name's Hess.'

At the war's end, William set up a medical laboratory that analysed blood samples for hospitals. As the Nuremberg Trials got under way, he tried to make a complete break with his Hitler past. He changed his name to William Stuart Houston and settled with his wife in Long Island. They would eventually have four sons.

William died in 1987 and was buried in anonymity in the same grave as his mother. And there the story might have ended, were it not for an American journalist named David Gardner who began investigating the Hitler family. He eventually stumbled across the strange story of William Hitler, and discovered that members of the Hitler clan were alive and well and living in America.

The family insist that William hated Hitler until his dying day and they proudly point to his unblemished war record, fighting against Nazi Germany.

Yet two enigmas remain. Why did William Hitler choose as his new name Stuart Houston, one that is strikingly close to the name of Adolf Hitler's favourite anti-Semitic author, Houston Stewart Chamberlain?

And why did William give his eldest son, Alexander, the middle name Adolf?

When Hitler Took Cocaine

The injections began shortly after breakfast. As soon as Adolf Hitler finished his bowl of oatmeal and linseed oil he would summon his personal physician, Theodor Morell.

The doctor would roll up his patient's sleeve in order to inject an extraordinary cocktail of drugs, many of which are these days classed as dangerous, addictive and illegal.

Every day for more than nine years, Dr Morell administered amphetamines, barbiturates and opiates in such quantities that he became known as the Reichsmaster of Injections. Some in Hitler's inner circle wondered if he wasn't trying to kill the Führer.

But Theodor Morell was far too devoted to Hitler to murder him. A grossly obese quack doctor with acrid halitosis and appalling body odour, he had first met the Führer at a party at the Berghof.

Hitler had long suffered from ill health, including stomach cramps, diarrhoea and such chronic flatulence that he had to leave the table after each meal in order to expel vast quantities of wind.

His condition was aggravated by his unconventional diet. He had forsaken meat in 1931 after comparing eating ham to eating a human corpse. Henceforth, he ate large quantities of watery vegetables, pureed or mashed to a pulp. Dr Morell watched the Führer eat one such meal and then studied the consequences. 'Constipations and colossal flatulence occurred on a scale I have seldom encountered before,' he wrote. He assured Hitler he had miracle drugs that could cure all of his problems.

He began by administering little black tablets called Dr Küster's Anti-Gas pills. Hitler took sixteen a day, apparently unaware that they contained quantities of strychnine. Although they alleviated his wind – temporarily – they almost certainly triggered the attention lapses and sallow skin that were to mark his final years.

Morell next prescribed a type of hydrolysed E. coli bacteria called Mutaflor, which seemed to further stabilize the Führer's bowel problems.

Indeed Hitler was so pleased with the doctor's work that he invited him to join the inner circle of Nazi elite. Henceforth, Morell was never far from his side.

Along with his stomach cramps, Hitler also suffered from morning grogginess. To alleviate this, Morell injected him with a watery fluid that he concocted from a powder kept in gold-foil packets. He never revealed the active ingredient in this medicine, called Vitamultin, but it worked wonders on every occasion it was administered. Within a few minutes, Hitler would arise from his couch invigorated and full of energy.

Ernst-Günther Schenck, an SS doctor, grew suspicious of Dr Morell's miracle cures and managed to acquire one of the packets. When tested in a laboratory, it was found to be amphetamine.

Hitler was untroubled by what he was given, just so long as the drugs worked. It was not long before he became so dependent on Morell's 'cures' that he placed all his health problems entirely in the doctor's hands, with disastrous long-term consequences. He directed the invasion of Soviet Russia while being pumped with as many as eighty different drugs, including testosterone, opiates, sedatives and laxatives. According to the doctor's medical notebooks, he also administered barbiturates, morphine, bull semen and probiotics.

The most surprising drug that Dr Morell prescribed to the Führer was cocaine. This was occasionally used for medical ailments in 1930s Germany, but always in extremely low dosages and at a concentration of less than one per cent. Morell began administering cocaine to the Führer by means of eye-drops. Aware that Hitler expected to feel better after taking his drugs, he put ten times the amount of cocaine into the drops. Such a concentrated dose may well have triggered the psychotic behaviour that Hitler was to experience in his later years.

The Führer found cocaine extremely efficacious. According to a cache of medical documents that came to light in America in 2012 (including a forty-seven-page report written by Morell and other doctors who attended the Führer), Hitler soon began to 'crave' the drug. It was a clear sign that he was developing a serious addiction. As well as the eye-drops, he now began to snort powdered cocaine 'to clear his sinuses and soothe his throat'.

Cocaine may have induced a feeling of well-being but it did nothing to boost the Führer's lack of sexual drive. To overcome this embarrassing condition, Morell began giving him virility injections. These contained extracts from the prostate glands of young bulls. Morell also prescribed a medicine called Testoviron, a medication derived from testosterone. Hitler would have himself injected before spending the night with Eva Braun.

The long-term effect of taking such drugs, particularly amphetamines, led to increasingly erratic behaviour. The most visible manifestation of this came at a meeting between Hitler and Mussolini in northern Italy. As Hitler tried to persuade his Italian counterpart not to change sides in the war, he became wildly hysterical. According to Third Reich historian Richard Evans: 'We can be pretty sure Morell gave some tablets to Hitler when he went to see Mussolini . . . [he was] completely hyper in every way, talking, gabbling, clearly on speed.'

As the war drew to a close, Hitler was in very poor health. Dependent on drugs, his arms were so punctured with hypodermic marks that Eva Braun accused Morell of being an 'injection quack'. He had turned Hitler into an addict. Yet the doctor continued to hero-worship his beloved Führer and remained with him in his Berlin bunker until almost the end.

Dr Morell was captured by the Americans soon after the fall of the Third Reich and interrogated for more than two years. One of the officers who questioned him was disgusted by his lack of personal hygiene.

Morell was never charged with war crimes and he died of a stroke in 1948, shortly after his release from prison. He left behind a cache of medical notebooks that reveal the extraordinary drug addiction of his favourite patient.

It is ironic that the man charged with restoring Hitler to good health probably did more than anyone else to contribute to his decline.

Part II
Jeez, It's Cold Out There

Insurance claims for pets on the *Titanic* who drowned
in icy seawater:

Robert W. Daniel
One pedigree French bulldog named Gamin de Pycombe: $750

William Carter
One King Charles Spaniel and one Airedale Terrier: $300

Ella Holmes White
Four roosters and hens: $207.87

Harry Anderson
One chow-chow: $50

A Corpse on Everest

The corpse was frozen and bleached by the sun. It lay face down in the snow, fully extended and pointing uphill. The upper body was welded to the scree with ice. The arms, still muscular, were outstretched above the head.

Mountaineer George Mallory had last been sighted on 8 June 1924, when he and Andrew Irvine went missing while attempting to become the first men to reach the summit of Everest. Whether or not they achieved this goal has been the subject of intense speculation for ninety years.

In the spring of 1999, an American named Eric Simonson set up the Mallory and Irvine Research Expedition. Five experienced mountaineers were sent high onto Everest with the aim of finding the bodies of one or both climbers.

They had a few clues to help them in their search. In 1975, a Chinese climber named Wang Hung-bao had stumbled across 'an English dead' at 26,570 feet (8,100 metres). Wang reported the find to his climbing partner shortly before being swept away by an avalanche. The precise location of the 'English dead' was never fixed.

Eric Simonson's five-strong team of experienced mountaineers were undeterred. Conrad Anker, Dave Hahn, Jake Norton, Andy Politz and Tap Richards were determined to succeed, even though the odds were stacked against them.

Their search was concentrated on a wide snow-terrace the size of twelve football pitches. Tilted at a crazy angle, the terrace lay above 26,000 feet. The men knew that if they lost their balance, the thirty-degree slope would carry them down a 7,000-foot drop to the Rongbuk Glacier.

On 1 May, Conrad Anker was combing the slope when he raised a cry. He had spotted a corpse, white as alabaster, sticking out of the ice. The rest of the team made their way towards him and began chipping the corpse from its frozen resting place. As they dug, they studied the body with care. The tibia and fibula of the right leg were broken, the right elbow was dislocated and the right side also badly damaged. The climbing rope had wrapped itself tightly around the ribcage.

It didn't take long to identify the body. When Tap Richards looked inside the clothing, he found a name-tag: *G Mallory*.

'Maybe it was the altitude and the fact that we'd all put aside our oxygen gear,' said Dave Hahn, 'but it took a while for reality to sink in. We were in the presence of George Mallory himself.'

The question that remained unanswered was whether or not Mallory and Irvine had made it to the summit. Did they die on their way up? Or on their way down?

The team hoped they might find Mallory's camera: experts at Kodak had said that the film, though old, might yet be developed. But when the men reached inside the pouch around Mallory's neck, they found only a metal tin of stock cubes: 'Brand & Co. Savoury Meat Lozenges'.

There was other evidence as well: a brass altimeter, a pocketknife, a monogrammed handkerchief and a pair of undamaged sun goggles in an inside pocket.

The goggles were potentially an important clue as to what had happened on that day in 1924. Just a few days before his attempt on the summit, Mallory's second climbing partner, Edward Norton, had suffered serious snow-blindness because he'd neglected to wear his goggles.

Mallory would not have dispensed with his goggles if climbing in daylight. The fact they were in his pocket suggested that the two men had completed their push for the summit in sunlight and were making their descent after dark.

No less interesting was an envelope found on Mallory's body. It was covered in numbers: pressure readings of the oxygen bottles they were carrying. It had long been believed that the climbers didn't have enough oxygen to get them to the summit. But the numbers showed that the two climbers were carrying five, perhaps six canisters – more than enough to get to the top of the mountain.

More tantalizing was an item that the searchers had expected to find on Mallory's body. He was known to have been carrying a photograph of his wife, Ruth, which he had vowed to leave on the summit. The photo was nowhere to be found, even though his wallet and other papers were intact.

The men who found Mallory were able to piece together a plausible scenario as to what happened on the fateful evening of his death. It is a story of adventure and tragic error – one that ultimately led to his doom.

It is late in the evening of 8 June, long after twilight, and the two climbers are still high on the mountain. Exhausted and with failing oxygen supplies, they are desperate to reach safety. As they cross a notoriously treacherous layer of marble and phyllite known as the 'Yellow Band', one of the two climbers slips.

It may well have been Mallory. If so, his fall is halted by the rope, which dashes him into a rocky outcrop. His ribs are instantly broken and his elbow is dislocated. But he is held there by the rope, dangling in a void.

And then, unexpectedly, the rope snaps and he plunges through the darkness. He lands on a steep shelf of snow, snapping his tibia and fibula. But still he doesn't stop. Gravity drags him down the North Face at tremendous speed.

He is terrified and in appalling pain, but still conscious and trying to save himself. In desperation, he clutches at frozen scree, digging his fingers into the ice. Faster and faster he slides until his forehead smashes into a jagged outcrop of rock. It punctures a hole in his head.

He comes to a standstill at the same time as he loses consciousness. Pain and hypothermia rapidly take over. Within minutes, George Mallory is dead.

Irvine, meanwhile, has almost certainly met with a similar fate. He has fallen, seriously injured, and is also suffering from hypothermia. Within a few minutes of Mallory's death he, too, has succumbed to the cold.

But had they already made it to the summit? Were they the first to scale Everest? It is a question that Eric Simonson's team was unable to answer with absolute certainty. The discovery of Mallory's body was a remarkable find, but the riddle is likely to remain unsolved unless or until the camera is found.

One person alone has felt able to say whether or not Mallory and Irvine deserve the title of 'conquerors of Everest'. Mallory's son, John, was just three years old when he lost his father. To him, George Mallory's failure to return home provided all the answers he needed. 'To me,' he said, 'the only way you achieve a summit is to come back alive. The job is only half done if you don't get down again.'

Drunk on the Titanic

It was 14 April 1912. Charles Joughin had finally fallen asleep after a hard day's work in the ship's kitchens. Suddenly, he was woken by a tremendous jolt. He felt the vessel shudder violently beneath him. Then, after a momentary pause, it continued moving forward.

Joughin was puzzled but not unduly alarmed. He knew that icebergs had been sighted in the water; he also knew that Captain Edward Smith had ordered a change of course, steering the *Titanic* onto a more southerly route in order to avoid potential disaster. Assuming that the danger had passed, Joughin tried to return to sleep. But at about 11.35 p.m., just a few minutes after the jolt, he was summoned to the bridge. Here, he was given some most unwelcome information.

Captain Smith had sent an inspection team below decks to see if anything was wrong. The men had returned with the terrible news that the ship had struck an iceberg and that the force of the blow had seriously buckled the hull. Rivets had been forced out over a length of some ninety metres and seawater was now gushing into the ship at a tremendous rate.

This news might have been expected to cause panic. Yet it didn't. Most people believed the *Titanic* to be unsinkable. She had watertight compartments that could be closed in the event of disaster. This meant that even the most serious damage to the ship's hull could be contained.

But now, in this moment of crisis, these watertight compartments were revealed to have a catastrophic design flaw. As they filled with water, so they weighed down the ship's bow, allowing water to pour into other areas of the stricken vessel. A fourth, fifth and then a sixth compartment had already filled with water: it became obvious to Captain Smith that the *Titanic* was doomed to sink.

Joughin, the *Titanic*'s chief baker, now swung into action. He aroused his fellow chefs from their beds and began to gather all the loaves of bread they could find. They then rushed back on deck and put four loaves into each lifeboat. They already knew that there were not enough boats for all the passengers. The *Titanic* had 2,223 people on board, yet there were only enough lifeboats for 1,178 people.

Charles Joughin realized that he, as a member of crew, would not be given a place in a lifeboat. As the ship began listing at an alarming angle, he decided to drink himself into oblivion. He descended into his cabin, downed a huge quantity of whisky (according to one account he finished off two bottles). He then returned to the deck and, with drunken energy, began pushing women into the lifeboats.

Once this was done, he staggered along the heavily listing promenade deck, wondering how long it would take for the ship to sink. He threw overboard some fifty deckchairs, along with other seats and cushions, in the hope that people in the water might be able to use them as rafts.

It was not long before he, too, found himself in the freezing Atlantic. 'I got onto the starboard side of the poop,' he later recalled, 'and found myself in the water. I do not believe my head went under the water at all. I thought I saw some wreckage.'

He swam towards this floating debris, not feeling the cold on account of all the whisky he had drunk, 'and found a collapsible boat B with Lightoller and about twenty-five men on it'.

There was no room for Joughin. 'I tried to get on,' he said, 'but was pushed off, but I hung around. I got around to the opposite side and cook Maynard, who recognized me, helped me and held on to me.'

By this time, it was a miracle Joughin was still alive. The water temperature was two degrees below freezing. Most passengers and crew who had jumped into the water had died of hypothermia within fifteen minutes.

Yet Joughin was to remain in the water for a further four hours before he was finally pulled aboard a lifeboat that came alongside collapsible boat B. Along with the other survivors, he was eventually rescued by the RMS *Carpathia*, which arrived at the wreck site at 4.10 a.m.

Joughin believed that his extraordinary survival was due to the vast quantity of whisky he had drunk. Not so fortunate were 1,517 of his fellow crew and passengers. They died in the water, sober and cold.

The *Titanic* catastrophe was not Joughin's last shipwreck. He was on board the SS *Oregon* when she sank in Boston Harbour. He survived that disaster as well, although it is not known if he had once again fortified himself with a bottle or two of whisky.

The Man Who Was Buried Alive

Augustine Courtauld, a young London stockbroker, was bored with his job. He was bored with the paperwork. He was bored with his colleagues. He was desperate to do something more exciting with his life.

In 1930, he learned that volunteers were being recruited for an expedition to conduct weather observations at Icecap Station, a purpose-built post on the Greenland ice sheet. It was 2,600 metres above sea level and 112 miles west of the expedition's main base. And it was very, very cold.

Weather data for Arctic Greenland was desperately needed. The quickest air route from Europe to North America was over the ice sheet, but no one knew what the weather was like, especially in the winter months. Augustine Courtauld went to find out.

He travelled from the coast with a party whose task was to supply the weather station with enough food and fuel for two men. 'But atrocious weather had so slowed down the journey that most of the food intended for the station was eaten on the way there. It looked as if the place would have to be closed down.' So wrote one of the men accompanying the supply party.

Courtauld thought that it would be a shame to abandon the expedition simply because there was not enough food. 'I worked out that I could last out alone for five months,' he later wrote. 'As I had frostbite in my toes, I had no wish to make the journey back. So I decided to stay on my own and keep the station going.'

Frostbitten toes is an eccentric reason for choosing to stay on the Greenland ice sheet in midwinter, but to Courtauld it had a certain logic. He could at least put his feet up for a few months.

Soon after settling into his new home it began to snow. Hard. His small tent was buried by drifting snow until only the tip of the ventilator pipe poked above the surface. Soon he was completely snowed in and effectively buried alive.

His supplies of food and fuel were rapidly depleted and he had no communication with the outside world. But he remained confident that a rescue team would eventually find him.

'As each month passed without relief, I felt more and more certain of its arrival,' he later wrote. 'By the time I was snowed in I had no doubts on the matter, which was a great comfort to my mind. I will not attempt any explanation of this, but leave it as a fact, which was very clear to me during that time, that while powerless to help myself, some outer force was in action on my side and I wasn't fated to leave my bones on the Greenland ice cap.'

Never once did he despair. Instead, he dreamed of roaring fires and his wife, Mollie, singing to him. He also prayed that Gino Watkins, with whom he had travelled to the base, would soon be coming to the rescue.

'I began to feel complete confidence,' he wrote. 'I knew that even if Gino was having to wait for better weather, he wouldn't let me down. I began to realize that I should not be left to die. I came to know that I was held by Everlasting Arms.'

On 5 May, exactly five months after he was left alone, the Primus gave its last gasp. 'Very soon, there was a noise like a football match overhead. They had come! A hole of brilliant daylight appeared in the roof. There was Gino's voice saying: "Put these on." He handed me a pair of snow-glasses. How different it was from the last time I had seen the outside world! It was May and now dazzling sunshine. I had not realized it would be like this.

'They lost no time in pulling me out and I found I was quite all right. My legs were a bit weak. We set out for home next day. I rode on a sledge the whole way, reading *The Count of Monte Cristo*. Conditions were good and we completed the journey in five days. It had taken us six weeks on the way up.'

Courtauld declined to return to his former life as a stockbroker after his Greenland experience. Instead, he undertook an extraordinary six-hundred-mile journey down the unmapped Greenland coastline, travelling in an eighteen-foot open whaleboat.

It was more interesting than sitting behind a desk in London.

Part III

Hell in Japan

Just before the collision it is essential that you do not shut your eyes for a moment so as not to miss the target. Many have crashed into the targets with wide-open eyes. They will tell you what fun they had.

Instructions to Second World War kamikaze pilots:
Kamikaze, by Albert Axell and Hideaki Kase

The Long War of Hiroo Onoda

His home was a dense area of rainforest and he lived on the wild coconuts that grew in abundance. His principal enemy was the army of mosquitoes that arrived with each new shower of rain. But for Hiroo Onoda there was another enemy, one that remained elusive.

Unaware that the Second World War had ended twenty-nine years earlier, he was still fighting a lonely guerrilla war in the jungles of the Philippines.

The Americans had landed on Lubang Island in February 1945. Six months later, the Second World War had come to an end. Yet Hiroo Onoda and his small band of men had never received any orders to lay down their weapons. Rather, they'd been instructed to fight to the bitter end. Onoda was still carrying out these orders in 1974: his story is one of courage, farce and loyalty gone mad.

Hiroo Onoda was born to be a soldier. He had enlisted in the Imperial Japanese Army at the age of twenty, receiving training in intelligence and guerrilla warfare. In December 1944, he and a small group of elite soldiers were sent to Lubang Island in the Philippines.

Their mission was to destroy the island's little airstrip and port facilities. They were prohibited, under any circumstances, from surrendering or committing suicide. 'You are absolutely forbidden to die by your own hand,' read Onoda's military order. 'So long as you have one soldier, you are to continue to lead him. You may have to live on coconuts. If that's the case, live on coconuts! Under no circumstances are you [to] give up your life voluntarily.'

Onoda was unsuccessful in destroying Lubang's landing facilities, enabling American and Philippine forces to capture the island in February 1945. Most of the Japanese soldiers were either taken prisoner or killed. But Onoda and three others fled to the hills, from where they vowed to continue the fight.

Lubang Island was small: sixteen miles long and just six miles wide. Yet it was covered in dense forest and the four Japanese soldiers found it easy to remain in hiding. They spent their time conducting guerrilla activities, killing at least thirty Filipinos in one attack and clashing with the police on several other occasions.

In October 1945, the men stumbled across a leaflet that read: 'The war ended on August 15. Come down from the mountains.' Onoda did not believe it: he was convinced it was Allied propaganda.

A couple of months later, the men found a second leaflet that had been dropped from the air. It was a surrender order issued by General Tomoyuki Yamashita, Commander of the Fourteenth Army. Once again, Onoda and his men did not believe it to be genuine and vowed to continue Japanese resistance.

Four long years passed and still the little band were living in the forest. But by now, one of the four – Yuichi Akatsu – had had enough. He abandoned his comrades, surrendered to the Filipino army and returned to Japan. He informed the army that three of his comrades still believed the war to be ongoing.

Another two years passed before family photographs and letters were dropped into the forest on Lubang Island. Onoda found the parcels but was convinced it was all part of an elaborate trick. He and his two companions remained determined to continue fighting until the bitter end. They had little equipment and almost no provisions. They survived by eating coconuts and bananas and occasionally killing a cow.

Their living conditions were abominable. There was tropical heat, constant rain and infestations of rats. All the while they slept in make-shift huts made from branches.

Years rolled into decades and the men began to feel the effects of age. One of Onoda's comrades was killed by local Filipinos in 1954. Another lived for a further eighteen years before being shot in October 1972. He and Onoda had been engaged in a guerrilla raid on Lubang's food supplies when they got caught in a shoot-out.

Onoda was now alone, the last Japanese soldier still fighting the Second World War, a conflict that had ended twenty-seven years earlier. By now his struggle had become a lonely one, yet he refused to lay down his arms. He was still conducting guerrilla raids in the spring of 1974, when a travelling Japanese student, Norio Suzuki, managed to track him down and make contact with him.

Suzuki broke the news that the war had ended a long time previously. Onoda refused to believe it. He told Suzuki he would never surrender until he received specific orders to that effect from his superior officer.

Only now did the Japanese government get involved in trying to bring Onoda's war to an end. They managed to locate his previous commanding officer, Major Taniguchi, who was fortunately still alive. The major was flown to Lubang Island in order to tell Onoda in person to lay down his weapons.

On 9 March 1974 he was finally successful. 'Japan', he said to Onoda, 'had lost the war and all combat activity was to cease immediately.'

Onoda was officially relieved from military duties and told to hand over his rifle, ammunition and hand grenades. He was both stunned and horrified by what Major Taniguchi had told him. 'We really lost the war!' were his first words. 'How could they [the Japanese army] have been so sloppy?'

When he returned to Japan, he was feted as a national hero. But Onoda disliked the attention and found Japan a mere shadow of the noble imperial country he had served for so many years. He felt sure that if more soldiers had been prepared to fight to the bitter end, just like him, then Japan might have won the war.

The Kamikaze Pilot Who Survived

They were almost the same age – two young Japanese pilots who had joined the elite Tokkotai Special Attack Squadron. Now they had volunteered their services as kamikaze fighters prepared to sacrifice their lives for Japan.

It was spring 1945. Shigeyoshi Hamazono and Kiyoshi Ogawa were about to embark on their final mission, a devastating attack on American warships based in the waters around Okinawa.

Operation Kikusui was planned as a rolling wave of kamikaze attacks involving more than 1,500 planes. But the mission did not go entirely to plan, as Shigeyoshi Hamazono was soon to discover.

Hamazono had volunteered to serve in the Japanese military after the bombing of Pearl Harbor in December 1941. His mother was appalled: 'She wrote me a letter with the only words she could manage: "Don't be defeated. Don't die."' This injunction seemed a forlorn one, for Hamazono was selected to take part in Operation Kikusui.

Service in the Special Attack Squadrons was supposed to be entirely voluntary. The pilots in Hamazono's group had previously been given a recruitment form and told to mark it with a circle if they volunteered, or a cross if they declined.

'Three men marked a cross,' recalled Hamazono, 'and they were forced to go anyway. I felt hatred towards those officers who made them go like that.'

Hamazono himself was given little choice when nominated for Operation Kikusui. He was called by the commander and told that he'd been selected for the following day's attack.

'As a military pilot, there was no way to say no . . . It was my duty. That night, all I thought about was my mission.'

He had already survived one abortive suicide mission: his plane had developed technical failure and he had been forced to return to base. Now he was despatched on what was supposed to be his final attack. He climbed into his Mitsubishi Zero fighter, knowing that he would never see his family again.

Before heading out towards the US fleet, he flew over his hometown and dropped a *hachimaki* headband with the words: 'Hope you are well, goodbye.' It was a symbolic farewell.

His comrade-in-arms, Kiyoshi Ogawa, was rather more enthusiastic. He had been desperate to join the kamikaze squadron and was looking forward to the attack. He had no second thoughts as he climbed into his plane for his final mission.

Ogawa was one of the first to approach the American ships. As he did so, his plane came under sustained anti-aircraft fire. Undaunted, he kept flying directly towards his target, the American aircraft carrier USS *Bunker Hill*. When he was overhead, he pushed his plane into a steep dive, simultaneously dropping a 550lb bomb.

The warhead penetrated *Bunker Hill*'s flight deck and exploded, setting fire to fuel. The flames spread to the refuelled planes on deck, which promptly exploded. Ogawa just had time to see the carnage he had caused before delivering his *coup de grâce*, crashing the plane into the ship's burning control tower.

There was utter devastation on board. The explosion killed many of *Bunker Hill*'s pilots waiting inside the 'ready room', burning up the oxygen and asphyxiating the men.

Hamazono was also intent on hitting his target ship. But as he neared the American fleet, he noticed that a squadron of US fighters had been scrambled to engage him.

There followed a dangerous thirty-five-minute dogfight, with Hamazono dodging the American bullets while at the same time trying to identify his target far below. 'At the end of the dogfight, I could see them coming at me again from a long way off. I was certain that I would be killed in a matter of seconds. But as they got closer, they banked and flew off. I still can't work out why they did that.'

Hamazono was by now flying an aircraft riddled with holes. He also had severe cuts and burns to both his face and hands. As darkness was approaching, he decided to limp back to the Japanese mainland rather than press on with his attack. 'I was burned all over and only had five of my teeth left.' His mission was at an end.

Hamazono was not selected for another kamikaze raid. The war was almost over and he had lost all desire to die inside his plane.

For many years afterwards, he and the handful of other surviving kamikaze pilots had to live with the stigma of having survived a mission that ought to have claimed their lives.

'They used to tell us that the last words of the pilots were: "Long live the Emperor!"' says Hamazono. 'But I am sure that was a lie. They cried out what I would have cried. They called for their mothers.'

Surviving Hiroshima and Nagasaki

Tsutomu Yamaguchi was travelling across Hiroshima on a public tram when he heard the droning sound of an aircraft engine in the skies above.

He thought nothing of it. After all, it was wartime and planes were forever passing above the city. He was unaware that the engines belonged to the US bomber *Enola Gay*, and that it was just seconds away from dropping a thirteen-kiloton uranium atomic bomb on the city.

As the plane approached its target at 8.15 a.m. on 6 August 1945, Yamaguchi was just stepping off the tram. He glanced at the sky and noticed a bomber passing overhead. He also saw two small parachutes. And then, quite without warning, all hell broke loose.

'[There was] a great flash in the sky and I was blown over.' The massive nuclear warhead had exploded less than three kilometres from the spot where he was standing.

The bomb was detonated at six hundred metres above Hiroshima. As Yamaguchi swung his gaze upwards he saw a vast mushroom-shaped pillar of fire rising high into the sky. Seconds later, he passed out. The blast caused his eardrums to rupture and the flash of light left him temporarily blinded.

The heat of the explosion was so intense that it left him with serious burns over the left side of his body. When he eventually regained consciousness, he crawled to a shelter and tried to make sense of what had happened. Fortunately, he stumbled across three colleagues, who had also survived. All were young engineers working for the shipbuilder Mitsubishi Heavy Industries. They had been unlucky enough to be sent to Hiroshima on the very day of the bombing.

They spent the night together in an air-raid shelter, nursing their burns and wounds. Then, on the following morning, they ventured out of their shelter and picked their way through the charred and molten ruins. As they approached the nearest functioning railway station they passed piles of burnt and dying bodies. Their aim was to catch one of the few working trains back to their hometown of Nagasaki, some 200 miles away.

Yamaguchi was in a poor state and went to have his wounds bandaged as soon as he reached Nagasaki. But by 9 August, after just two days of convalescence, he felt well enough to struggle into work.

His boss and his co-workers listened in horrified amazement as he described the unbelievable destruction that a single bomb had managed to cause. He told them how the explosion had melted metal and evaporated entire parts of the city. His boss, Sam, simply didn't believe him.

'You're an engineer,' he barked. 'Calculate it. How could one bomb destroy a whole city?'

At the exact moment he said these words – 11.02 a.m. – there was a blinding white flash that penetrated to the heart of the room. Yamaguchi's tender skin was once again pricked with heat and he crashed to the ground. 'I thought that the mushroom cloud followed me from Hiroshima,' he said later.

The US Air Force had dropped their second nuclear warhead – Fat Man – named after Winston Churchill. It was much larger than the Hiroshima device, a twenty-five-kiloton plutonium bomb that exploded in the bowl of the valley where Nagasaki is situated.

The destruction was more confined but even more intense than at Hiroshima. Some 74,000 were killed and a similar number injured.

Yamaguchi, his wife and his baby son miraculously survived and spent much of the following week in an air-raid shelter near what was left of their home. Five days later, they heard the news that Emperor Hirohito had announced Japan's surrender.

Yamaguchi's survival of both nuclear explosions was little short of miraculous. Yet it was later discovered that he was one of 160 people known to have lived through both bombings.

In 1957, he was recognized as a *hibakusha* or 'explosion affected person'. But it was not until 2009 that he was officially allowed to describe himself as an *eniijuu hibakusha* or double bomb survivor.

The effects of the double bombing left its scars, both mental and physical. Yamaguchi lost the hearing in his left ear as a result of the Hiroshima explosion. He also lost his hair temporarily. His daughter would later recall that he was swathed in bandages until she reached the age of twelve.

Yamaguchi became an outspoken opponent of nuclear weapons until he was well advanced in years, at which point he began to suffer from the long-term effects of the exposure to radiation. His wife developed liver and kidney cancer in 2008 and died soon after. Yamaguchi himself developed acute leukaemia and died in 2010 at the age of ninety-three. His longevity was extraordinary, as he knew only too well. He viewed his long life as a 'path planted by God'.

'It was my destiny that I experienced this twice and I am still alive to convey what happened,' he said towards the end of his life.

Part IV

Ladies in Disguise

In final effect my outfit might deceive any eye; it revealed a thick-set and plump figure, finished by a somewhat small head and a boyish face.

Dorothy Lawrence admires her disguise as a
First World War soldier

Agatha Christie's Greatest Mystery

At shortly after 9.30 p.m. on Friday 3 December 1926, Agatha Christie got up from her armchair and climbed the stairs of her Berkshire home. She kissed her sleeping daughter Rosalind, aged seven, good-night and made her way back downstairs again. Then she climbed into her Morris Cowley and drove off into the night. She would not be seen again for eleven days.

Her disappearance would spark one of the largest manhunts ever mounted. Agatha Christie was already a famous writer and more than one thousand policemen were assigned to the case, along with hundreds of civilians. For the first time, aeroplanes were also involved in the search.

The Home Secretary, William Joynson-Hicks, urged the police to make faster progress in finding her. Two of Britain's most famous crime writers, Sir Arthur Conan Doyle, creator of Sherlock Holmes, and Dorothy L. Sayers, author of the Lord Peter Wimsey series, were drawn into the search. Their specialist knowledge, it was hoped, would help find the missing writer.

It didn't take long for the police to locate her car. It was found abandoned on a steep slope at Newlands Corner near Guildford. But there was no sign of Agatha Christie herself, nor was there any evidence that she had been involved in an accident.

As the first day of investigations progressed into the second and third – and there was still no sign of her – speculation began to mount. The press had a field day, inventing ever more lurid theories as to what might have happened.

It was the perfect tabloid story, with all the elements of an Agatha Christie whodunnit. Close to the scene of the car accident was a natural spring known as the Silent Pool, where two young children were reputed to have died. Some journalists ventured to suggest that the novelist had deliberately drowned herself.

Yet her body was nowhere to be found and suicide seemed unlikely, for her professional life had never looked so optimistic. Her sixth novel, *The Murder of Roger Ackroyd*, was selling well and she was already a household name.

Some said the incident was nothing more than a publicity stunt, a clever ruse to promote her new book. Others hinted at a far more sinister turn of events. There were rumours that she had been murdered by her husband, Archie Christie, a former First World War pilot and serial philanderer. He was known to have a mistress.

Arthur Conan Doyle, a keen occultist, tried using paranormal powers to solve the mystery. He took one of Christie's gloves to a celebrated medium in the hope that it would provide answers. It did not.

Dorothy Sayers visited the scene of the writer's disappearance to search for possible clues. This proved equally futile.

By the second week of the search, the news had spread around the world. It even made the front page of the *New York Times*.

Not until 14 December, fully eleven days after she disappeared, was Agatha Christie finally located. She was found safe and well in a hotel in Harrogate, but in circumstances so strange that they raised more questions than they solved. Christie herself was unable to provide any clues to what had happened. She remembered nothing. It was left to the police to piece together what might have taken place.

They came to the conclusion that Agatha Christie had left home and travelled to London, crashing her car en route. She had then boarded a train to Harrogate. On arriving at the spa town, she checked into the Swan Hydro – now the Old Swan Hotel – with almost no luggage. Bizarrely, she used the assumed name of Theresa Neele, her husband's mistress.

Harrogate was the height of elegance in the 1920s and filled with fashionable young things. Agatha Christie did nothing to arouse suspicion as she joined in the balls, dances and Palm Court entertainment. She was eventually recognized by one of the hotel's banjo players, Bob Tappin, who alerted the police. They tipped off her husband, Colonel Christie, who came to collect Agatha immediately.

But his wife was in no hurry to leave. Indeed, she kept him waiting in the hotel lounge while she changed into her evening dress.

Agatha Christie never spoke about the missing eleven days of her life and over the years there has been much speculation about what really happened between 3 and 14 December 1926.

Her husband said that she had suffered a total memory loss as a result of the car crash. But according to biographer Andrew Norman, the novelist may well have been in what is known as a 'fugue' state or, more technically, a psychogenic trance – a rare condition brought on by trauma or depression.

Norman says that her adoption of a new personality, Theresa Neele, and her failure to recognize herself in newspaper photographs were signs that she had fallen into psychogenic amnesia.

'I believe she was suicidal,' says Norman. 'Her state of mind was very low and she writes about it later through the character of Celia in her autobiographical novel *Unfinished Portrait*.'

She soon made a full recovery and once again picked up her writer's pen. But she was no longer prepared to tolerate her husband's philandering: she divorced him in 1928 and later married the distinguished archaeologist Sir Max Mallowan.

We will probably never know for certain what happened in those lost eleven days. Agatha Christie left a mystery that even Hercule Poirot would have been unable to solve.

Dressed to Kill

Dressed in khaki fatigues and splattered in mud, Private Denis Smith looked little different from his thousands of other war-weary comrades.

The boyish face and cropped hair provoked few comments from those at the battlefront. Indeed, no one in the 51st Division of the Royal Engineers (British Expeditionary Force) knew that Private Smith was hiding an extraordinary secret.

He was actually a woman, Dorothy Lawrence, who had come to the battlefield to see with her own eyes what was taking place. In doing so, Lawrence became the only female soldier to fight on the Western Front in the First World War.

Dorothy's story began in Paris at the outbreak of war in 1914. She was desperate to become a war correspondent, but was told that it was a man's world in which she could play no part. Determined to witness the bloody fighting in northern France, she decided to disguise herself as a soldier and make her own way to the front.

'I'll see what an ordinary English girl, without credentials or money, can accomplish,' she wrote.

She befriended two English soldiers in Paris – she later referred to them as her 'khaki accomplices' – and asked them to smuggle her a uniform. They agreed to help and within a week Dorothy was kitted out with military boots, khaki trousers, braces, jacket, a shirt and puttees.

There still remained the problem of how to disguise her feminine form. She knew that she would be arrested and sent home with immediate effect if anyone discovered that she was a woman.

'Enveloping myself in swathes of bandages, like a mummy, I pulled these swathes taut around my body.' But her womanly curves remained visible, 'so I padded my back with layers of cotton wool . . . my outfit . . . revealed a thick-set and plump figure, finished by a somewhat small head and a boyish face'.

The men also helped her obtain an all-important travel pass that would enable her to reach the town of Béthune, which was right on the front line.

Concerned that she still looked too feminine, Dorothy had one of her accomplices crop her hair and shave her face. 'Vainly I hoped that boyish bristles would sprout,' she wrote. A born tomboy, she was disappointed when this failed to happen.

To complete her disguise before setting off for the front line, Dorothy coated her face in diluted Condy's fluid. Bronzed, and looking decidedly shabby, she now headed for the battlefront.

It was not easy to reach the fighting. On several occasions she was stopped by officers who demanded to know what she was doing so far from her supposed regiment. Yet none of them ever imagined she was a woman.

Dorothy eventually secured the services of a tunnel expert named Sapper Tom Dunn who was serving with a Lancashire unit of the Royal Engineers. She admitted her secret to him and asked for his help.

Sapper Tom was amused by her daring and touched by her courage. He and a few comrades agreed to help get her into active service. They found her a secret hiding place where she could rest up during the day. Only when it became dark did she venture out with the other sappers, digging tunnels underneath the German lines and filling them with high explosive. The charges would then be set, blowing the German trenches and control centres high into the sky.

Hygiene was impossible and Dorothy was soon crawling with fleas and lice. 'Every inch of my body tickled and irritated,' she wrote. 'Fleas jumped in all directions.'

Although she faced terrible discomfort, she was soon actively involved in tunnelling underneath enemy lines. Shells and mortars rained down on her, yet she never once flinched. Her closest male comrade, Sapper Tom, was extraordinarily impressed by her bravery. He later described how she spent ten continuous days and nights '400 yards from the Boche front line, under rifle fire and trench mortars'.

The incessant fire, poor food and contaminated water rapidly took their toll. Dorothy fell ill and suffered a series of fainting fits. Fearing that her ruse would be discovered, she presented herself to her commanding sergeant and admitted her deception. He immediately arrested her on suspicion of being a spy.

Intense interrogation followed. Six generals and twenty officers were involved in cross-questioning Dorothy, but failed to prove anything other than the fact that she was a woman who wanted to join the dangerous world of men.

They forced her to sign an affidavit to the effect that she would never write about her story. And then she was despatched back to London.

Dorothy did eventually write about her adventures and Sapper Dunn even signed an affidavit to vouch for the fact that it was true. Yet few believed her story and she died in obscurity in 1964.

Mission into Danger

Irena Sendler aroused no suspicion as she left the Warsaw ghetto with a parcel under her arm. As her dog barked noisily, she gripped the parcel more tightly and gave a friendly wave to the Gestapo guards. What they did not know – and they would have killed her if they had – was that she was smuggling Jewish babies to safety.

Sendler was a Polish Catholic social worker living in occupied Poland. She was permitted by the Nazi authorities to enter the Jewish ghetto in order to check for signs of typhus, for the Nazis were terrified of the disease spreading across the city.

Gestapo officials had no idea that they were being duped and that Irena Sendler was actually involved in one of the greatest rescue missions of all time. In the guise of an employee of the Social Services Department, she managed to smuggle some 2,500 Jewish children to safety.

Her work was extremely dangerous. Warsaw, in 1942, was full of Gestapo officers constantly searching for Jews who had managed to escape from the ghetto.

'Transporting weapons . . . planning sabotage against the Germans, none of it was as dangerous as hiding a Jew,' said Wladyslaw Bartoszewski of the Polish Resistance. 'You have a ticking time bomb in your home. If they find out, they will kill you, your family and the person you are hiding.'

Under the pretext of inspecting conditions in the ghetto, Sendler smuggled out babies and small children in packages, suitcases, boxes and trolleys. Older children were taken out through the city's sewers.

Irena always went into the ghetto with a dog, which she had trained to bark whenever German soldiers were about. This enabled her to cover any noises that the babies might make while they were wrapped up in her parcels. Once the children were safely out of the ghetto, they were given Catholic birth certificates and forged identity papers. These were signed by priests or officials who worked for the Social Services Department.

The children were then taken to orphanages and convents in the countryside around Warsaw.

By mid-1942, the SS were rounding up large numbers of Jews and transporting them to Treblinka extermination camp. Sendler begged Jewish parents to release their children, knowing it was their only hope of survival. In an interview recorded before her death in 2008, she spoke vividly of her conversations with the parents of these children.

'Those scenes over whether to give a child away were heart-rending . . . Their first question was: "What guarantee is there that the child will live?" I said, "None. I don't even know if I will get out of the ghetto alive today."'

Sendler kept a list of all those she had rescued and she secretly buried their names in jars. It was hoped that they would be reunited with their parents when the war was over.

In 1943, Sendler was arrested by the Gestapo. They had grown suspicious of her activities and realized she was working on behalf of Warsaw's Jews. She was beaten, severely tortured by her guards (they broke her legs and arms) and then sentenced to death for refusing to give them any information.

News of her impending execution reached Żegota, the secret Council to Aid Jews, which managed to save her by bribing a German guard as she was being led away to be killed. She was listed on the bulletin boards as among those who'd been executed; this enabled her to live in hiding for the rest of the war.

At the war's end, Irena dug up jars containing the 2,500 children's identities in the hope of reuniting the youngsters with their parents. But almost all of the adults had been executed in Treblinka.

Irena found herself persecuted by Poland's post-war Communist authorities because of her relations with the Polish government-in-exile. Not until 1965 did she receive recognition for her extraordinary bravery. She was honoured as a 'righteous gentile' by the Israeli Holocaust Memorial Centre, Yad Vashem.

With the fall of Communism came recognition in her own land: many of Poland's highest honours were bestowed on her. In 2007, she was even nominated for the Nobel Peace Prize. But she did not win: the prize went to former Vice President Al Gore for his work on climate change.

Irena remained modest to her dying day. When asked about her work, she said simply: 'Every child saved with my help is the justification of my existence on this Earth, and not a title to glory.'

Part V

Man's Best Friend

America entered the war . . . and Stubby came to the conclusion that he ought to do his bit by his country.

New York Times obituary of Sergeant Stubby, the most decorated dog in American history, April 1926

The Real War Horse

He stood fearless and proud in readiness for the battle ahead. He had already braved four years of warfare, including the Battle of the Somme in 1916. He had also survived the muddy hell of Passchendaele. Now, on 30 March 1918, Warrior was to face his toughest assignment. The ten-year-old chestnut-brown gelding was to lead one of the last great cavalry charges in history.

His mission was to stop the German Spring Offensive of 1918 and his adventures were to prove every bit as extraordinary as those of Michael Morpurgo's fictional warhorse.

Warrior was one of the million horses sent to France between 1914 and 1918. Only 62,000 of them ever returned home. They are forgotten victims of a conflict that pitted defenceless animals against tanks and machine guns.

Warrior belonged to General John Seely, one of Churchill's closest friends, and both he and his horse were born survivors. Warrior had proved his mettle on numerous occasions since arriving in France in the summer of 1914. That autumn, he narrowly escaped capture by the advancing German army. In the following year, the horse next to him was killed when a shell exploded and ripped it in two. Warrior was fortunate to escape unscathed.

A few days later, his stable was destroyed within seconds of him leaving it. On another occasion, he had to be dug out of mud that was several feet deep.

In February 1915, General Seely (and Warrior) were put in command of the Canadian Cavalry, a ragbag force of ranchers, Mounties, Native Americans and a thousand horses. After three years proving their worth on the battlefield, they were given a mission of vital strategic importance. The German war machine had broken through the Allied front line and taken more than 100,000 prisoners, many of them members of the British Fifth Army. Buoyed by this victory, the Germans were intent on pushing even further west.

It was vital that their advance should be checked as soon as possible. Allied forces were to take the offensive at Moreuil Wood on the banks of the Avre river. Victory here would not only secure the river but also stop the German thrust westwards.

The woodland attack was to take place on 30 March and to be led by Warrior and eleven other horses. Their initial task was to plant a red pennant on the hill above the river. This would act as a guide for the rest of the cavalry.

'[Warrior] was determined to go forward,' wrote Seely, 'and with a great leap started off. All sensation of fear vanished from him as he galloped at racing speed. There was a hail of bullets from the enemy as we crossed the intervening space and mounted the hill, but Warrior cared for nothing.'

Warrior made it to the hilltop and the pennant was planted. Seconds later, there was a loud thundering as a thousand other horses followed him into battle.

Squadron after squadron rode into the chaos. Shells rained down on them and gunfire came spurting from every angle.

Warrior and his fellow horses advanced under protective covering fire from men of the Royal Flying Corps. More than 17,000 rounds were fired at the Germans. But it was to little avail: hundreds of horses were mown down by the German machine guns.

The battle continued into the late afternoon. Rain sluiced down from the metal-grey sky and the light soon began to fade. Warrior continued to lead the mounted brigade forward under constant fire until the battle slowly began to turn.

By nightfall, the wood had been captured and the Germans forced back. But victory came at a heavy price. A quarter of the men and more than half the horses had been killed in the bloodbath.

There was no respite for Warrior. He was called back into action on the following day in order to lead an attack close to the village of Gentelles. But he soon suffered such injuries that he had to be withdrawn. General Seely was also wounded and unable to continue the fight.

Warrior made a remarkable recovery and lived until 1941, too old to re-enter service in the Second World War. Besides, warfare had changed beyond all recognition in the intervening years. Cavalry charges belonged to the past and there was no longer a place for warhorses like Warrior.

He remains one of the unsung heroes of the Great War: a faithful, devoted and extraordinarily courageous warhorse who helped to secure victory on the Western Front.

Pigeon to the Rescue

Major Charles Whittlesey knew that the situation was desperate. Just twenty-four hours earlier, on 2 October 1918, he and his men had been ordered to advance against heavily fortified German positions in the Argonne Forest in northern France. It was part of the biggest operation undertaken by the American Expeditionary Force in the First World War.

Charles Whittlesey was serving in the 77th Division, a motley band who were known as the Metropolitans, a reference to the fact that they had been drawn from New York's multi-ethnic Lower East Side. Between them they spoke forty-two languages.

The linguistic diversity did not hide the fact that most of the men were inexperienced soldiers. After a brief but intensive training at Camp Upton in New York, they had been shipped to France. Some had not even learned how to throw a hand grenade.

Major Whittlesey was in command of 554 soldiers attacking the German front line. The strength of the enemy made this a perilous task, but what made it even more deadly was the hostile terrain.

The Argonne is an area of deep ravines and high bluffs of rock. It is easy to defend and almost impossible to attack. Whittlesey sniffed at the danger and sensed a tough time ahead. But orders were orders. On 2 October, he and his men moved forward.

They proved remarkably successful in penetrating the Argonne's ravines. Indeed, their initial success was to prove their downfall. The Allied units on their flanks were unable to make such rapid progress and it was not long before Major Whittlesey's men found themselves cut off. They had made the classic mistake of advancing too far.

The German counter-attack was devastating. Soldiers hidden on the high bluffs began firing downwards on Whittlesey's exposed positions, picking off the men below. They had no chance of firing back because the rocky pinnacles were two hundred feet high.

Whittlesey knew that any attempt to retreat would be tantamount to suicide. His men would be cut down by German machine guns. His only option was to sit tight until American forces could come to their aid.

His wireless equipment was unable to function in the gorge and his only means of contacting battlefield headquarters was to use one of the three carrier pigeons he had brought with him. When he learned that three hundred of his men had been killed, he sent one of the pigeons to headquarters with the message: 'Many wounded. We cannot evacuate.'

The pigeon was immediately shot down by the Germans. They were determined to prevent additional troops coming to Whittlesey's rescue.

The major sent his second pigeon: 'Men are suffering. Can support be sent?' It was all to no avail: the second bird was also shot down.

Whittlesey had just one pigeon left, his prize bird, Cher Ami. He now desperately needed to send a message, for as well as being attacked by the Germans, his men were also coming under friendly fire from American artillery.

Whittlesey placed a note inside a canister and then attached it to Cher Ami's leg. 'We are along the road parallel to 276.4. Our own artillery is dropping a barrage directly on us. For heaven's sake, stop it!'

The men watched anxiously as Cher Ami began flying out of the ravine. He represented their last hope of salvation.

He was scarcely above the line of trees when he was spotted by German gunners. There was a burst of gunfire as they turned all their weaponry on him, firing wildly in an attempt to bring him down.

Cher Ami continued flying through the hail of bullets until disaster struck. The bird was hit and could be seen dropping to the ground. Major Whittlesey's men were devastated. They now knew that they were destined to die in this Argonne hellhole.

But no sooner had the gunfire stopped when there was a collective gasp. Cher Ami had struggled back into the air and was once again flying through the ravine. This time, he made it out alive.

Sixty-five minutes later, divisional headquarters sighted a carrier pigeon approaching its loft. It was Cher Ami. When they went to look for the message, they discovered he had been shot through the breast and was blinded in one eye. One of his legs, the one carrying Major Whittlesey's message, was hanging from a single tendon. Divisional headquarters read it and acted within seconds, ordering an immediate halt to the bombardment.

The troops in the ravine managed to hold out for a further four days before the Allies finally sent in a relief force. The Germans retreated and Whittlesey's Lost Battalion, as it was already being called, was finally safe. Whittlesey returned to America a war hero. His stand in the Argonne became the stuff of legend.

Cher Ami was also to become a national hero. One of six hundred pigeons used by the United States Army Signal Corps, he had already delivered twelve important messages at Verdun. Now, his rescue of the Lost Battalion was his finest hour.

His leg was so damaged that it had to be amputated; a wooden leg was specially carved for him. And then he sailed back to America, with General John J. Pershing seeing him off personally.

On arrival, he was awarded the Croix de Guerre medal with a Palm Oak Leaf Cluster; he would later become an exalted member of the Racing Pigeon Hall of Fame.

Cher Ami died on 13 June 1919, from wounds received in battle. He was stuffed by a taxidermist and placed on display in the Smithsonian, alongside another famous hero from the First World War, the mongrel dog Sergeant Stubby. Both of them remain there to this day.

Barking for Victory

It was a most unusual way to join the US Army. But then again, he was a most unusual recruit. Stubby sauntered onto the Connecticut training ground of the 102nd Infantry Division, wagged his tail and signalled his desire to serve in the First World War. It was the beginning of a long and illustrious canine military career.

Stubby was a brindle puppy with a short tail. Homeless and apparently ownerless, he was adopted by Private J. Robert Conroy and began training with the 102nd Infantry's 26 Yankee Division.

He proved quick to learn. Within weeks he knew all the bugle calls and drills and had even learned to salute his superiors, placing his right paw on his right eyebrow.

The time soon came for the Infantry Division to sail for France. Stubby ought to have been left behind, but Private Conroy smuggled him aboard the SS *Minnesota*. He was kept hidden in a coal bin until the ship was far out at sea; he was then brought out and introduced to the sailors, who were amused by his canine salutes.

When the ship arrived in France, Private Conroy smuggled him ashore. His commanding officer was minded to have the dog sent back on board, but he changed his mind when Stubby gave him a full military salute.

The Yankee Division headed for the front lines at Chemin des Dames, near Soissons, in the first week of February 1918. Stubby was allowed to accompany them as the division's official mascot. Under constant fire for over a month, he soon became used to the noise of shelling.

His first injury came not from gunfire but from poison gas. He was rushed to a field hospital and given emergency treatment. The gassing left him sensitive to even minute traces of the substance in the atmosphere. When the Infantry Division was the target of an early morning gas attack, the men were asleep and their lives were at great risk. But Stubby recognized the smell and ran through the trench barking and biting the soldiers in order to wake them. In doing so, he saved them from certain death.

Stubby also proved extraordinarily talented at finding wounded soldiers lying out in no man's land between the trenches of the opposing armies. He would stand by the body, barking loudly until stretcher bearers were able to rescue the injured person.

On one occasion, while serving in the Argonne, Stubby stumbled across a German soldier-spy who was in the process of mapping the layout of the Allied trenches. He understood what the man was doing and began barking wildly.

The German spy realized that his cover was blown and started to run back to his own trenches. But Stubby chased after the man, gnawing his legs and causing him to fall to the ground. He then pressed home his attack until American troops arrived and captured the spy.

Stubby's heroism in the face of extreme danger caused a sensation. He was immediately promoted to the rank of sergeant by the commander of the 102nd Infantry.

A few months later, Sergeant Stubby was badly injured during a grenade attack and received a large amount of shrapnel in his chest and leg. He was rushed to a field hospital for emergency surgery, then taken to a Red Cross hospital for additional treatment. When he was well enough to wander through the wards, he visited wounded soldiers, boosting their morale.

By the end of the war, Stubby had served in seventeen battles and four major offensives. He also played an important role in liberating Château-Thierry. The women of the town were so grateful that they made him a special chamois coat on which he could pin his many medals.

His military decorations included three service stripes, the French Battle of Verdun Medal, New Haven World War I Veterans Medal, Republic of France Grande Guerre Medal and the Château-Thierry campaign medal. He was also made a life member of the American Legion, the Red Cross and the YMCA. When the Humane Education Society awarded him a gold medal in 1921, it was presented by General John Pershing.

After the war, Stubby became a national celebrity, attending military parades up and down the country. He even got to meet three presidents: Wilson, Harding and Coolidge.

In 1926, he died peacefully in Private Conroy's arms. Brave, but also lucky, he was the most decorated dog of the First World War. He was also the only dog to be promoted to the rank of sergeant through combat.

His remains were stuffed, preserved and put on display in the Smithsonian, alongside the pigeon Cher Ami.

Part VI

Guilty Until Proven Innocent

I have nothing to say.

Amelia Dyer, as the noose was placed around her neck
in preparation for her execution, 10 June 1896

Angel of Death

It began with an advert in the Bristol *Times and Mirror*. 'Wanted,' it read, 'respectable woman to take young child.' The advertisement had been placed in the newspaper by Evelina Marmon, a twenty-five-year-old barmaid.

Two months earlier, in January 1896, Evelina had given birth to a baby girl named Doris. Unable to meet the cost of feeding and clothing the child, and abandoned by the man who made her pregnant, Evelina had no option but to find a foster home.

As she read through the advert she had placed in the newspaper, her eye happened to fall on another advertisement on the same page. 'Married couple with no family would adopt healthy child, nice country home. Terms, £10.'

Foster families were not unusual in Victorian Britain. Unwanted pregnancies and poverty had led to a veritable foster industry, with thousands of illegitimate children being discreetly farmed out to charitable families. The mother of the unwanted child would pay a fee – it was either a one-off payment or a monthly advance – and find herself free of the stigma of having a child born out of wedlock.

Evelina, a vivacious blonde, read the advert and had the feeling that she was at last in luck. She immediately wrote to the lady – a Mrs Harding from Oxford Road in Reading – and asked for more information.

A reply was quickly forthcoming. 'I should be glad to have a dear little baby girl, one I could bring up and call my own,' wrote Mrs Harding. She also provided a little more information about her love of children. 'We are plain, homely people, in fairly good circumstances. I don't want a child for money's sake, but for company and home comfort. Myself and my husband are dearly fond of children. I have no child of my own. A child with me will have a good home and a mother's love.'

Evelina was thrilled by what she read: it was the answer to all her prayers. Mrs Harding even described the enchanting place where she and her husband lived. There was a large garden and an orchard. It was the perfect place to raise a young child.

There was only one detail that caused Evelina a moment's hesitation. Mrs Harding said she could not accept a weekly fee for caring for baby Doris. Rather, she wanted a one-off payment of £10. She said she would take entire responsibility for the child and that Evelina would never have to trouble herself about the illegitimate baby.

Evelina felt uneasy. As with any young mother, the idea of being separated for ever from her newborn was extremely painful. But she was in such desperate straits that she agreed to Mrs Harding's terms. A week later, Mrs Harding arrived in Cheltenham to pick up baby Doris.

And this was the point when Evelina got a most unwelcome surprise. She was expecting Mrs Harding to be youthful and maternal. Instead, she turned out to be an elderly woman with a rough-looking face.

Evelina was somewhat reassured by the loving way Mrs Harding picked up the baby. She wrapped Doris tightly in a shawl, professing to be concerned about the chill evening air. After chatting about the wonderful home in which the baby would be brought up, she turned to leave. Evelina shed a quiet tear as she waved farewell.

A few days later Evelina wrote to Mrs Harding for news of baby Doris and was relieved to learn that all was well. But it was to be the last news she ever heard of her baby. All of her subsequent letters went unanswered – and with good reason. Baby Doris was dead.

Only much later would the grisly story emerge: one that would cause shock and revulsion throughout Victorian Britain. Mrs Harding was not who she claimed to be: her real name was Amelia Dyer. Under the pretence of being a foster mother, she took in illegitimate babies (for a sizeable fee) and then murdered them.

Amelia Dyer did not take baby Doris home to Reading as she had promised. Instead, she went directly to Mayo Road in Willesden where her daughter lived. In the room upstairs, she took some white edging tape from a box and wound it tightly around baby Doris's neck, slowly strangling the child. She pawned Doris's baby clothes, thereby earning herself a few more shillings, and then wrapped the corpse in a napkin.

On the following morning, she took delivery of another child, a thirteen-month-old boy named Harry Simmons. He, too, was strangled.

The next evening, Dyer shoved the two corpses into an old carpet bag and threw it into a lonely spot by the weir at Caversham Lock. Unknown to her, it did not sink.

Nor did she know that she was already under police surveillance. Just days before killing baby Doris, the police had recovered a parcel in the Thames, near Reading. On opening it, they found the remains of a baby. Crucially, they also found the smudged remnants of an old label on the parcel. After a clever piece of detective work, police found themselves on the trail of Amelia Dyer.

Suspecting Dyer of murdering babies, the police began dragging a stretch of river. They pulled out three baby corpses, followed by the bag that contained the remains of Doris Marmon and Harry Simmons.

In the third week of May, Amelia Dyer was put on trial for murder. She pleaded guilty to one of the killings, baby Doris, and claimed insanity as her defence.

This was swiftly rejected. The jury took just four and a half minutes to find her guilty and Amelia was hanged two weeks later. To the surprise of many, her daughter escaped prosecution.

The police never discovered how many other babies Amelia had killed, but the vast collection of baby clothes and letters found at her house suggested that she had murdered many more. Indeed, some believed her to have killed more than four hundred babies, making her the most prolific murderess in history.

Who Killed Rasputin?

The frozen corpse was spotted in the River Neva on the last day of December 1916. A river policeman noticed a fur coat lodged beneath the ice and ordered the surface crust to be broken.

The frozen body was immediately recognizable as belonging to Grigori Rasputin, 'holy' adviser to the tsar and tsarina of Russia. Tsar Nicholas and his wife, Alexandra, believed Rasputin to be blessed with semi-magical powers that brought temporary relief to their haemophiliac son.

Others took a rather different view. Rasputin was widely hated as a dissolute fraudster who was manipulating the affairs of state to his own advantage. Many in the Russian capital had long wished him dead.

The corpse was prised from its icy sepulchre and taken to Chesmenskii Hospice. Here, a post-mortem was undertaken by Professor Dmitrii Kosorotov. Rumours about Rasputin's death were already circulating around Petrograd, rumours that would later be fuelled by one of the murderers. Prince Felix Yusupov, in whose palace Rasputin had died, not only admitted to being involved, but also justified the killing by arguing that Rasputin was bad for Russia. He bragged about having poisoned him with cyanide before shooting him through the heart.

'He rushed at me, trying to get at my throat, and sank his fingers into my shoulder like steel claws. His eyes were bursting from their sockets, blood oozed from his lips.'

From the outset there were good reasons to doubt Yusupov's account. The professor conducting the post-mortem noted that the corpse was in a terrible state of mutilation. 'His left side has a weeping wound, due to some sort of slicing object or a sword. His right eye has come out of its cavity and falls down onto his face . . . His right ear is hanging down and torn. His neck has a wound from some sort of rope tie. The victim's face and body carry traces of blows given by a supple but hard object.'

Rasputin had been repeatedly beaten with a heavy cosh.

More horrifying was the damage to his genitals. At some point his legs had been wrenched apart and his testicles had been 'crushed by the action of a similar object'.

Other details gleaned by Professor Kosorotov suggest that Yusupov's account was nothing more than fantasy. The story of the poisoned cakes was untrue: the post-mortem found no trace of poison in Rasputin's stomach.

Kosorotov also examined the three bullet wounds in Rasputin's body. 'The first has penetrated the left side of the chest and has gone through the stomach and liver. The second has entered into the right side of the back and gone through the kidney.'

Both of these would have inflicted terrible wounds, but the third bullet was the fatal shot. '[It] hit the victim in the forehead and penetrated into his brain.' Professor Kosorotov noted, significantly, that the bullets 'came from different calibre revolvers'.

On the night of the murder, Yusupov was in possession of a pocket

Browning, as was fellow conspirator Grand Duke Dmitrii. Vladimir Purishkevich, also present, had a Savage.

These weapons could have caused the wounds to Rasputin's liver and kidney. But the fatal gunshot wound to Rasputin's head could only have come from a revolver. Ballistic experts now agree that the grazing around the wound is consistent with that left by a lead, non-jacketed bullet fired at point-blank range.

All the evidence points to the fact that the gun was a British-made .455 Webley revolver. This was the gun that belonged to Oswald Rayner, a close friend of Yusupov since the days when they had both studied at Oxford University.

Unknown to anyone except the small group of conspirators, Rayner had also been present on the night of Rasputin's murder. Sent to Russia more than a year earlier, he was a British agent working for the Secret Intelligence Service (now MI6).

Prince Yusupov was circumspect about Rayner when he wrote his memoirs. He mentions meeting him on the day after Rasputin's murder but presents their meeting as a chance encounter. 'I met my friend Oswald Rayner . . . he knew of our conspiracy and had come in search of news.'

Yusupov did indeed meet with Rayner after the murder, but Rayner had not needed to 'come in search of news' for he had fired the fatal shot.

Rayner would later tell his family that he was present in the Yusupov palace that night, information that would eventually find its way into his obituary. Surviving letters from his fellow agents also shed light on his role. 'A few awkward questions have already been asked about wider involvement,' wrote one. 'Rayner is attending to loose ends.'

The tsar was quick to hear rumours of British involvement in Rasputin's murder. Anxious to know more, he asked the British ambassador if Rayner had had a hand in the killing.

The ambassador denied any knowledge of Rayner's involvement. So, too, did Samuel Hoare, the head of the British espionage bureau in Petrograd. 'An outrageous charge,' he said, 'and incredible to the point of childishness.'

Yet Hoare was remarkably quick to learn of Rasputin's death. Indeed he telegrammed London with news of the murder many hours before it was publicly known in Petrograd.

Till Death Us Do Part

The letter begins as an intimate billet-doux. 'Oh Harry, my own precious darling, your letter today is one long yearning cry for your little love.'

But within a few lines, a more sinister story begins to emerge. 'Yesterday, I administered the powder you left me . . . the result? Nil.'

The powder – arsenic – had not worked.

The writer of the letter was an Edwardian housewife named Augusta Fullam, who lived in Agra in central north India. Her 'precious darling' was Lieutenant Henry Clark, a surgeon. Together, in 1911, the two lovers decided to poison Augusta's husband Edward. Once he was dead, they would then kill Mrs Clark, Henry's wife. And then they would get married.

But they found themselves with a significant problem when they tried to kill Edward: he stubbornly refused to die. Each day, Augusta sprinkled arsenic powder onto his supper or slipped it into his tea, but all to no avail. 'My hubby returned the whole jug of tea saying it tasted bad,' she wrote in one letter to her lover.

On Friday 16 June 1911, Augusta managed to administer a massive dose to her husband. This time he ate the lot. But once again, it failed to kill him. 'Since 4pm [he's] vomited eight times . . . vomited ten times at a quarter to nine . . . vomited 12 times at ten pm.'

Augusta began to fear that he was indestructible. 'I give him half a tonic powder every day in his Sanatogen, lovie darling, because it lays on the top of the white powder quite unsuspiciously.'

For month after month, Augusta fed her husband arsenic. And for month after month Edward clung to life, despite vomiting many times each day. But eventually he fell seriously ill. As he lay in bed with a raging fever, Lieutenant Clark decided to finish him off with a huge dose of poison, administering it himself. Within hours, Edward Fullam was dead.

In his capacity as surgeon, Lieutenant Clark was able to sign the death certificate: it recorded the cause of death as heart failure.

The lovers were halfway to their goal. All they now had to do was murder Mrs Clark. This time, they decided not to waste months in administering arsenic. Instead, Lieutenant Clark hired four assassins who broke into the house and struck Louisa Clark with a sword, smashing her skull. The noise of the brutal attack woke the Clarks' daughter, Maud, who screamed, causing the robbers to flee.

Agra police began their investigations that same day and their suspicions immediately fell on Lieutenant Clark and Augusta Fullam. Their love affair had not gone unnoticed in the local community and they clearly had a motive for both murders. But the detectives assigned to the case could find no conclusive proof.

None, that is, until Inspector Smith called at Augusta Fullam's house and noticed a large metal box hidden under the bed. When he asked what was inside, Augusta turned bright red 'and fell like a heap into a chair'.

Inspector Smith had the box prised open: inside there were 370 love letters that set down in great detail how Augusta and Lieutenant Clark had planned their terrible crime.

The ensuing trial proved a sensation: colonial India had never before seen such a spectacular double murder. Every sordid detail was splashed across both the Indian and British newspapers.

The two lovers were tried separately and both were convicted. Lieutenant Clark was hanged on Wednesday 26 March 1913. Augusta Fullam, who was pregnant at the time of the trial, was sentenced to life. She served just fifteen months before dying of heatstroke the following year.

'My very own precious lovie,' she had written when she and Clark first started administering the arsenic, 'don't you think our correspondence rather risky?'

But Lieutenant Clark assured her it was fine. He said they would never be caught.

Part VII

Big-Time Adventure

I was listening to the radio when [the newscasters] told about it. I cut my iron off and I run to my neighbors house and said: 'Did you hear what was on the radio? My brothers have escaped from Alcatraz.'

Marie Widner, sister of escaping prisoners,
John and Clarence Anglin

By Balloon to the North Pole

At exactly 2.30 p.m. on 11 July 1897, a gigantic silk balloon could be seen rising into the Arctic sky above Spitsbergen. Inside the basket were three hardy adventurers, all Swedish, who were taking part in an extraordinary voyage.

Salomon Andrée was the instigator of the mission. Charismatic and confident, he managed to persuade Nils Strindberg and Knut Fraenkel to accompany him on his historic balloon flight over the North Pole.

Andrée was confident of success. His balloon, the *Eagle*, used advanced hydrogen technology and he claimed to have developed a revolutionary steering system using drag-ropes.

A disastrous test flight suggested that Andrée's confidence was seriously misplaced. The much-vaunted rope-steerage system had numerous glitches and hydrogen was found to be seeping out of the balloon's 8 million little stitching-holes.

The expedition ought to have been abandoned before it even took off. But Andrée overruled all objections and the launch was scheduled for the second week of July.

The problems began within minutes of getting airborne. As the balloon drifted across the sea to the north of Spitsbergen, it was weighed down by the drag-ropes – so much so that at one point the balloon actually dipped into the water.

Andrée jettisoned 530 kilograms of ropes, along with 210 kilograms of ballast. This lightened the balloon so much that it now rose too high. The change in air pressure caused huge quantities of hydrogen to escape through the stitching-holes. Andrée remained optimistic, releasing a carrier pigeon with the message: 'All well on board.'

This was far from true. The first ten hours of troubled flight were followed by forty-one hours in which the balloon, soaked in a rainstorm, flew so low that it kept bumping into the frozen sea.

The *Eagle* eventually crash-landed onto sea-ice some fifty hours after taking off from Spitsbergen. No one was hurt, but it was clear that the balloon would never fly again. The men were stranded, many miles from anywhere and lost in an Arctic wilderness.

They were well supplied with safety equipment, including guns, sleds, skis, a tent and a small boat. Yet returning to the relative safety of Spitsbergen involved a gruelling march across shifting, melting ice.

The men spent a week at the crash site before setting out on their long hike. They had a reasonable quantity of food, including meat, sausages and pemmican, but found it impossible to transport so much weight across the rucked-up ice. Much of the food had to be abandoned. Henceforth, they were to rely on hunting for their survival.

They left their makeshift camp on 22 July and initially headed for Franz Josef Land. But the ice soon became impassable so they headed instead towards the Seven Islands, a seven-week march, where there was known to be a depot of food.

The terrain was so gruelling that they were reduced to advancing on all fours. But they eventually reached a place where the sea-ice had melted sufficiently for them to use their collapsible boat.

'Paradise!' wrote Andrée in his diary. 'Large even ice floes with pools of sweet drinking water and here and there a tender-fleshed young polar bear!'

Their route soon became impassable once again, forcing them to change direction. Aware that winter would soon be upon them, they built a hut upon an ice floe. But the ice broke up beneath them and they were lucky to struggle ashore onto desolate Kvitøya Island.

'Morale remains good,' reported Andrée. 'With such comrades as these, one ought to be able to manage under practically any circumstances whatsoever.' It was the last coherent message he ever wrote. Within a few days, all three men were dead.

Their fate was to become one of the great mysteries of Arctic exploration. What happened to them? They had shelter, food and ammunition and ought to have been able to keep themselves alive. In the absence of any news, the world's media began to speculate on their fate.

It was not until 1930, fully thirty-three years after the men were lost, that their remains were finally found. Far from answering questions, the discovery of their bodies only deepened the mystery.

The most plausible theory is that the men died of trichinosis, contracted after eating undercooked polar bear meat. They certainly had the symptoms of the disease, and larvae of the *Trichinella* parasite were found in a polar bear carcass at the site. But recent scientific evidence has thrown doubt on this theory.

Other suggestions include vitamin A poisoning from eating polar bear liver, lead poisoning from the food cans or carbon dioxide poisoning from their Primus stove.

By the time they struggled ashore they were living off scant quantities of canned goods from the balloon stores, along with portions of half-cooked polar bear meat.

They were suffering from foot pains and debilitating diarrhoea and were constantly cold and exhausted. Indeed they were so weary on their arrival at Kvitøya Island that they left much of their valuable equipment down by the water's edge.

Nils Strindberg, the youngest, was the first to die. His corpse was wedged into a crack in the cliff. Analysis of his clothing suggests he was killed by a polar bear.

The other two men seem to have weakened dramatically in the days that followed Strindberg's death. As the Arctic winter struck in earnest, they lost the will to live.

It will never be known how many days they survived in their makeshift Arctic shack. By the time they were eventually found, all that remained was their diaries, a few spools of undeveloped film and a heap of bleached bones.

Escape from Alcatraz

It was a routine inspection by the prison warders. On the morning of 12 June 1962, the guards at Alcatraz high security prison made their morning check on the prisoners in their cells.

When they came to Cell Block B, they quickly realized that something was not quite right. The men were in their beds but they were showing no signs of life.

The guards unlocked the cells and were stunned by what they found. Frank Morris, John Anglin and Clarence Anglin were missing: in their place were elaborately made papier-mâché heads with real hair and painted eyes. Three of Alcatraz's most dangerous prisoners had escaped.

Neither the guards nor the other prisoners could believe that they'd managed to get away. Alcatraz, after all, was one of the world's most closely guarded prisons. Situated on a rocky island in San Francisco Bay, it was washed by cold and hazardous waters, making escape almost impossible.

In its twenty-nine years as a federal prison, from 1934 to 1963, no one had ever made it out alive. Forty-one inmates tried. Of those, twenty-six were recaptured, seven were shot dead and at least three were known to have drowned.

This proved no deterrent for the three new escapees. In fact, they saw the island's isolation as a challenge.

All three men were hardened criminals. Frank Morris had first been convicted at the age of thirteen. Since that time, he'd been involved in a number of serious crimes ranging from armed robbery to dealing in narcotics. He had been transferred to Alcatraz in 1960.

John Anglin was also an infamous criminal. He had robbed the Columbia Alabama Bank in 1958, together with his two brothers. It had earned him a thirty-five-year prison sentence.

Clarence Anglin had been involved in a number of other bank robberies and had also been caught escaping from the Atlanta State Penitentiary. It was decided to send him to Alcatraz, in order to prevent him from making any more escape attempts.

All the men were highly resourceful and extremely motivated. They discovered that there was an unguarded three-foot-wide utility corridor behind their cells. This led to an air vent and thence to the outside world. The prisoners began to chisel away at the moisture-damaged concrete. For tools, they used metal spoons stolen from the canteen and an electric drill that they improvised from the motor of a stolen vacuum cleaner. They did most of the work during music hour, when the noise of accordions covered the sound of their hacking at the concrete.

They also made dummy heads from soap, toilet paper and real hair in order to fool the guards; there were constant checks on the prisoners throughout the night.

It took a year to tunnel through the wall of the service tunnel. The men then had to steal a long piece of cord in order to reach the manhole that covered the air vent. When they finally lifted the manhole cover, they replaced the metal bolts with fake ones made of soap. Finally, on the night of 11 June, all was ready. It was time to make their escape.

Everything went exactly to plan. They crawled into the utility corridor, climbed the air vent and reached the prison roof. Then they clambered down to the rocky ground and began pumping air into a raft that they'd previously made from rubber raincoats. They had even managed to make oars.

What happened next is a complete mystery. The three men disappeared and were never seen again. They were never captured, despite an extraordinary FBI manhunt, nor were their bodies ever found.

Their raft was washed up the following day on Angel Island, some two miles from Alcatraz, and there were footprints leading away from the raft. But there the trail went cold. Did they drown? Did they get away? These are questions that no one has ever been able to answer.

A recent investigation discovered that a car was stolen on the very night of the escape: the prisoners had always intended to make their getaway by car. But despite an exhaustive investigation, detectives are no closer to solving the mystery.

If they survived, the escapees would now be in their eighties. This does not mean that the case has been closed. According to US Marshal Michael Dyke, 'there's an active warrant and the Marshals Service doesn't give up looking for people . . . There's no proof they're dead, so we're not going to quit looking.'

And so the search goes on. The FBI website requests anyone with any information regarding the prison's greatest escape to call (415) 436-7677.

A Lonely Trek Through the Andes

There was a sickening crunch and a violent jerk. The right wing of the plane was ripped off by the mountain peak and flung backwards into the rear of the fuselage. The plane, wildly out of control, smashed into a second peak, which tore off the left wing.

Inside the cabin, the terrified passengers expected the shattered plane to plunge them to their deaths. But the plane's crash-landing miraculously spared some of those on board. The fuselage hit a snow-covered mountain slope and slid downwards before coming to a halt in a deep drift.

As a wall of silence descended over the wreckage, the injured and groaning survivors came to their senses. They were lost in the wilds of the High Andes. But they were alive.

There had been forty-five people on board Uruguayan Air Force Flight 571 when it took off on Friday 13 October 1972. Among the passengers was the Old Christians Club rugby team from Montevideo, en route to Chile.

As the injured survivors clambered from the wreckage they found that thirty-eight of them were still alive, although several were suffering from such injuries that they would clearly not survive for long.

Their pitiful plight soon struck home. They were lost in the snow-bound Andes at an altitude of more than 3,600 metres with no food or winter clothing. Worse still, they lacked any medical supplies – a major handicap given that many of them were suffering from wounds sustained in the crash.

They gathered together the remaining food on board. It did not amount to much: some snacks, a little chocolate and a few bottles of wine. There was nothing to eat on these windswept mountains, nor any animals to hunt.

'At high altitude, the body's caloric needs are astronomical . . .' wrote Nando Parrado, one of the survivors. 'We were starving in earnest, with no hope of finding food, but our hunger soon grew so voracious that we searched anyway . . . again and again we scoured the fuselage in search of crumbs and morsels . . . Again and again I came to the same conclusion: unless we wanted to eat the clothes we were wearing, there was nothing here but aluminium, plastic, ice, and rock.'

It became clear that if they were to survive, they would have to eat their dead loved ones. It was a decision that was not taken lightly. Many of those aboard the plane were strict Roman Catholics who had serious reservations about resorting to cannibalism. But they also knew they had little choice. Unless they ate, they would die.

Among the crash survivors was Roberto Canessa, a young medical student. He was convinced that a small party should try to hike over the mountains and seek help. This would involve a gruelling trek over

68

some of the world's most inhospitable terrain. They would have to climb peaks of almost 5,000 metres. They would also face extreme temperatures with no winter clothing. Worse still, they would have almost no food.

After waiting eight weeks for the temperatures to rise a little, Roberto Canessa and two comrades, Nando Parrado and Antonio Vizintin, set off on their long march. It was 12 December.

The lack of oxygen was their first hazard. The constant climbing left them dizzy and desperately short of breath. The cold, too, was hard to endure. They had made a makeshift sleeping bag, but the nights were nevertheless bitter.

Parrado was the fittest: he reached the peak of the first high mountain before the other two. From the top, he got the shock of his life. He thought they had crashed just a few miles from the Chilean border and was expecting to see some distant signs of civilization. Instead, he saw nothing but a barren vista of ice-bound mountains and valleys stretching for as far as the eye could see.

Only now did the men realize that they had crashed in the middle of the High Andes and were a vast distance from the nearest human habitation.

Aware that the rescue hike would be even more arduous than anticipated, Vizintin chose to head back to the crash site. The others continued on their long trek. For day after day they crossed lonely peaks and valleys. They were freezing at night and constantly starved. But they eventually found a stream that led them out of their frozen hell. After nine days of gruelling marching along the banks of the Rio Azufre, they saw cows – a sure sign of human habitation.

As they prepared to make a fire that evening, Canessa looked up and noticed a man on the far side of the river. He shouted and waved, trying to show that they desperately needed help. Over the roar of the water they heard him shout 'tomorrow'.

The two survivors slept soundly that night, aware that their ordeal was almost at an end. On the following day, the Chilean horseman brought them some bread and hurled it across the river, along with a pen and paper. They wrote down what had happened and flung it back.

The horseman went back to raise the alarm and get help for Canessa and Parrado. Shortly afterwards they were finally rescued and given much needed shelter, food and water.

That same day, 22 December, two helicopters set off for the crash site. Despite atrocious weather they eventually plucked the remaining survivors from the mountain. They were in a desperate state: cold, starving and suffering from extreme malnutrition.

But sixteen of them had survived seventy-two days without food and supplies in one of the bleakest spots on earth.

Part VIII

I'm a Celebrity

One of Captain Loewenstein's secretaries came into my cabin
and handed me a piece of paper on which I read:
Mr Loewenstein has fallen out of the plane.

Pilot Donald Drew, interviewed by *The Times*, July 1928

The First Celebrity Kidnap

At around 10 p.m. on 1 March 1932, nursemaid Betty Gow went to make a final check on twenty-month-old Charles Lindbergh, son of the famous aviator of the same name.

To her surprise, she found that baby Charles was missing from his cot. She went straightaway to seek out his mother, Anne, to see if she had taken him.

Anne didn't have the baby, so Betty went to see Charles, who was in his study.

He didn't have the baby either and he was alarmed to hear that Charles junior was missing from his crib. He rushed up to the nursery to check for himself. Betty was right. The baby was missing.

As he looked around the room his eyes alighted on a white envelope that had been left close to the windowsill. Written in poor English it read:

> Dear Sir! Have 50.000$ redy 25.000$ in 20$ bills 15.000$ in 10$ bills and 10.000$ in 5$ bills After 2–4 days we will inform you were to deliver the mony.

The letter also warned him not to notify anyone of the abduction.

Lindbergh ignored the last warning and immediately called the police. They arrived twenty minutes later.

A thorough search of the kidnapping scene revealed smudged footprints underneath the nursery window. Two sections of ladder had been used to reach the window; these were found near the house.

One of the sections was split, suggesting that the ladder had broken during the descent. There were no bloodstains in or about the nursery, nor were there any fingerprints.

The Lindberghs were understandably distraught and desperate to get their baby back. Charles Lindbergh gave the police investigation every support, but he also made contact with a number of underworld characters in the hope that they would be able to trace his child. Two of these, Salvatore Spitale and Irving Bitz, immediately offered their services. But they also approached the *New York Daily News* in the hope of selling advance information on the baby-snatch.

On 6 March, five days after the kidnapping, Charles received a second ransom note. This increased the ransom demand to $70,000. It was followed by a third and fourth ransom note, at which point a trusted local ex-headmaster named Dr John F. Condon offered his services. He suggested trying to make direct contact with the kidnapper by placing a series of adverts in local newspapers. If the kidnapper responded to his adverts, he could act as an intermediary in any ransom negotiations.

It was a long shot but to everyone's surprise it worked. The kidnapper responded and, from this point on, all his notes were sent directly to Dr Condon.

One of these contained instructions for him to meet with an unidentified man called 'John' at Woodlawn Cemetery in New York. Dr Condon duly went along, met with 'John' and discussed payment of the ransom money. In return, the stranger handed Dr Condon the baby's sleeping suit, proof enough that he had little Charles. When the Lindberghs saw the sleeping suit, they immediately recognized it as belonging to their baby.

After an exchange of yet more notes, Dr Condon once again met with 'John'. He handed over $50,000 and was told that the kidnapped child could be found on a boat named *Nellie* near Martha's Vineyard, Massachusetts. An extensive search and rescue mission failed to find any boat of that name.

On 12 May, almost ten weeks after the kidnapping, the body of a baby was found, partly buried and decomposed, some five miles from the Lindberghs' home. Its head was crushed, there was a hole in the skull and the left leg and both hands were missing.

The body was positively identified as Charles Lindbergh and was cremated, at the Lindberghs' insistence, on the following day. The coroner concluded that the child had been dead for some two months and that the cause of death was a blow to the head.

The New Jersey State police were no nearer finding the murderer, despite offering a ransom of $25,000. They knew that the most likely means of capturing the kidnapper was to ensnare him while trying to spend the ransom money, which had been paid in so-called gold certificates whose numbers had been noted by the police.

One suspicious gold certificate was spotted by a teller at a bank in the Bronx. It had a New York number plate, 4U-13-14-N.Y., pencilled in the margin. This helped police track the bill to a petrol station in Upper Manhattan. The station manager, Walter Lyle, recalled writing down the number because he thought the customer looked 'suspicious'.

The number plate led the police to a blue Dodge owned by a certain Bruno Hauptmann, aged thirty-five, a native of Saxony in Germany. He was arrested and when police searched his home they found almost $2,000 in those same gold certificates.

They also found a great deal of additional evidence. There was a notebook containing a sketch for the construction of a collapsible ladder similar to that found at the Lindbergh home and the wood in his loft was found to be identical to the wood used to make the ladder. They also found Dr Condon's telephone number in his house.

The trial of Hauptmann began in January 1935. He was charged with extortion and murder. The evidence that had been found in his home, together with handwriting samples from the ransom notes, quickly secured his conviction. Although the defence appealed, the verdict was upheld and Hauptmann was electrocuted at 8.47 p.m. on 3 April 1936.

There have been many attempts to prove that he was duped, framed or otherwise innocent, but the most authoritative recent account, written by the former FBI agent Jim Fisher, concludes that 'Hauptmann is as guilty today as he was in 1932 when he kidnapped and killed the son of Mr. and Mrs. Charles Lindbergh.'

Sir Osman of Hyderabad

His personal fortune was said to be more than double the annual revenue of India and he owned enough pearls to pave Piccadilly from one end to the other. His jewels alone were worth a staggering £400 million.

Sir Osman Ali Khan, autocratic ruler of the princely state of Hyderabad, was once the richest man in the world and also a contender for one of the richest people in history.

He was worth more than £2 billion in 1940 and had an array of sumptuous palaces filled with rare and wonderful treasures: oriental carpets, priceless manuscripts and rare gemstones. He shared his wealth with his seven wives, forty-two concubines and vast numbers of children and dependants.

Every statistic about Sir Osman is eye-watering. He ruled a state that was just a fraction smaller than the UK and he held absolute power over the lives of 16 million people.

He had dozens of Rolls-Royces and owned the rare Jacob diamond, valued today at £100 million. He was also a fanatical ally of the British during the Raj and donated all the fighter planes that made up the Royal Flying Corp's 110 Squadron in the First World War.

The British responded by awarding him with the titles 'His Exalted Highness' and 'Faithful Ally of the British Government'.

Sir Osman had succeeded his father as ruler of Hyderabad on the latter's death in 1911. Already fabulously wealthy, he expanded the family coffers by developing the mining industry in the state of Hyderabad. The mines were a rich source of diamonds and other precious stones. The famous Koh-i-Noor diamond came from Hyderabad.

By 1941, Sir Osman had founded his own bank, the Hyderabad State Bank. His fiefdom became the only state on the subcontinent that issued its own currency, quite different from that of the rest of India. Often benevolent, and always erratic, Sir Osman spent much of the family fortune on education, railways and electrification. But there was plenty of spare cash for him to indulge his passion for racehorses, rare cars and regal uniforms.

Huge sums of money were also spent on a lavish beautification programme that included public buildings, a high court, hospitals and the Osmania University. But Sir Osman's real passion remained his palaces, which were scattered across his realm. The biggest were staffed by many thousands of servants, retainers and bodyguards, all jostling for position alongside scheming eunuchs and jealous concubines.

Sir Osman's favourite palace was said to be the Falaknuma, built on a hilltop above Hyderabad with a panoramic view across the city. Known as 'Mirror of the Sky', it was constructed in the classical style out of imported Italian marble.

There was also the Chowmahalla Palace, another rambling edifice that had been started in 1750 and took another 120 years to complete. It became famous for its pillared Durbah Hall, a vast marble salon lit by chandeliers made of Belgian crystal. There were huge drawing rooms, courtyards and an elegant clock tower.

Sir Osman seemed to have had it all: a fortune, palaces and a peaceful dominion that managed to escape integration into the new Indian state. But everything was soon to turn sour. After months of failed negotiations with India, Sir Osman's fiefdom was invaded in 1948. There were five days of fighting before he reluctantly agreed to join the union. His autocratic rule was replaced by India's parliamentary democracy.

A quarter of a century later, Sir Osman's titles were abolished and he was subjected to crippling taxes.

His death in February 1967 was always going to result in a complex battle over inheritance. There were hundreds of would-be claimants to his land and property.

His grandson, Mukarram Jah, was his official successor, but he rapidly found himself in deep financial trouble. He inherited not only huge debts, but also an enormous number of servants, retainers and hangers-on. These included nearly 15,000 palace staff and dependants, along with the forty-two concubines and their numerous offspring.

The family's oldest and most prestigious palace, the Chowmahalla, still had 6,000 employees. Thirty-eight of them were employed solely to dust the chandeliers.

Thus began a complex and highly rancorous legal battle over Sir Osman's fortune, which had shrunk to a mere £1 billion at the time of his death. Mukarram Jah eventually tired of the wrangling and left India altogether. He divorced his first wife, the Turkish-born Princess Esra, and emigrated to Australia, where he became a sheep farmer.

And there the story ended, at least for more than twenty years. But in 2001, Princess Esra returned to India in a bid to sort out her grandfather-in-law's complex will. With the help of a gifted lawyer, the competing claims over the inheritance were finally resolved.

The beautiful Chowmahalla Palace was eventually re-opened as a museum and the Falaknuma became a luxury palace hotel. The many descendants of Sir Osman are now free to come back and reflect on the former glories of their once-noble family.

But these days, they have to pay like everyone else.

The Very Strange Death of Alfred Loewenstein

In the early evening of 4 July 1928, a fabulously wealthy businessman named Alfred Loewenstein boarded his private plane at Croydon Airport. It was a routine flight that would take him across the English and French coastlines before landing at Brussels, where Loewenstein lived with his wife, Madeleine.

Loewenstein was instantly recognizable to the staff at the airport. Indeed he was recognizable wherever he went. He was a spectacularly wealthy entrepreneur: so wealthy that he was widely known as the world's richest man.

Already rich before the First World War, his fortune had increased dramatically in the peace that followed. His various companies provided electric power for developing countries and before long he was being sought out by presidents and prime ministers around the globe.

But he also had many enemies. In 1926, he established International Holdings and Investments, which raised huge amounts of capital from wealthy investors. By 1928, these investors wanted some return on their money. And they wanted it sooner rather than later.

Loewenstein was pleased to be flying home on that July day in 1928. It was a fine evening for flying with scarcely a cloud in the sky. The pilot, Donald Drew, assured him that it would be a smooth flight.

There were a total of six people on the plane, in addition to Alfred Loewenstein. Pilot Drew stood by the doorway of the aircraft as the passengers and crew boarded. The other people in the cabin included Fred Baxter, Loewenstein's loyal valet, and Arthur Hodgson, his male secretary. There were also two women, Eileen Clarke and Paula Bidalon, his stenographers.

In the cockpit were Drew and Robert Little, the aircraft mechanic. The cockpit was a sealed unit with only a porthole connecting it to the rest of the plane. Once the Fokker had taken off, Drew and Little had no direct access to the cabin.

Shortly after 6 p.m., the Fokker FVII, a small monoplane, set off down the grass runway. Within minutes the plane was airborne and climbing to its cruising altitude of 4,000 feet. Before long, everyone on board could see the Kent coastline below. A minute or so later, they were flying over the English Channel.

At the rear of the Fokker's cabin there was a windowless door that led into a small toilet. This room also had an exterior door. This door was clearly marked EXIT and was equipped with a spring-loaded latch controlled from inside. It took two strong men to open it in mid-air, owing to the pressure of the slipstream against it.

Loewenstein spent the first half of the flight making notes. Then, as the plane headed out over the Channel, he went to the toilet compartment at the rear.

According to statements later made by Baxter, ten minutes passed and he had still not returned to his seat. Baxter grew concerned and knocked on the toilet door. There was no answer.

Worried that Loewenstein might have been taken ill, he forced open the door. The toilet was empty. Alfred Loewenstein had disappeared into thin air.

An obvious course of action would have been for the plane to divert to the airstrip at St Inglevert, which lay between Calais and Dunkirk. Here, the pilot could have alerted the coastguard to Loewenstein's disappearance. Instead, Donald Drew landed the plane on what he believed to be a deserted beach near Dunkirk.

In fact, the beach was being used for training by a local army unit. When the soldiers saw the Fokker coming in to land, they began running along the beach to meet it. It took them six minutes to arrive at the stationary plane, by which time the passengers and crew had disembarked.

They were initially questioned by Lieutenant Marquailles, but he was unable to make any sense of what had happened. Pilot Drew behaved particularly strangely, evading his questions for half an hour until finally admitting that they had lost Alfred Loewenstein somewhere over the English Channel.

Drew was next interrogated by a professional detective named Inspector Bonnot. The inspector confessed to being extremely puzzled by what he was told. 'A most unusual and mysterious case,' he said. 'We have not yet made up our minds to any definite theory, but anything is possible.'

He didn't arrest anyone and even allowed the plane to continue its flight to St Inglevert and then back to Croydon.

The ensuing investigation was bungled from the outset. Loewenstein's body was finally retrieved near Boulogne on 19 July, more than two weeks after his disappearance. It was taken to Calais by fishing boat where his identity was confirmed by means of his wristwatch.

A post-mortem revealed he had a partial fracture of the skull and several broken bones. Forensic scientists concluded that he had been alive when he hit the water.

The mystery of how he fell to his death remained unanswered, though there are many theories. Some said the absent-minded Loewenstein had accidentally opened the wrong door and fallen to his death. This was most unlikely, given that it was virtually impossible to open the door in mid-flight.

Others said he'd committed suicide, perhaps because his corrupt business practices were about to be exposed.

A far more plausible and sinister explanation is that Loewenstein was forcibly thrown out of the plane by the valet and the male secretary, possibly at the behest of Loewenstein's wife, Madeleine. She had a very frosty relationship with her husband and was desperate to get her hands on his fortune.

One thing is clear: all six people on board were almost certainly privy to the murder. Indeed, they had probably planned it carefully in advance.

One theory as to why the Fokker landed on the beach was so that a new rear door – already stowed on board the plane – could be fitted to replace the one jettisoned over the Channel. This fits neatly with the story of a French fisherman who recalled seeing something like a parachute falling from the sky at precisely the moment Loewenstein went missing. This 'parachute' was quite possibly the rear door.

If the door and Loewenstein were jettisoned over the Channel, it was the perfect crime. No one was ever charged with the murder, nor even directly accused. As for Loewenstein, he was so unpopular that he ended up being laid to rest in an unmarked grave.

Even his 'grieving' widow, Madeleine, didn't show up. She doubtless had more important matters to attend to, organizing and investing the fortune that she had just inherited.

Part IX

When Stalin Robbed a Bank

He stayed in bed most mornings and shaved slowly in the kitchen with a cut-throat razor. His favourite treat was seed toffee and I bought him some daily.

Recollections of Arthur Bacon, a thirteen-year-old who looked after Joseph Stalin during his 1907 visit to London

The Mysterious Death of Joseph Stalin

Stalin was feeling weak on account of his unusually high blood pressure. He was also complaining of dizziness. Yet his temper was as fiery as ever on the evening of 28 February 1953.

He had invited a few of his closest comrades to his dacha at Kuntsevo, near Moscow. After a few glasses of diluted Georgian wine, he launched a blistering attack on his personal physician, who had urged him to step down as head of the government on account of his poor health.

He then extended his tirade to the prominent Moscow doctors who had recently been arrested on trumped-up charges as part of the so-called Doctors' Plot. Stalin demanded that they make public confessions of their guilt.

Among the guests at the dacha that night was Lavrenti Beria, one of Stalin's most loyal henchmen. He was used to the ill humour of 'The Boss', yet he became deeply alarmed when Stalin unexpectedly turned his fire on those who were present. He lambasted them for basking in past glories and began issuing vague yet ominous threats against them. The implication was clear: Beria and the other guests were next on his hit list.

No one was allowed to leave the dacha until Stalin had given his blessing. But he was in no hurry for them to depart. He kept up his tirade for some considerable time, drinking wine as he pressed home his attack. It was 4 a.m. on 1 March by the time he finally allowed his guests to leave.

Stalin was not left alone in the dacha. There were three duty officers in the building that night – Starostin, Tukov and Khrustalev. There was also the dacha's deputy commandant, Peter Lozgachev. He was to be a key witness in the disturbing events that followed.

The official account of that night records that Stalin spoke to his guards before retiring to his room. 'I'm going to bed,' he told them. 'I shouldn't be wanting you. You can go to bed too.'

But the deputy commandant, Peter Lozgachev, later declared that he never actually heard Stalin speak those words. It was Khrustalev, one of the three guards (and a close comrade of Beria), who brought the message from Stalin. 'Well, guys, here's an order we've never been given before. The Boss said: "Go to bed, all of you, I don't need anything. I am going to bed myself. I shouldn't need you today."'

Khrustalev took Stalin at his word, leaving the dacha as soon as he had passed on the message.

Stalin slept late the next morning. The clock struck eleven, then twelve, and the three men who had stayed behind at the dacha began to get concerned. Starostin turned to Lozgachev and said: 'There's something wrong. What shall we do?'

But there was very little they could do. Stalin had issued categorical orders that he was never to be disturbed when sleeping. The men were expressly forbidden from entering his room.

The guards waited many more hours until the light in Stalin's room was finally switched on. 'We thought, thank God, everything was OK,' recalled Lozgachev.

Yet still there was no movement and by 11 p.m. the guards were once again concerned. When an important parcel arrived from the Central Committee, Lozgachev felt he had the excuse he needed to enter the room. 'All right then,' he said, 'wish me luck, boys.'

He pushed open the door and was horrified by what he saw. Stalin was lying on the floor, soaked in urine and with his right arm outstretched. He was conscious but dazed.

'I said to him: "Should I call a doctor?" He made some incoherent noise – like "Dz . . . Dz . . ."'

Lozgachev called Starostin and the two men lifted Stalin onto the sofa and then phoned Beria and Malenkov, a prominent Politburo member who had also been present the previous evening.

They expected the two men to come immediately, yet four crucial hours were to pass before they pitched up at the dacha. Beria was extremely irritated when he finally inspected Stalin.

'What are you panicking for? The Boss is sound asleep.' He ordered the guards to leave Stalin undisturbed and also warned them that he didn't expect to be called out again.

Lozgachev and Starostin now took matters into their own hands, alerting several key doctors to what had happened, along with other members of the inner circle.

When the doctors finally arrived on the morning of 2 March, at least thirteen hours had passed since Stalin had been taken ill. By now he was vomiting blood and in an extremely serious condition.

'The doctors were all scared stiff,' said Lozgachev. 'They stared at him and shook. They had to examine him but their hands were too shaky.' They eventually concluded that he was suffering from an internal haemorrhage.

Stalin's daughter, Svetlana, was summoned to the dacha when it was realized that he would not recover. 'The death agony was terrible,' she recalled. 'It was a horrible look – either mad or angry and full of fear of death.'

Significantly, she also recorded Beria's jubilant reaction when Stalin finally breathed his last on 5 March. 'Beria was the first to run out into the corridor and in the silence of the hall, where everyone was standing quietly, came his loud voice, ringing with open triumph: "Khrustalev, the car!"'

It was unusual behaviour on the part of Beria, especially given the context. Beria was surrounded by key members of Stalin's inner circle, yet the first person he summoned was Khrustalev, the guard who had originally warned his dacha comrades that Stalin was not to be disturbed.

A possible explanation for Beria's behaviour is to be found hidden in the post-mortem report on Stalin's corpse, a report that has only recently become available. The doctors who conducted the autopsy said that Stalin had suffered a haemorrhage in the brain, the cardiac muscles and the lining of the stomach. They concluded that his known high blood pressure had triggered the haemorrhages.

But modern analysis suggests otherwise. High blood pressure might indeed have caused a brain haemorrhage, but it would not have caused Stalin to vomit blood, nor would it have necessarily provoked the gastrointestinal haemorrhage.

A far more likely trigger for such internal bleeding is the tasteless transparent chemical warfarin, a blood thinner, which had just become available in 1950s Russia. It is now believed that Lavrenti Beria administered warfarin to Stalin's diluted wine on the evening of 28 February.

He had every reason to do so, for he was fearful of being the next on Stalin's hit list. And he later told the Soviet inner circle that they should thank him for killing Stalin. He even bragged to Vyacheslav Molotov, the first deputy minister: 'I did him in. I saved all of you.'

He was aided in his work by Khrustalev, the dacha guard. His warning that the other guards were not to disturb Stalin guaranteed that no one would discover Uncle Joe until it was too late for anything to be done.

Red Frankenstein

In the spring of 1926, an elderly Russian scientist could be seen stepping ashore in the steaming African port of Conakry, in French Guinea. Professor Ilya Ivanov had travelled from Moscow in order to conduct a sensational biological experiment, one that was funded by the Soviet regime and approved by the Soviet Academy of Scientists.

Ivanov was hoping to breed a bizarre human-ape hybrid by means of artificial insemination. If successful, he knew that he would go down in history as one of the greatest scientists of all time. He would also earn himself the adulation of Joseph Stalin.

He had good reason for conducting his experiment in French Guinea: the Institut Pasteur in Paris had offered him free access to the chimpanzees at their facility in the inland town of Kindia. But Ivanov had another reason for travelling to Africa, one that he was keeping to himself. As well as artificially inseminating female chimps, he hoped to inseminate local Guinean women with monkey sperm.

Ivanov had been fascinated by the idea of breeding a human-ape hybrid for many years. He had first discussed it publicly at an Austrian zoology conference in 1910. He had also conducted many experiments on animals, extracting the sex glands of horses in an attempt to produce super-stallions.

Increasingly fascinated by the potential of artificial insemination, he began to play God, breeding a series of strange hybrid animals, the like of which had never been seen before.

He produced a zeedonk (a zebra-donkey cross), a zubron (a bison-cow cross) and endless hybrids of rabbits, rats and mice. By the early 1920s, he was convinced that the blood cells of humans were so similar to those of chimpanzees, gorillas and orang-utans that producing an ape-man hybrid would also be possible.

Ivanov's first trip to Guinea was a failure. None of the chimpanzees were sexually mature enough to breed. He returned to Paris and continued his research alongside the notorious surgeon, Serge Voronoff, who had successfully grafted monkey testicle tissue into ageing men seeking to regain their youthful virility.

The two scientists never once questioned the ethics of these operations. Indeed they dreamed up ever more bizarre experiments. During the long summer of 1926, they succeeded in transplanting a woman's ovary into a chimpanzee called Nova. They then inseminated Nova with human sperm from an unknown donor. But despite all their best efforts she failed to fall pregnant.

In November, Ivanov headed back to Conakry and paid locals to capture a number of mature chimpanzees. He was by now hungry for results and managed, with considerable difficulty, to inseminate three of the chimps.

But he remained convinced that he would have far greater success if he could experiment on humans, impregnating African women with chimpanzee sperm.

He quickly discovered that local women had no desire to take part in his monstrous experiment. So he took the momentous decision to start inseminating them without their knowledge, performing his work during routine gynaecological examinations.

The governor general of French Guinea, Paul Poiret, was horrified when he learned of Ivanov's intentions. He rejected the plan out of hand – before Ivanov had started his work – and made it clear that he would never sanction such immoral behaviour.

Ivanov was bitterly disappointed: the governor general had dealt a big blow to his experiment. A further setback came when his three female chimps failed to conceive. Soon afterwards, the disappointed Russian professor left Guinea for good. He departed with twenty chimps; they were to stock a new ape laboratory being established in the Soviet republic of Abkhazia.

Only four of Ivanov's chimps survived the journey, but they were soon joined by a new contingent that included six more chimps, five orang-utans and twenty baboons. All were supplied by the German firm Rueh.

Astonishingly, Ivanov managed to persuade five Soviet women to volunteer to be impregnated by primate sperm, even though the risks to their health were completely unknown.

But by the time the professor was ready to begin his experiment, the chimps and baboons had all died. The only sexually active survivor was an adult male orang-utan named Tarzan.

Once again, fate was to intervene in Ivanov's work. Tarzan suffered an unexpected brain haemorrhage and also expired. 'The orang has died and we are looking for a replacement,' wrote a distressed Ivanov in a cable to the women volunteers.

By now, his original plan to inseminate African women without their consent had been leaked to the press. Ivanov was first condemned by the Soviet Academy of Sciences, which promptly withdrew its funding. He then fell foul of Stalin, who had been persuaded by scientists that genetic research was bourgeois and imperialist.

On 13 December 1930, Ivanov was arrested by Stalin's secret police and convicted of being a counter-revolutionary. He was banished to Kazakhstan, where he died of a stroke two years later.

Ivanov's bizarre experiment was to be forgotten for more than six decades. It was not until the 1990s that his attempt to breed a human-ape hybrid was rediscovered in the archives. He was immediately dubbed the Red Frankenstein by the Russian press. There were even reports, never substantiated, that Stalin himself had ordered the creation of an ape-man super-warrior.

Although Ivanov's work came to an end with his death in 1932, it was not quite the end of the story. Indeed one aspect of the professor's work continues to this day. His primate laboratory still exists in the republic of Abkhazia, where it is now part of the Abkhazian Academy of Science, although it struggles from chronic underfunding.

After an exchange of scientists in the 1950s, Professor Ivanov's bizarre laboratory-cum-zoo also became the model for the US National Primate Research Centers programme.

The one big difference is that there is no longer any talk of attempting to breed a human-ape hybrid.

When Stalin Robbed a Bank

The two heavily armed carriages rattled slowly into the central square of Tiflis (now known as Tbilisi), the state capital of Georgia. Seated resplendent in one of the carriages was the State Bank's cashier. The other carriage was packed with police and soldiers. There were also numerous outriders on horseback, their pistols cocked and ready.

It was shortly before 11 a.m. on 13 June 1907, and there was good reason for the security. The carriages were transporting an enormous sum of money, more than 1 million roubles (£7 million), to the new State Bank.

Unknown to anyone on board the carriages, the transportation of the money had been brought to the attention of Georgia's criminal underworld. Now, one of its most audacious leaders, Josef Djugashvili – better known as Stalin – was intending to pull off a dazzling heist. The money was urgently needed to finance the Bolsheviks' political movement and Stalin had discussed the planned robbery with Lenin, who had given his approval.

Stalin knew it would require great daring to stage such a coup. He also knew he would need the help of a dependable gang of fellow criminals. These were easy enough to find in Tiflis: Stalin had already been involved in previous robberies and had a trusty band of individuals whose services could be called upon.

The robbery was meticulously planned. Twenty heavily armed brigands loitered in the city's central square, awaiting the arrival of the carriages. Lookouts were posted on all the street corners and rooftops.

A further band was hiding inside one of the taverns close to the square. Stalin had also enlisted the services of two girls, trusted accomplices, who took up position nearby. All were watching and waiting.

Stalin himself remained curiously aloof. In the aftermath of the heist, no one could say whether or not he was actively involved. One witness said that he threw the first bomb from a nearby rooftop, the signal for the attack to begin. Another said he had been merely the architect of the robbery. A third claimed he was at the railway station, preparing to make a quick getaway if things went wrong.

The carriages swung into the square exactly as expected. One of the gangsters slowly lowered his rolled newspaper as a sign to his fellow brigands. Seconds later, there was a blinding flash and deafening roar as Stalin's band hurled their hand grenades at the horses.

The unfortunate animals were torn to pieces. So, too, were the policemen and soldiers. In a matter of seconds, the peaceful square was turned into a scene of carnage. The cobbles were splattered with blood, entrails and human limbs.

As the gangsters ran towards the carriages, one of the horses – maimed but not killed – reared up and began dragging the money-bearing cavalcade across the square. It picked up speed and there was a real danger it would get away.

One of Stalin's men chased after the horse and frantically hurled another grenade under its belly. It exploded beneath the animal, with devastating effect. The horse was shredded and the damaged carriages were brought to a halt.

Before anyone could make sense of what was happening, the robbery began in earnest. Stalin's most faithful accomplice, a bandit named Captain Kamo, rode boldly into the square. The gangsters hurled the banknotes into his carriage and then Kamo took off at high speed. He disappeared before anyone was able to give chase.

The carnage caused by the attack was spectacular. Six people were killed by the grenades and gunfire and a further forty were wounded. Amazingly, none of the gangsters was killed.

The stolen money was taken to a safe house where it was quickly sewn into a mattress and later smuggled out of Georgia.

Neither Stalin nor any of the others involved in the heist were ever caught, even though scores of detectives were sent to investigate. It was the perfect robbery.

But if the crime itself had proved a spectacular success for Stalin, the aftermath was not so triumphant. The stolen roubles included a large number of 500-rouble notes whose serial numbers were known to the authorities. It proved impossible to cash them.

Nevertheless, the robbery was extraordinarily audacious and was to be the making of Stalin. He had proved himself a skilful organizer of men and utterly ruthless in action.

That ruthlessness would come to the fore when he took the reins of power in the Soviet Union. The six innocent civilians killed in Tiflis's main square were not his last victims.

Part X

It'll Never Happen to Me

Smoking is confined to the smoking saloon,
where all accessories for the smoker are at hand
and where there are no restrictions.

The smoking rules for passengers aboard the *Hindenburg*,
kept airborne by 7 million cubic feet of highly flammable
hydrogen gas

Cabin Boy on the Hindenburg

Werner Franz was stocking a cupboard aboard the airship *Hindenburg* when he heard an ominous thud. The airship shuddered violently, pitching all the crockery onto the floor. As he knelt down to pick up the broken plates there was a sickening roar.

Franz looked up and was appalled by what he saw. A massive ball of fire was rushing towards him at high speed. He knew that he would be engulfed by flames.

It was Thursday 6 May 1937, and the giant Zeppelin airship was in the process of docking at its mooring mast at Lakehurst Naval Air Station in New Jersey. The flight from Frankfurt had taken longer than usual due to the strong headwinds in the mid-Atlantic.

Fourteen-year-old Franz, employed as a cabin boy, knew that the *Hindenburg* had originally been scheduled to land in mid-morning. He was hoping he would have time to make a quick tour of New York before re-boarding for the return flight to Germany. But poor weather and thunderstorms had delayed the landing by many hours and it was early evening by the time Captain Max Pruss was able to steer the craft towards its docking station.

It was to be a 'flying moor landing', so called because the airship would drop its landing ropes while still in the air and then be winched down to its mooring.

Franz was busily tidying the kitchens as they came in to land. At 7.10 p.m., he heard the signal for landing stations being sounded throughout the airship.

Ten minutes later, radio operator Franz Eichelmann relayed an order from the control car: six men were to go to the ship's bow immediately. The captain was having difficulty in landing the craft. It was hoped that the weight of the crew would help bring the airship into trim.

Young Franz wanted to join them, because the windows in the bow of the *Hindenburg* offered a magnificent panorama of the ground. But he still had dishes to put away and was obliged to remain in the kitchen.

At 7.17 p.m. the wind suddenly shifted direction, forcing Captain

Pruss to make a sweeping sharp turn. A minute later, he dumped hundreds of tons of water ballast because the airship was still too heavy at the stern end. At 7.21 p.m., the first of the mooring lines were dropped and all seemed well.

A further four minutes were to pass before it became apparent that something was seriously wrong. Several of the crew noticed that the outer fabric of the craft, just above the upper fin, was fluttering in a strange way. There was also a strange blue discharge that looked like static electricity. And then – quite without warning – all hell broke loose.

A massive wall of yellow flame burst from the top fin, ripping through the fabric of the airship at devastating speed.

Franz was jolted by the thud and glanced up, only to see the flame advancing towards him. Before he had a chance to react, he was drenched in cold water. One of the water ballast tanks above him had ruptured, sending gallons of water crashing down on him.

On the ground, a crowd of spectators had gathered to watch the *Hindenburg* docking. There were also a number of journalists at the airbase, for this was the first transatlantic passenger flight of the year (the airship had previously made a return flight from Germany to Brazil).

Among the journalists was Herbert Morrison, a radio broadcaster for WLS Station based in Chicago. He was in mid-broadcast when he saw the *Hindenburg* erupt into a ball of fire.

'It's burst into flames,' he screamed down the microphone, 'and it's falling, it's crashing! Watch it; watch it! Get out of the way. Get out of the way!'

His broadcast would later become famous for the sheer drama of his reporting.

'It's burning and bursting into flames . . . and it's falling on the mooring mast. And all the folks agree that this is terrible. This is one of the worst catastrophes in the world,' he said. 'Crashing . . . it's a terrific crash . . . it's smoke and it's in flames now and the frame is crashing to the ground . . . Oh, the humanity!'

It was a hideous spectacle for the onlookers, but it was far more terrible for Werner Franz and his fellow crew and passengers. Although the burst water tank had soaked Franz's clothes and afforded him some protection from the heat, the fire was rapidly advancing towards him.

Like the other ninety-six passengers and crew Franz was trapped. There seemed to be no way out of the burning Zeppelin.

He looked around in desperation and noticed that there was a hatch just in front of him; it was used to load the airship with food. He couldn't reach it while the ship was hanging at such an angle in the sky, but as the bow slowly began to tilt downwards, he had the presence of mind to pull himself towards it.

The fire was burning like a furnace but Franz kicked the hatch out. As it fell away, he saw the ground hurrying up fast. He leapt from the burning airship, at great risk of having the blazing machine come down on top of him.

Just as he hit the ground, the airship rose up as it rebounded off the landing wheel. Franz ran – ran for his life – and escaped from the wreck at the very moment it crashed back down to the ground.

He was extremely lucky to escape. Many of his fellow crew were not so fortunate. When the rescue teams were finally able to approach the smouldering wreckage and count the cost of the disaster, it was discovered that 22 crew and 13 passengers had lost their lives. One of the ground crew was also killed. Yet it was a miracle that 62 people escaped from the burning inferno.

The *Hindenburg* disaster was never satisfactorily explained, despite numerous investigations. It marked the end of travel by airship: the famous Zeppelin was consigned to history.

Franz eventually got passage by ship back to Germany, arriving on his fifteenth birthday. And there he lives to this day, now in his nineties and the only living survivor of arguably the most spectacular air disaster of the twentieth century.

Attack by Killer Whale

Doug Robertson had just replaced the sextant in its box when he was knocked sideways by a massive crash that came from underneath the boat. 'Sledgehammer blows of incredible force,' is how he later described them, 'hurling me against the bunk.' It was 15 June 1972, a date that was to change the lives of the Robertson family for ever.

Doug quickly lifted the hatch of the family's schooner to see what was wrong. He found himself gazing at a massive hole that had been punched in the hull by a killer whale, 'through which water was pouring in with torrential force'.

It was immediately clear that nothing could be done to save the boat. The *Lucette*, a 43-foot pleasure craft, was sinking. The Robertson family was about to find themselves adrift and alone in the middle of the Pacific Ocean.

The Robertsons had set sail on their round-the-world voyage in January 1971: Doug, his wife Lyn, and their children, Douglas, Neil, Sandy. Also on board was Robin, a twenty-two-year-old graduate who had joined the family in Panama for the leg of the journey that would take them across the Pacific to New Zealand.

They were 200 miles west of the Galapagos Islands, and far from land, when the killer whale attacked. As seawater gushed into the *Lucette*, Doug managed to release the stricken schooner's little dinghy, *Ednamair*, and salvage some food and supplies. It was just as well: within a few minutes the *Lucette* slipped beneath the surface of the Pacific.

Thus began an ordeal of survival that was to last thirty-eight days. The family faced an enormous challenge. They had precious little food or water and were adrift in the middle of the biggest ocean on earth. Few castaways in history have survived such challenging circumstances.

'Breakfast consisted of one quarter-ounce biscuit, a piece of onion and a sip of water,' wrote Doug. But even these scant supplies soon dried up. The family knew that if they were to have any hope of survival, they would have to live off the ocean.

A rain shower brought their first supply of water. Soon after, a huge dorado fish plopped in the bottom of the boat. Doug grabbed his knife and 'plunged it into the head, just behind the eye'. They had secured their first meal from the ocean depths.

The family's ordeal was made worse by the heat of the tropical sun, which beat down on their dinghy. 'We lay gasping in the torrid heat, sucking at pieces of rubber trying to create saliva to ease the burden of our thirst.' By the end of the first week, they were all suffering from skin eruptions caused by constant exposure to saltwater. By the end of the second, they were seriously malnourished.

'Turtle!' yelled one of the boys. They managed to grab it and heave it aboard, plunging a knife into its throat in order to drain the blood. 'I felt', wrote Doug, 'as if I'd just drunk the elixir of life.'

As the days passed, the family grew more confident that they could survive. They made tools, kept themselves reasonably healthy and relied on each other psychologically.

They also became increasingly adept at plucking food from the ocean. They managed to kill thirteen turtles, using a spear fashioned from a paddle, and they even dispatched (and ate) a five-foot shark.

Yet they still faced great dangers, including both extreme heat and terrible cold. Violent storms flung their dinghy from peak to trough and at one point they were caught in a ferocious tempest that threatened to sink their little boat. 'The rain doubled and redoubled until a frenzy of water fell from the sky; above the noise of the storm, I could hear Sandy sobbing and Lyn praying,' wrote Doug, in his account of the disaster.

Lyn, who had trained as a nurse, instigated an undignified (but efficacious) technique to keep them all hydrated with the scant rainwater they had collected in the boat. The water was contaminated by turtle blood and offal and would be poisonous if drunk. Aware of this, she insisted her family take enemas using tubes made from the rungs of a ladder. She knew that if the water was taken rectally, the poisons wouldn't work their way into the digestive system.

On the thirty-eighth day of their ordeal, Doug gazed towards the horizon and caught sight of something. 'A ship!' he said, half wondering if his eyes were playing tricks. 'There's a ship and it's coming towards us!'

It was indeed. The *Toka Maru II* was a Japanese vessel and its crew were astonished by the sight of the wild-looking Robertson family, adrift in their dinghy. They were even more amazed when they heard the account of their ordeal.

After four days aboard the *Toka Maru II*, the Robertsons reached Balboa in Panama, where they landed to a welcome fit for heroes. Their achievement was truly remarkable. They had survived thirty-eight days at sea with almost no water or supplies.

Doug would later write an account of the family's experiences entitled *Survive the Savage Sea*. First published in 1973 – and still in print – it ranks as one of the great survival stories of all time. But according to one of Doug's sons, Douglas, the book only tells half the story.

He, too, has written an account of what happened, *The Last Voyage of the Lucette*, and it's rather more explosive. 'Dad was a bit of a tyrant and we lived under his command,' he says. 'He gave us a good thrashing every time we stepped out of line, and he had hands like spades.'

Doug's larger-than-life personality did much to keep the family alive, but it didn't always make him easy to live with. Douglas reveals that at one point on the voyage his father was washed overboard. Douglas grabbed his legs to save him, but before hauling him aboard he extracted a vow: 'Promise you'll never hit me again, ever . . . or I'll dump you over the side right now.'

His father had little option but to agree.

Template for 9/11

On Christmas Eve 1994, four men in Algerian police uniforms boarded the Air France flight as it sat on the tarmac in Algiers. They said they needed to check the passengers' passports, but their nervous behaviour and the fact they were armed raised the suspicions of one of the flight attendants.

Algerian troops based at the airport were also suspicious: they had not been told that the plane was to be searched. They came out onto the tarmac and surrounded the aircraft, at which point the four 'police' revealed they were terrorists. The plane had been hijacked.

But it was a hijacking with a difference. There were no political demands and no negotiations over hostages. The hijackers had a far more sinister plan for Air France Flight 8969, one that was to provide a blueprint for the al-Qaeda attacks of 11 September 2001.

The first thing they did was to make all the women on board cover their heads. They then broadcast a chilling message over the intercom: 'Allah has selected us as his soldiers. We are here to wage war in his name.'

The airport control tower attempted to negotiate, but the terrorists expressed no interest in talking. All they said – ominously – was that they intended to fly the plane to Paris.

The Algerian authorities refused to remove the landing stairs, thereby preventing the plane from taking off. The hijackers therefore decided to force the issue. They singled out one of the passengers, an Algerian police officer, and shot him in the head.

'Don't kill me. I have a wife and child.' They were his last words.

It was not long before a second passenger was selected to be killed. Bui Giang To, a commercial attaché from the Vietnamese Embassy in Algiers, was also shot in the head.

The leader of the hijackers, Abdul Yahia, was proving to be a ruthless fanatic. Equally terrifying was his sidekick, a man named Lofti. The hijacked passengers would later refer to him as 'Madman' because his behaviour was as violent as it was unpredictable. A third hijacker was known as 'the Killer', because it was he who carried out the shootings.

As night fell the situation grew extremely tense. Everyone was wondering who would be next to be shot. When dawn broke on the following morning, Christmas Day, the French Interior Minister learned some terrible news. A mole in the Algiers Islamic Group, who had planned and executed the hijack, informed him that the group on board intended to crash the plane in Paris. In fact, they intended to fly it into the Eiffel Tower, thereby destroying one of the great symbols of France.

The terrorists once again demanded clearance for take-off. When this was refused, they shot a third passenger. The French government now pleaded with its Algerian counterpart to allow the plane to get airborne, but with only enough fuel to reach Marseilles.

On 26 December, the plane finally took off, touching down in Marseilles at 3.30 a.m. The hijackers demanded an additional 27 tonnes of fuel from the airport authorities, far more than the 9 tonnes needed to reach Paris. The inevitable conclusion was that the plane was to be turned into a deadly fireball.

By now, a crack French military unit was on standby, waiting to storm the aircraft. The moment for action came at 5 p.m., when Yahia was about to order the death of another passenger.

The special forces rapidly moved the air-stairs towards the plane.

They then forced the doors and entered the aircraft in a burst of gunfire. The hijackers returned fire and bullets were soon flying through the cabin. Grenades were also detonated, filling the plane with dense smoke.

The dramatic shoot-out was described by one of the flight attendants as 'an apocalypse'. But it was an effective apocalypse. Within twenty minutes all four hijackers were dead and the 166 passengers and crew were escorted to safety. They were shocked, stunned and exhausted from their ordeal. But at least they were alive.

The hijackers never attained their ultimate goal of destroying the Eiffel Tower. But they provided the template for a very similar, and far more deadly hijacking, on 11 September 2001. On that occasion nearly 3,000 innocent people lost their lives.

Part XI
Escape from Hell

946: number of Allied casualties in Exercise Tiger, the rehearsal for D-Day.

200: number of Allied casualties on Utah Beach on D-Day.

Escape from Auschwitz

The prisoners had been engaged in hard labour for hours. They were working in an area of Auschwitz that lay between the two perimeter fences. It was some distance from the gas chambers, but the stench of death was nevertheless hanging in the air.

In the early afternoon of 7 April 1944, two of the prisoners – Rudolf Vrba and Alfred Wetzler – began surreptitiously monitoring their brutal guards. Both men were extremely nervous, and with good reason. They were about to place themselves in the greatest possible danger.

At around 2 p.m., the two men noticed that the guards had briefly turned their backs. It was the moment they had been waiting for. In a flash, they ran at high speed towards a nearby woodpile. It had a hollowed out space in the middle with just enough room to hide two men. As soon as they were inside their comrades concealed the hole with wooden planks.

Vrba and Wetzler had been prisoners in Auschwitz for almost two years. They had first-hand experience of the brutality of the guards who ran one of the Nazi regime's most notorious extermination camps.

Vrba, a Slovakian Jew, had been arrested by the Nazi authorities while trying to flee his homeland. Sent to Auschwitz, his first job was to dig up corpses that the camp commanders wanted to incinerate.

He soon managed to get himself transferred to one of the camp storehouses, known to inmates as Canada. It contained clothing, food and medicine. Vrba began pilfering supplies and, in this way, managed to keep himself reasonably healthy.

In January 1943, he was transferred to nearby Auschwitz II Birkenau. While there he kept a careful count of the number of prisoners arriving and also noted the belongings of those who had been gassed. In this way, he was able to calculate the number being killed.

By the spring of 1944, he reckoned that 1,750,000 Jews had already been exterminated.

He noticed that most of the arriving Jews brought their possessions with them. This alarmed him, for it implied that they genuinely believed the Nazi fiction that they were going to be resettled. He realized he had to warn Europe's Jewish population that stories of resettlement were a lie: all of them, without exception, were being transported to death camps.

Vrba and Wetzler knew their absence would be noted at the evening roll call. They also knew that the SS would undertake an intensive search that would last for at least three days. They therefore decided to remain in the woodpile, between the perimeter fences, for more than seventy-two hours before making their dash for freedom.

Their plan began well. On 10 April – their fourth night in hiding – they broke out of the woodpile, cut through the outer perimeter fence and made their escape, wearing Dutch clothes and boots they had stolen from the storehouse. They headed directly for the Polish border with Slovakia, some eighty miles to the south.

After a fortnight on the run, they reached the Slovakian town of Čadca, where the two men met the chairman of the underground Jewish Council, Dr Oscar Neumann.

Neumann encouraged them to write a detailed report of everything they had seen and experienced. This they duly did: it would later become known as the Vrba-Wetzler Report. It contained a meticulous description of Auschwitz, along with an account of how prisoners were housed and selected for work. It also provided detailed information about the shootings and gassing of inmates.

The report was soon being circulated in Hungary: shortly afterwards, in mid-June 1944, it reached American intelligence and was made public. Parts of it were broadcast by the BBC World Service.

The report horrified Allied leaders. They appealed to Miklós Horthy, regent of Hungary, to stop the deportation of Hungarian Jews to Auschwitz. They said that he would be held personally responsible for the killings, which had already claimed the lives of 437,000 Hungarian Jews.

Horthy, trapped in an uneasy alliance with Hitler, had to tread with care. Nevertheless, he ordered the deportations to stop with immediate effect.

The news brought some comfort to Rudolf Vrba and Alfred Wetzler. They had risked everything in making their escape from Auschwitz and would have been executed immediately if captured. Instead, their bold dash for freedom had proved the means by which tens of thousands of Budapest Jews were saved from certain death.

Trapped in a Firestorm

The first siren was sounded at shortly after 7.30 p.m. on 23 February 1945. More than 370 British planes were heading towards Pforzheim, a provincial town in south-west Germany. They had already crossed the Rhine and were flying low and fast. The town's inhabitants had less than five minutes to take shelter.

One teenage girl, Hannelore Schottgen, was cycling across town when the sirens sounded. She was immediately stopped by an air-raid warden and ordered into the nearest shelter.

Hannelore did as she was told, descending into a cellar where eight Reich Labour Service girls and a warden had already taken cover. They were huddled around a wireless and listening to the announcement: 'Big groups of enemy planes are coming nearer our area.'

And then, just moments later, the initial attack began. Thump. Thump. Thump. Overhead, hundreds of Lancaster bombers began dropping their bombs. Their aim was not just to destroy the town below, which was wrongly suspected of being a centre for precision bomb-making, but they were also tasked with creating a firestorm that would obliterate the entire historic centre of Pforzheim, along with all its inhabitants.

'All we could hear was bomb after bomb,' recalled Hannelore. 'Screaming and screeching and noises of things breaking down. The whole house seemed to be moving. A bit of ceiling fell in. Was the house going to collapse on top of us? Was it going to bury us alive?'

On the ground above, Pforzheim was a vast sheet of flame. More than 90 per cent of buildings in the town centre were already ablaze. In the eye of the firestorm, the temperature was approaching a staggering 1,600° Centigrade, so hot that metal girders were turned to liquid.

It was a terrifying experience for Hannelore and the other girls. 'The walls were moving and chunks of plaster kept falling into the room. Dust and smoke. We put wet cloths over our mouths and noses.'

There was now a real danger that the building above them would collapse, crushing them all to death. The exit door was blocked by fallen masonry and thick smoke began pouring into the cellar. In desperation, the warden began tapping the wall, hoping to find a weak point and smash his way through to an adjoining cellar. But there was no escape. 'The only thing we can now do is pray,' he said.

As the heat and smoke became insufferable, the warden made one more attempt to break a hole through the cellar wall. This time, a brick gave way. And then a second. And finally the hole was big enough for the girls to squeeze through.

No sooner had they reached the relative safety of the adjoining cellar than the one they had just vacated slumped in on itself, bringing down tons of masonry.

Many of the 17,000 Pforzheimers who died that night had already been killed. Pulverized by bombs, crushed by collapsing buildings or starved of oxygen, their end was terrible but mercifully swift.

The warden looking after Hannelore and the other girls grew increasingly concerned about the risk of being poisoned by toxic gas. He managed to force open a door that led to the street and ordered them all out. Hannelore followed him outside, but the others were too scared and stayed behind.

'Massive flames everywhere – a sea of fire, like a hot tempest. Walls completely red hot and enormous pieces of rubble that were also red hot.'

The streets were blocked with burning rubble and people were running in desperation through the burning streets, looking for a way to escape.

Some ran towards Hannelore: 'You can't get through here,' they said. 'It's too hot.' She turned back, only to be met by more refugees. 'There's no way out,' they cried. 'Just heat, heat.'

The warden now took a decision that was to save both their lives. He told Hannelore to cover her hands and face with her coat and make a charge through the burning street towards the river. It was their last hope of survival.

'Keep going,' he shouted as they ran through the flames. 'Step by step.'

At long last they reached the river and slumped onto the bank where they were shielded from the worst of the heat. Hannelore lay on her front, placed her nose just above the water and focused on getting oxygen into her lungs.

She had made it. She was alive.

Captured by North Korea

Captain Lloyd Bucher was in command of the most sensitive mission he had ever undertaken. On 22 January 1968, a North Korean assassination squad had attempted to kill President Park Chung-hee of South Korea. Now Bucher was ordered to sail his ship, USS *Pueblo*, to the North Korean coast and eavesdrop on the country's secret communications. America urgently required intelligence about one of the most unpredictable regimes in the world.

As the USS *Pueblo* approached Korea's territorial waters, Captain Bucher realized that his ship was being trailed by a North Korean chaser vessel. Soon after, the chaser vessel was joined by four torpedo boats, a second chaser and two MiG-21 fighters. Bucher received a message ordering him to submit to a search or risk attack.

He knew that there was no question of the *Pueblo* putting up a fight. Her ammunition was stored below decks and her machine guns were wrapped in cold weather tarpaulins. At the very time when they were urgently required, the weapons were unprepared for action.

The North Korean vessels attempted to send boarding parties to the *Pueblo*, but Captain Bucher skilfully manoeuvred his ship in order to prevent this. His evading action came at a price. One of the North Korean chasers opened fire with a 57mm cannon, blasting directly into the pilothouse, the nerve centre of the ship. One member of the crew was killed.

The smaller vessels also turned their guns on the *Pueblo*, forcing Captain Bucher to come to terms. Outgunned and surrounded, he had little option but to comply with the North Korean demand to search the vessel. Bucher hurriedly ordered his men to destroy as much sensitive material as possible.

The US Navy authorities based in Kamiseya, Japan, had managed to keep in radio contact with the *Pueblo*. As a result, the commander of the Seventh Fleet was aware of the ship's situation. Yet nothing was done.

The USS *Enterprise* was within striking distance of the *Pueblo* and had four F-4B planes on board. But the captain had neglected to prepare their air-to-surface weapons and it would take almost two hours to get the aircraft into the air, too late to help the *Pueblo*.

Captain Bucher's ship was by now being boarded by men from one of the North Korean vessels. They bound the hands of the American crew and proceeded to blindfold them. The men were then beaten and prodded with bayonets.

The North Koreans took control of the *Pueblo* and manoeuvred her into the country's territorial waters. The vessel was once again boarded, only this time by senior-ranking officials. They ordered the ship to be towed into the port of Wonsan.

It was the beginning of a terrible ordeal for the crew, who were now escorted off their ship and interned in POW camps. During their imprisonment they were starved and regularly tortured.

The treatment got even worse when the North Koreans examined the staged propaganda photographs they had taken and discovered that the American crewmen were sticking one finger up at the camera. Captain Bucher was singled out for particularly unpleasant treatment. He was psychologically tortured and put through a mock firing squad in an effort to induce him to confess to being engaged in espionage.

The North Koreans eventually threatened to execute all of the captives, at which point Bucher reluctantly agreed to 'confess to his and the crew's transgression'. He read out his confession in front of the television cameras, but managed to keep his sense of humour. He repeatedly said: 'We paean North Korea. We paean their great leader Kim Il Sung.'

The North Koreans were delighted by the use of the word paean: they thought that Bucher was venerating their country and leader. In fact, he pronounced it with a strong American accent and was actually saying: 'We pee on North Korea. We pee on their great leader Kim Il Sung.'

The American government eventually admitted that the *Pueblo* had been engaged in espionage and offered an apology. In response, the North Korean regime released the *Pueblo*'s eighty-two crew.

On 23 December 1968, they were taken by bus to the border with South Korea and told to walk in single file across the Bridge of No Return that spanned the frontier.

Eleven months after being taken prisoner, Captain Bucher led his crewmen into the safety of South Korea. As soon as the men were free, the American government verbally retracted its admission of espionage, along with its apology.

USS *Pueblo* remains in North Korean custody to this day. The American government continues to state that the return of the vessel is a priority. But enduring political tensions suggest that the vessel is unlikely to be returned in the foreseeable future.

Rehearsal for D-Day

It was three minutes past two on the morning of 28 April 1944. A flotilla of American warships was approaching Slapton Sands on the Devon coast in south-west England, a crucial practice exercise in advance of the D-Day landings.

Exercise Tiger was a 300-vessel, 30,000-men dress rehearsal for the biggest amphibious landing in history. It would enable Allied commanders to fine-tune their Normandy battle plan.

Angelo Crapanzano was one of those involved in the operation. He was in the engine room of his vessel, named LST 507, when it was suddenly rocked by a tremendous explosion. 'I got this sensation of flying up, back, and when I came down I must have bumped my head someplace and must have been out for a few seconds, because I felt cold on my legs,' he later recalled.

As he recovered consciousness, he wondered if his ship had been hit by a torpedo. This was indeed the case. A German naval squadron had encountered the Allied flotilla by chance and immediately opened fire.

'The ship was burning,' said Crapanzano. '[It] was split in half . . . fire went from the bow all the way back to the wheelhouse.' The sea also was on fire, because the fuel tanks had ruptured and poured oil into the water.

LST 507 was not the only ship to be hit. Crapanzano witnessed a second landing vessel, LST 531, coming under attack. She sank in ten minutes, killing almost everyone on board. A third ship also burst into flames, another victim of the German ambush.

By about 2.20 a.m., the captain of Crapanzano's vessel realized that she was fatally damaged. 'The tank deck was burning fiercely. It [was] just like a gas jet stove. And all the heat going up to the top deck.' The order was given to abandon ship.

Crapanzano braced himself for the forty-foot jump into the sea, hitting the water at high speed and plunging deep beneath the surface. 'It was frigid. It was like unbelievable, unbelievable cold.' But he didn't think of the chill for long. He was too busy trying to escape the burning fuel on the water's surface.

Of the twelve life rafts on the LST, only one had been lowered into the water. It was completely burned, but Crapanzano and ten others managed to cling to it. They desperately kicked themselves away from the ship so as not to get sucked under when it sank.

Crapanzano witnessed scenes that would haunt him for years. 'I saw bodies with arms off, heads off, heads split open, you wouldn't believe what the hell goes on.'

Nine German E-boats had attacked the Allied fleet as it headed for Slapton Sands. Their assault had come hard and fast. Three LSTs were totally crippled and a fourth was badly damaged by friendly fire. The E-boats had got away before the Allies could return fire.

A staggering 638 servicemen were killed in a matter of minutes and many more were flailing around in the burning water, desperately hoping to be rescued. But there was to be no help for Crapanzano and his comrades. The practice landing operation was set to continue, despite the German attack, and the remaining ships pressed on at full speed towards Slapton Sands, leaving the dead and dying in the water.

The beach landings were to prove the setting for the day's second tragedy. General Eisenhower, the Supreme Allied Commander, had ordered that real ammunition be used, in order that men could experience actual battlefield conditions. It was a disastrous decision, one rendered even more dangerous by the fact that the entire exercise was mistimed. The British cruiser HMS *Hawkins* was still shelling the beach as the soldiers stormed ashore, killing a further 308 men. The landings rapidly turned into a bloodbath.

At the same time that men were coming ashore under heavy friendly fire, Angelo Crapanzano was still struggling to keep alive in the icy water. He was acutely aware of the dangers of hypothermia and tried to keep up the spirits of the ten men clinging to the raft.

'I kept saying to them: "Don't fall asleep, whatever you do. If you fall asleep you're dead."'

But one by one they slipped into unconsciousness and were swallowed by the sea. Soon there was no one left alive except for Crapanzano and one of his comrades.

They had been in the water for four and a half hours when Crapanzano noticed a faint light. 'I see this light, going up and down, and it seems to be getting bigger. I immediately assume that help is coming.'

Help was indeed at hand. The light came from LST 515, one of the ships that had belatedly put back to sea in order to search for survivors. The crewmen were scanning the water when they spotted Crapanzano's head. At first they thought it was yet another corpse, but then one of them noticed it move. Crapanzano was still alive.

He was plucked from the sea, wrapped in blankets and eventually transferred to a Dorset hospital where he made a full recovery. It was several days before he learned the full extent of the Slapton Sands disaster. Exercise Tiger had cost the lives of 946 American servicemen.

Everyone involved in the operation was sworn to secrecy. It was vital that the Germans knew nothing of the practice landing. The massive loss of life was also highly embarrassing for the Allied high command, who wanted to keep it firmly under wraps.

And so it remained for many years, an episode of the war that was deliberately expunged from the records. Not until four decades later, in 1984, was a memorial finally erected to the memory of the men who lost their lives in the practice landings for D-Day.

Part XII

Just Plain Weird

Charlie would have thought it ridiculous.

Lady Oona Chaplin, on the theft of her late husband's corpse

Ice Man

Helmut and Erika Simon had been hiking all day in the warm, high-altitude sunshine. It was late in the afternoon of Thursday 19 September 1991, and they were exhausted. Anxious to return to their lodgings, they decided to begin their descent from the frozen peaks of the Ötztal Alps, on the border between Italy and Austria.

They took a short cut, leaving the marked footpath and following a rocky gully that cut a trail down the mountain. It was strewn with ice and meltwater, making the descent treacherous.

As they paused to catch their breath, they noticed something brown in the gully bed. At first they thought it was rubbish left behind by a careless climber, but when they went over to inspect it more closely, they discovered to their horror that it was a human corpse.

He was in a terrible state of decay and still half buried in ice. Only his head, his bare shoulders and a part of his back were jutting out of the glacier. The Simons assumed it was the body of an unfortunate climber who had fallen from one of the surrounding peaks. He lay with his chest against a flat rock and beside him there were several scraps of rolled-up birch.

The couple raised the alarm when they reached the valley below. On the following day, an Austrian team climbed up to the corpse and tried to extract it from the glacier. Using a pneumatic drill, they attempted to break the ice that entombed the lower part of the body. But as the weather worsened they were forced to abandon their efforts.

Several more attempts were made to free the frozen corpse but it was not until the following Monday, four days after the initial discovery, that it was finally hacked from the ice by a specialist team from Innsbruck University's Institute of Forensic Medicine.

The corpse was placed in a body bag, along with numerous pieces of leather and hide, string, straps and clumps of hay. Everything was then flown by helicopter to the town of Vent in the Austrian Ötz Valley, before being transferred by hearse to Innsbruck.

Scientists who examined the corpse knew immediately that it was very old but its identity was as yet unknown. It was some time before they became aware of the extraordinary significance of the find.

The Ice Man, soon to become known as Ötzi, had lain in the mountain gully for fifty-three centuries, protected from decay by ice and snow. His corpse, his DNA, his clothing and the contents of his stomach would provide forensic scientists with an extraordinary glimpse of life some 3,000 years before the birth of Christ.

More remarkable still was the discovery (in 2012) that Ötzi still had intact red blood cells, the oldest blood cells ever identified.

Science was to reveal a great deal about Ötzi, but one key question remained unanswered. How did the forty-six-year-old die? Numerous theories abounded. Some scientists suspected he had succumbed to hypothermia after being caught outside in a winter storm. A few thought that he had been the victim of a human sacrifice.

But the latest research has revealed an even more harrowing story of Ötzi's final hours. His death was violent, bloody and extremely painful, and it was preceded by the slaughter of several other individuals.

It was springtime when Ötzi set out on his fateful final journey and he and his companions had just undertaken a raid on a rival tribal community. The raid had turned violent and Ötzi found himself engaged in hand-to-hand combat. By the time the fight came to an end, his animal-skin clothes and his weapons were smeared with four different types of human blood.

Ötzi was wounded in the fight. The wounds were not fatal but they were certainly serious. He had been stabbed several times while attempting to defend himself against one or more assailants.

A sharp object, possibly a flint-tipped dagger, had punctured the base of his thumb, shredding the skin and muscle down to the bone. He possibly received the wound as he was fleeing up the nearby mountain: it certainly happened soon before he died, for it never had time to form into a scar.

Ötzi pressed on up the mountain, climbing higher and higher. When he looked back, he saw that his assailants were hot on his trail and fast closing the gap. He must have realized that he was in serious trouble and in danger of being caught. He was still clutching his bow, his arrows and his copper axe, but these were to prove useless to him. As he reached an altitude of 3,200 metres (10,500 feet), an arrow struck him so hard that it pierced his left collarbone and punctured a hole in an artery. This led to a massive loss of blood as well as severe internal bleeding.

He collapsed onto the ice still conscious and able to feel an excruciating thumping pain in his chest. The shock of the wound and the blood loss had triggered a serious heart attack.

As he lay there clutching his chest in agony, one of his assailants flipped him onto his stomach and attempted to wrench the arrow from his body. The hole in his artery widened significantly and the internal bleeding proved fatal. Özti's fate was sealed.

It will never be known how long he took to die, but it was probably mercifully fast. His final view would have been a close-up of the dirty ice of the glacier. And then nothing.

The snowstorm came soon after, entombing him in a natural freezer that was to preserve him intact for the next 5,300 years. And there he might have remained into eternity, had it not been for Helmut and Erika Simon.

Stealing Charlie Chaplin

It was a moonless night and the rain was being driven horizontal by the wind. The villagers of Corsier-sur-Vevey, on the shores of Lake Geneva in Switzerland, were already in their beds, unaware that a macabre crime was about to be committed on their doorstep. 1 March 1978 was to be a night of grave-robbery, deception and ransom.

Two criminals dressed in black scuttled into the little village cemetery. One of the men, Roman Wardas, was a twenty-four-year-old petty criminal from Poland. The other, thirty-eight-year-old Gancho Ganev, was from Bulgaria. Together, they had hatched a plot intended to net them a fortune.

The two men stumbled in the darkness as they picked their way through the 400 graves. Most of the tombs were marked with simple wooden crosses, but one was far grander. Sculpted from white stone, it was engraved with the words: 'Charles Chaplin 1889–1977'. The world's most famous comedian, who owned a mansion in the village, had died just two months earlier, on Christmas Day.

As the rain sluiced down, Wardas and Ganev pulled out a pickaxe and started to dig their way around the grave. The soil was still loose, even though the rain had made it wet and heavy. It took them almost two hours to reach their goal.

Shortly after midnight they managed to prise Charlie Chaplin's coffin from its resting place. They heaved it across the churchyard and loaded it into the back of their estate car. They then drove it to a cornfield at the eastern end of Lake Geneva, dug a shallow grave and reburied the coffin. It was the perfect hiding place.

The villagers of Corsier-sur-Vevey noticed that something was amiss early on the following morning. A mound of freshly dug earth and an empty grave was evidence of the terrible crime that had taken place.

'The grave is empty. The coffin has gone,' a police official told the growing number of reporters who began to converge on the village.

At the Chaplin mansion, one of the domestic staff commented: 'Lady Chaplin is shocked. We all are. We can only wonder why; why should this happen to a man who gave so much to the world?'

Why indeed? The crime was a complete mystery. No one came forward to admit to having exhumed the body and for the next ten weeks precious few clues came to light.

Swiss police launched a major investigation. They also asked Interpol to help them solve the crime. But it proved a hopeless task.

In the absence of any hard news, people began to devise theories as to what had happened. Some said that the corpse had been stolen by fanatical admirers. Others said that Chaplin had long expressed a desire to be buried in England.

A third theory revolved around the claim that Chaplin was actually Jewish. This was the story promoted by a Hollywood newspaper, which suggested Chaplin's body had been removed because he was buried in a Gentile cemetery.

The true reason for the crime would not become apparent until May 1978, ten weeks after the body had been stolen. The Chaplin family began to receive strange phone calls demanding ransom money. The blackmailers revealed they had exhumed Chaplin's body and that it would not be returned until they received the massive sum of $600,000.

The two criminals, Wardas and Ganev, were extremely aggressive on the phone. The Chaplins' butler, Giuliano Canese, took the calls on several occasions and was frightened by their threats.

Geraldine Chaplin, the comedian's actress daughter, also took a few of the calls. She was deeply shocked when Wardas threatened to shoot Geraldine's younger brother and sister unless his demands were met.

The family consistently refused to negotiate, forcing the bodysnatchers into a corner. They now lowered their ransom to $250,000.

The police had been monitoring the Chaplin family phone line ever since the empty grave had been discovered. When the two grave robbers announced that they would give their final demand by telephone at 9.30 a.m. on a certain morning, the police monitored all of the 200 telephone kiosks in the Lausanne area.

It was to prove the criminals' undoing. That very morning Wardas was captured making his ransom demand. Ganev was arrested soon after.

The last major hurdle for the police was to find Chaplin's corpse. The two grave robbers had forgotten the place where they had reburied it and it took some time to locate the exact spot. But after two and a half tense months, Charlie Chaplin was back in safe hands.

Wardas and Ganev were convicted of disturbing the peace of the dead. They were also convicted of trying to extract a ransom. Wardas was sentenced to four and a half years of hard labour. Ganev, his inept accomplice, was given a suspended sentence of eighteen months.

Charlie Chaplin's body was taken back to the little cemetery of Corsier-sur-Vevey and given a second burial. This time, his final resting place was to be just that. It was sealed with a thick slab of concrete.

The Man Who Never Died

His heart stopped at exactly 1.15 p.m. on 12 January 1967.

Dr James Bedford, who had been slowly dying of kidney cancer, had finally expired. But his death was to be the starting point of an extraordinary medical adventure. For Dr Bedford had donated his corpse to a team of cryonic scientists. Their task was to preserve it intact in a state of suspended animation, with the aim of one day bringing it back to life.

It sounds like the plot of a horror movie, but James Bedford was a real person with a long-held fascination in cryonics. Almost five decades after his death, his body is still preserved in a deeply frozen state.

Bedford had plenty of warning of his impending demise. As his condition worsened, he had himself moved to a nursing home in California in order that the cryonic procedure of 'suspension' could begin within seconds of his death. It was vital to preserve cell structures before they succumbed to decay.

The Cryonics Society of California had a 'suspension team' on hand, yet they were nevertheless caught by surprise on the day of Bedford's death. Robert Nelson, president of the society, was nowhere to be found and several vital hours were lost before he was able to reach the deathbed.

In the intervening time, the 'suspension' process had been begun by others. Bedford's physician, Dr Able, was present at the moment of death. He immediately began artificial respiration and heart massage in an attempt to keep the brain alive while the body was cooled with ice. To aid this process, heparin was injected into Bedford's arteries to prevent the blood from coagulating.

Within a very short space of time, the corpse had been entirely packed in crushed ice and the internal organs injected with dimethyl sulfoxide, a chemical that prevents cell decay.

Robert Nelson had by now arrived. He attempted to circulate the chemical solution into Bedford's carotid arteries and then pass it through the entire corpse using a bag-valve respirator.

He later reported that within two hours of Bedford's 'deanimation', he was transferred to a foam-insulated box and coated with one-inch-thick slabs of dry ice.

Within forty-eight hours of Bedford's death, Nelson informed the world's media that 'the patient is now frozen with dry ice, minus 79°C, and will soon be stored in liquid nitrogen, minus 196°C'. He was to be kept frozen until such time as medical science would be able to bring him back to life.

Dr James Bedford was not the first person, nor will he be the last, to dream of being resurrected from the dead. As long ago as 1773, Benjamin Franklin expressed his regret at being born into the world 'too near the infancy of science'. He wished to be preserved and later revived in order to fulfil his 'very ardent desire to see and observe the state of America a hundred years hence'.

Others have also dreamed of having their bodies frozen. But it was not until the scientific advances of the 1960s that cryopreservation became a reality.

In the spring of 1991, some twenty-four years after Bedford's death, his corpse was cut out of its sealed cryogenic capsule in order that it could be examined.

The official report revealed that he was in a good state and 'appears younger than his 73 years'. There were a few problems. 'The skin on the left side of the neck is distended . . . [and] there is frozen blood issuing from the mouth and nose.'

The report added that Bedford's eyes 'are partially open and the corneas are chalk-white from ice'. His nostrils were somewhat flattened against his face, 'apparently as a result of being compressed by a slab of dry ice during initial freezing'.

After thorough inspection, Bedford was transferred to a new capsule and placed back into storage in the Alcor Life Extension Foundation in Arizona.

And there he remains to this day, a frozen corpse who hopes one day to be resurrected from the dead.

Part XIII
Die-Hard Nazis

Twenty seconds – and the job was done.

KGB officer Vladimir Gumenyuk, on burning Hitler's remains

How to Survive an SS Massacre

Their last radio contact with brigade headquarters came at shortly after 11.30 a.m. on 27 May 1940. It brought bad news. In the mass retreat of the British Expeditionary Force, the soldiers of the 2nd Battalion, Royal Norfolk Regiment, had inadvertently found themselves cut off from the main body of troops. They were more than thirty miles to the south of Dunkirk and surrounded by elite divisions of the German army.

The men decided to dig themselves into their positions close to Cornet Farm, just outside the village of Le Paradis. They numbered more than a hundred and had a reasonable quantity of guns and ammunition. But they were up against a force that was not only far larger, but also a good deal better equipped.

A barrage of mortar fire began the German attack. The Royal Norfolks fought defensively and with considerable skill, holding their position for the next six hours.

The Germans responded by attacking the farm with even heavier mortars that steadily reduced the farmhouse and surrounding barns to rubble. By 5.15 p.m. the ninety-nine surviving defenders had no more ammunition. Their commander, Major Lisle Ryder, ordered them to surrender under a white flag.

As they emerged from their positions, dazed and shell-shocked, they made a grave error, one that was to cost them dearly. Instead of surrendering to the unit they had been fighting, they accidentally gave themselves up to a fanatical SS Division known as Totenkopf, or Death's Head. This was commanded by Fritz Knoechlein, an SS ideologue with a deep-seated hatred of the British.

Knoechlein had already received the surrender of a small band of Royal Scots. These men were never seen again and were almost certainly murdered in cold blood. Knoechlein now decided on the same course of action for the ninety-nine Royal Norfolks.

The captives were disarmed and marched down the country lane that led away from Le Paradis. Ominously, Knoechlein ordered his men to set up two machine guns in one of the nearby fields.

Among the surrendered British troops was a young private named Albert Pooley. He would never forget the appalling events that were to follow. Indeed Pooley's testimony was to prove crucial when the time for retribution arrived.

'We turned off the dusty French road, through a gateway and into a meadow beside the buildings of a farm,' he recalled. 'I saw – with one of the nastiest feelings I have ever had in my life – two heavy machine guns inside the meadow.'

The guns were pointing directly towards him and his comrades. Suddenly, all hell broke loose. 'The guns began to spit fire . . . for a few seconds the cries and shrieks of our stricken men drowned the crackling of the guns. Men fell like grass before a scythe.'

Pooley himself felt a searing pain in his body and was pitched violently forward: 'My scream of pain mingled with the cries of my mates.' But he was lucid enough to vow to himself that 'if [I] ever get out of here, the swine that did this will pay for it'.

In total, Knoechlein's men killed ninety-seven prisoners-of-war in defiance of all the rules of war. There were two survivors. One was Pooley, who miraculously escaped death even though he was bleeding heavily. The other was Private William O'Callaghan, who also survived the shooting.

The SS forces soon left the scene of the massacre, unaware that two men were still alive. Pooley and O'Callaghan hid themselves in a nearby pigsty and spent the next three days living off raw potatoes and rainwater.

Both were later captured by the Wehrmacht. O'Callaghan was sent to a prisoner-of-war camp in Germany and did not return to England until the war came to an end.

Pooley was marginally more fortunate. He spent three years in a German military hospital recuperating from the appalling wounds he had suffered at Le Paradis. He was eventually repatriated to England in 1943.

He informed the British authorities about the SS massacre but no one believed his account of what had taken place. It was not until after the war, when O'Callaghan corroborated his story, that the authorities swung into action.

In 1947, Knoechlein was tracked down by Allied investigators and charged with having committed a war crime. He pleaded not guilty and claimed that he hadn't even been present at the massacre. But there were two key witnesses who proved otherwise. The evidence of Private Arthur Pooley, along with that of Private William O'Callaghan, was more than enough to convict Knoechlein.

He was found guilty and sentenced to death by hanging: the judge rejected all calls for clemency.

Knoechlein is said to have 'turned grey' when the verdict was read out to the court. But there was nothing he could do to save himself. He was hanged at Hameln Prison on 29 January 1949.

Target America

The men were landed under the cover of darkness, four Nazi saboteurs who were specially trained to destroy civilian targets. Their task was to undertake a series of daring strikes on America's infrastructure, blowing up railway bridges, power stations and tunnels. The aim was to paralyse industrial facilities vital to the American war effort.

Hitler himself had dreamed up the plan to attack America from within. According to Albert Speer, he was obsessed with the idea of 'the downfall of New York in towers of flames'.

But Operation Pastorius was to run into trouble from the very outset and to have an ending no one expected, least of all Adolf Hitler.

The operation began in the small hours of 13 June 1942, when the German submarine U-202 managed to land four Nazi agents at the village of Amagansett on Long Island. They were led by George Dasch, a thirty-nine-year-old saboteur equipped with enough explosives and incendiary devices to wage a two-year campaign of destruction across the United States. His three accomplices were Ernst Burger, an American citizen, Richard Quirin and Heinrich Heinck.

A second party of four men was successfully landed at Ponte Vedra Beach, Florida, a few days later. They were also carrying large quantities of explosives.

All had been specially trained for their mission. Just a few months earlier, in the spring of 1942, they had been sent on an intensive, three-week course at Gut Quenzsee, near Berlin. Military instructors taught them how to use explosives, timed detonators and hand grenades. By the end of May, they were considered ready for action.

The mission got off to an unfortunate start. George Dasch and his Long Island party almost drowned on the night of 13 June while struggling to get ashore in their inflatable raft.

The U-boat that had carried them to the American coastline also got into difficulty. It ran aground in shallow water less than two hundred metres from the shore and it was only due to the skill of the commander, Captain Hans-Heinz Lindner, that it was manoeuvred off the sandbank before the first light of day.

The four saboteurs eventually made it to the beach, where they buried their stash of explosives amidst the sand dunes. Dasch got accidentally separated from the others and was spotted wandering among the dunes by an American coastguard named John Cullen.

When Cullen approached him and started to ask questions, Dasch pretended to be a fisherman. But he realized that his interrogator was not fooled and shoved $260 into his hand, telling him not to breathe a word. Then he ran off down the beach.

Cullen had no intention of keeping silent about his strange encounter. He immediately informed his comrades and they instigated a search of the shoreline. Before long they had dug up four large crates of explosives and some German uniforms that had been buried in the sand. They immediately alerted the FBI, who launched a manhunt for the four suspected terrorists.

Dasch's comrades were still on the beach and they eventually managed to regroup. Dasch then led them inland and onto a train to New York. His hope was to use the city as a base and start their terror campaign as soon as possible.

Shortly after their arrival, Dasch set off alone for Washington in order to make a study of potential targets. But instead of staking out bridges, railways and power stations, he dramatically turned himself in to the FBI.

Why he did this remains unclear. He must have feared that the coastguard would report their encounter of a few days earlier. He must also have known that he would be treated more leniently if he gave himself up.

The FBI initially dismissed him as a madman suffering from a psychological disorder. It was only when he produced the mission's budget of $84,000 (the Florida saboteurs had been supplied with an identical sum) that he was taken seriously. Interrogated for hours, he showed FBI agents the tissues on which he had written down his targets in invisible ink.

Using the information supplied by Dasch, FBI agents soon rounded up his fellow saboteurs in New York (the third, Ernst Burger, had also turned himself in). Shortly afterwards, the four Nazis in Florida were also arrested.

All eight men were put on trial before a military tribunal, on the orders of President Roosevelt. They were charged with violating the laws of warfare and conspiracy to commit sabotage.

All eight were found guilty and sentenced to death. But Roosevelt commuted Burger's sentence to life imprisonment and Dasch's to thirty years, on the grounds that the two men had cooperated. On 8 August 1942, the other six saboteurs were led to the electric chair of the District of Columbia jail.

Dasch and Burger were fortunate to have avoided the death penalty and their luck was to continue. In 1948, President Truman granted them clemency on condition that they were deported to the American Zone of occupied Germany.

With hindsight, the Nazi saboteurs were almost certainly too unreliable to have been successful. Edward Kerling, leader of the Florida team, couldn't resist telling an American friend about his mission. And Herbert Haupt, another of the saboteurs, took some of the money to his Chicago-based father and asked him to buy a black Pontiac sports car.

Hitler was disappointed with the failure of Operation Pastorius. He continued to harbour dreams of destroying America with sabotage and took a keen interest in the development of the so-called 'Amerika rocket', a weapon designed to reach the United States.

But the war was already over by the time such long-range weapons were nearing the production stage.

The Double Life of Doctor Aribert Heim

He was known to his friends and neighbours as Uncle Tarek, a genial and good-looking individual who was a familiar sight in the narrow streets of 1980s old Cairo.

There was just one thing strange about Uncle Tarek. Although he was a keen amateur photographer and rarely stepped outside without having a camera around his neck, he never allowed himself to be photographed.

There was a good reason for this. Uncle Tarek was hiding a dark and terrible secret. His real name was not Tarek Hussein Farid, as he claimed, but Aribert Ferdinand Heim, one of the most brutal and evil of Hitler's henchmen.

An SS doctor stationed at Mauthausen concentration camp, he was infamous for torturing and killing numerous victims, taking a sadistic pleasure in watching their gruesome deaths.

He also performed operations on his prisoners without using anaesthetic, removing organs from healthy inmates and then leaving them to a lingering death on the operating table. He injected various poisons, including petrol, into the hearts of others.

One of his victims, an eighteen-year-old Jewish man, was said to have gone to the camp's clinic with an infected foot. When Heim asked him why he was so fit, he said that he had been a top swimmer.

Heim gave him an anaesthetic, ostensibly in order to operate on his foot. But no sooner was the man asleep than he cut him open, took apart one kidney, removed the second and then castrated him. He then cut off the man's head so that he could use the skull as a paperweight.

Dr Heim was captured by the Americans at the end of the war and briefly imprisoned. But the prison guards were unaware of his crimes and released him shortly afterwards.

Less than a year later, US war crimes investigators were appalled to discover that the man they had set free stood accused of a truly horrific catalogue of murders. According to Josef Kohl, a former inmate at Mauthausen, he was the camp's worst Nazi butcher.

'Dr Heim had a habit of looking into inmates' mouths to determine whether their teeth were in impeccable condition,' said Kohl. 'If this were the case, he would kill the prisoner with an injection, cut his head off, leave it to cook in the crematorium for hours, until all the flesh was stripped from the naked skull, and prepare the skull for himself and his friends as a decoration for their desks.'

Heim kept a very low profile after his release by the Americans, yet he remained in Germany, living in Baden-Baden under an assumed name and working as a gynaecologist.

In 1962, German police discovered his whereabouts after a lengthy investigation and prepared to swoop. Heim was tipped off about his imminent arrest and fled the country that very day. He was never seen in public again. According to his son, Heim drove through France and Spain before crossing into Morocco and eventually settling in Egypt.

It was a clever move. Unlike the majority of Nazis on the run, who ended up in South America, Heim elected to remain in the Middle East. Here, he lived an unassuming life.

He knew that if he was to avoid capture, he needed to construct a convincing new identity for himself. He changed his name to Tarek Hussein Farid and converted to Islam. Each day, he would walk through the Egyptian bazaars to the Al-Azhar mosque. He would also frequent the famous Groppi cafe, where he bought cakes and sweets for the children of his friends.

German and Israeli investigators continued to pursue leads but they always followed the wrong scent, believing that he lived in South America. In fact, Heim was by now living in Cairo with the Doma family, who ran the Kasr el Madina hotel. It was here that he spent the last decade of his life, until his death from cancer in 1992.

His secret double life was not exposed for many years. But in 2009, his old briefcase was discovered and opened. The paperwork revealed that Uncle Tarek and Dr Heim were one and the same person. For although some of his papers were in the name of Tarek, and others in the name of Heim, they all bore the same date and place of birth: 28 June 1914, in Radkersburg, Austria.

Dr Heim's son later confessed that he had learned of his father's whereabouts through his aunt, who is also now dead. He said that he had declined to inform the authorities of his father's existence because he did not want to upset his many friends.

Instead, he buried his father in an unmarked and anonymous grave, where he remains to this day. One of the last of Hitler's butchers, and the most high-profile Nazi to have escaped capture in recent decades, he never paid the price for his hideous crimes.

Part XIV

A Trio of Monsters

He was very affectionate. He loved children.
He loved children a lot.
And for that reason, he had about fifty kids.

Jean Serge Bokassa, one of the many sons of the
'cannibal' Emperor Bokassa

The African Cannibal

He was charged with the most horrific crimes: cannibalism, mutilation, sadism, embezzlement and thirty-eight murders. The ex-emperor of the Central African Republic, Jean-Bédel Bokassa, found himself in the dock in December 1986, two months after returning from exile.

It was reckoning time. He was about to come face to face with those he had tortured when he was the absolute dictator of one of Africa's poorest countries.

Bokassa had seized power in a military coup in 1966, declaring 'a new era of equality' for this landlocked country in central Africa. In fact, there was to be equality for one man only – himself. With the help of Libya and France, he embarked on a thirteen-year orgy of excess.

The opening session of his trial began on 15 December 1986, and took place in the stiflingly hot chambers of the Palais de Justice in Bangui, the capital of Bokassa's former fiefdom. The world's media had turned out in force, eager to report every lurid detail of his grotesque reign as emperor.

Bokassa hired two top French lawyers, aware that he would need the very finest legal team if he were to escape the death penalty.

The sixty-five-year-old former emperor cut a strange figure in court. He wore a smart double-breasted suit, yet his gout-ridden right foot was clad in an open slipper. He followed the proceedings intently, losing his temper on occasions and interjecting strange comments and apologies.

The prosecution witnesses shed much light on his regime of monstrous cruelty. One of his former cooks, Philippe Linguissa, recalled how he had been ordered to prepare a special feast for Bokassa. The main course was a human corpse that the emperor kept stored in his walk-in refrigerator.

Other witnesses described how they had broken into Bokassa's palace shortly after he was ousted from power. They were searching for relatives who had been missing for years and were appalled to find corpses and human limbs stacked in the palace refrigerators.

One female witness testified that Bokassa had executed her husband,

General M'bongo, when he had refused to allow Bokassa to sleep with her. When Bokassa heard her speaking in court, he displayed sudden contrition. 'I take moral responsibility in the death of this general,' he said as he begged the woman's forgiveness.

One of the most damning testimonies came from a group of 27 youngsters, the only survivors of 180 children who were killed in April 1979 after they threw rocks at Bokassa's passing Rolls-Royce. They had been protesting over being forced to wear expensive school uniforms that they were obliged to purchase from a factory owned by one of Bokassa's wives.

Several of the children revealed that Bokassa visited them on their first night in prison and ordered the prison guards to club them to death. They also recounted how he had participated in smashing the skulls of five children with his ebony walking stick.

The trial gave a grim insight into life inside Bokassa's notorious Ngaragba Prison, where inmates routinely had hands and feet chained to the floor. Under prison director Joseph Mokoa, prisoners either died of starvation or were strangled. Some were killed with repeated hammering.

Bokassa continually interjected during the trial. He expressed his dismay at being accused of such appalling crimes. He also denied ever personally ordering the torture of any of his subjects. Nor did he admit to keeping corpses in his palace.

As the evidence against him mounted, he tried to shift the blame away from himself and onto various ministers in his former cabinet. When he came to present his defence, he caused incredulity by stating: 'I'm not a saint. I'm just a man like everyone else.'

As more and more alleged crimes came to the surface, Bokassa grew increasingly angry. At one point, he leapt to his feet and harangued the chief prosecutor. 'The aggravating thing about all this is that it's all about Bokassa, Bokassa, Bokassa! I have enough crimes levelled against me without you blaming me for all the murders of the last twenty-one years!'

On 12 June 1987, Bokassa was found guilty of all charges, with the exception of those relating to cannibalism. There was insufficient evidence to convict him of eating his own subjects. Nor was it ever determined whether or not he served human flesh at a banquet held for French president Giscard d'Estaing. The ex-emperor wept silently as Judge Franck sentenced him to death.

But he was destined to escape the gallows, for his sentence was commuted to life imprisonment in solitary confinement. In 1989, this was reduced to twenty years and in 1993, as part of a general amnesty, Africa's most notorious leader was set free.

In 1996, shortly after proclaiming himself the thirteenth apostle, the former emperor died of a heart attack. He was survived by his seventeen wives and more than fifty children.

The Mad Baron of Mongolia

The bonfires began to light the sky shortly after dusk on 31 January 1921. The Chinese garrison soldiers of Urga (now Ulan Bator), the capital of Mongolia, were horrified to see that the entire city was ringed with fire.

They had known for days that they would soon come under attack from a small band of mercenaries. Now, seeing the number of fires that had been lit, they realized that they were about to face a huge army.

The leader of that army was one of the most monstrous commanders of the twentieth century, a sadistic psychopath with a megalomaniacal streak. His name was Baron Roman Nikolaus Fyodorovich von Ungern-Sternberg and he saw himself as the reincarnation of Genghis Khan. Not only did he want to rebuild a mighty empire in Central Asia, he also intended to destroy Lenin's Bolsheviks and restore a tsar to the throne of Russia.

Over the previous twelve months, the 'Mad Baron' had roved through Central Asia with his freelance mercenaries, attacking towns and villages with impunity. In the chaos that followed the Bolshevik Revolution, the remote outposts of the old tsarist empire were at the mercy of anyone who could raise an army. The Mad Baron, whose eccentricities included a conversion to mystical Buddhism, seized his chance.

Baron von Ungern-Sternberg had been born into a thousand-year-old dynasty of Baltic noblemen who claimed descent from Attila the Hun.

He fought with distinction in the First World War, winning a score of medals for valour. But he also began to display an alarming psychopathic streak, perhaps as the result of a serious sabre wound he had received to his head.

'His broad forehead bore a terrible sword cut which pulsed with red veins,' recalled one who served with him.

At the war's end, he began to recruit a freelance army in order to fight his two principal enemies, Bolsheviks and Jews. His soldiers were either White Russians or Mongolian troops who had been displaced by the occupying Chinese.

One who watched the baron inspecting a batch of new recruits was shocked by his ruthlessness. 'All men with physical defects were shot, until only the able-bodied remained. He killed all Jews . . . hundreds of innocent people had been liquidated by the time the inspection was closed.'

Many of his recruits were homeless and destitute: they joined the Mad Baron in the hope of booty and plunder. In this they were not disappointed. Baron von Ungern-Sternberg sacked a string of towns as he swept across Mongolia.

Anyone who resisted was sadistically punished. Enemies were whipped to death, strangled, roasted alive and tied behind cars. By January 1921, his terrifying army had conquered much of Mongolia and reached the capital, Urga.

Although his fighters were ferocious, they were relatively small in number. As he prepared to attack Urga the baron had fewer than 2,000 men and he faced an enemy that was far more numerous. It was in order to trick the defenders into thinking he had a huge army that he lit numerous bonfires. He was playing a game of psychological warfare, hoping to intimidate them before launching his army on their citadel.

The assault began with a grenade attack on the city gates. Once these gates were destroyed, the baron's men stormed the Chinese garrison and attacked the defenders with machine guns, rifles and bayonets. Some even used meat cleavers. The soldiers then went on the rampage, slaughtering Jews and raping women.

'Mad with revenge and hatred, the conquerors began plundering the city,' wrote one. 'Drunken horsemen galloped through the streets, shooting and killing at their fancy.'

These freelance soldiers unleashed violence and lust on everyone they could find. One poor boy, suspected of being 'Red', was roasted alive.

After three days, the baron ordered the violence to stop. Only Jews continued to be targeted, because 'in my opinion, the Jews are not protected by any law'.

Some three weeks after the city's capture, the Bogd Khan, the hereditary ruler of Mongolia, was restored to his throne. It was part of the baron's policy to restore monarchies to the lands he conquered. In return, he was rewarded with a string of honorary titles.

Military success soon went to the baron's head. He now proclaimed himself Emperor of all Russia and set off northwards towards Soviet territory in order to attack Lenin's Bolsheviks. After initial success, he suffered several serious reverses at the hands of the Red Army.

His magic seemed to have deserted him. As his ragbag army retreated towards Chinese Turkestan, a group of rebellious soldiers turned their wrath on the baron himself. He was shot several times, but not fatally. Bleeding heavily, he rode off into the night and was eventually captured by a Red Army patrol.

He was taken in chains to Siberia where he was tried by a people's court. His fate was never in doubt: Lenin himself wanted him executed. After bragging about his thousand-year-old dynasty and attempting to justify his actions, the Baron von Ungern-Sternberg was found guilty of countless crimes and killed by firing squad.

It was the cleanest death in his long reign of terror.

How to Kill a Dictator

On the morning of 21 December 1989, Nicolae Ceauşescu, Romania's communist leader, addressed the crowds gathered in central Bucharest.

The previous days had seen disturbances in several provincial centres. Now Ceauşescu himself decided to calm the unrest with a conciliatory speech heralding the achievements of communist Romania. To ensure a favourable reception, busloads of workers were driven to Palace Square and ordered (on pain of losing their jobs) to cheer and wave red banners.

His speech was the usual monologue of party rhetoric and it didn't impress the crowd. After eight minutes, they began chanting 'Ti-mi-şoa-ra!' – a reference to the city that had witnessed serious disturbances.

Ceauşescu was stunned. He had been expecting the usual adoring crowd of party faithful. Nothing had prepared him for a hostile and angry reception. In his confusion, he panicked. After attempting to offer concessions, he paused again in mid-speech. The crowd grew increasingly restless. There was the sound of gunfire.

The bodyguard realized that something was seriously wrong and jostled him back into the building just as the situation turned sour.

If he had fled straight away Ceauşescu might have saved his skin. Instead, he chose to remain inside the Central Committee building, unsure how to react to a moment of national crisis. He spent the night sheltering in the building wondering what to do.

On the following morning, 22 December, he attempted to address the crowd once again. This time, rocks were hurled at him and he was forced to flee inside once again. He was now in grave danger of becoming trapped inside the building.

At around 10 a.m., a group of protesters managed to break into the Central Committee building. They overpowered Ceauşescu's body-guards and then headed for the balcony. They were not aware of it at the time, but they came within a whisker of capturing Ceauşescu and his wife, Elena. The couple had escaped into the lift and were now hiding on the roof of the building.

At precisely 11.20 a.m., Ceauşescu's personal pilot, Vasile Maluţan, was ordered to rescue the Ceauşescus by helicopter. He landed with difficulty on the roof of the building and the couple were bundled into the chopper. They were taken to Snagov, some 40 kilometres to the north of Bucharest. For the moment, they were out of danger.

Ceauşescu told his pilot to contact military headquarters and order more helicopters and armed guards. Maluţan did as he was told, only to be informed by his commander: 'There has been a revolution. You are on your own.' He then added the words: 'Good luck!'

Ceauşescu panicked when he heard this and ordered Maluţan to fly to Titu in southern Romania. But Maluţan was by now tiring of helping the Ceauşescus to escape. He sent the helicopter into a series of dives, informing his passengers he was dodging gunfire. A terrified Ceauşescu ordered him to land.

The flight of Ceauşescu and his wife now had to continue on the ground. A car was flagged down and the couple clambered in. But the driver, a doctor, had no desire to help them. He pretended there was engine trouble and told them he could go no further.

A second car was flagged down and the driver, Nicolae Petrişor, said that he had the perfect hiding place, a farming institute on the edge of town. He took them there and once they were safely inside, he locked the door. He then informed local police, who came to arrest the Ceauşescus shortly afterwards. They were taken to a local barracks while their fate was decided in Bucharest.

Less than forty-eight hours after their capture, the head of the newly formed Council of the National Salvation Front signed a decree establishing an Extraordinary Military Tribunal. Its first trial was to be that of Ceauşescu and his wife, held in secret in a shabby lecture hall at the Târgovişte barracks.

The trial began at 1 p.m. on Christmas Day. There were five military judges and two prosecutors. Ceauşescu protested that the proceedings were unlawful and remained defiant. 'I am not the accused,' he snarled. 'I am the President of the Republic.'

His crimes were read out to the court: genocide, sabotage of the economy and a string of other abuses. Ceauşescu merely looked at his watch and said impatiently: 'Let's get this over with.'

The couple were quickly found guilty and – although they did not yet know it – were sentenced to immediate execution. As their hands were roped behind their backs, Elena screamed at her captors: 'Don't tie us up. It's a shame, a disgrace. I brought you up like a mother.'

One of the captors gloated: 'You're in big trouble now.'

Not until they were led outside did they realize they were about to be shot.

'Stop it, Nicu,' screamed Elena. 'Look, they are going to kill us like dogs.'

Three paratroopers had been selected to carry out the execution, using AK-47 automatic rifles. They took a few paces backwards before turning their guns on the couple. 'I put seven bullets into him and emptied the rest of the magazine into her head,' recalled one of the paratroopers.

As the couple slumped to the ground, all the soldiers watching the execution now reached for their guns and began pumping bullets into the hated Ceaușescus.

The execution had been brutal but efficient. The only flaw was the fact that the cameraman arrived too late to film it. But he managed to obtain footage of the two bullet-ridden corpses, which was immediately broadcast to a jubilant nation and world.

Part XV

I Am a Hero

HANS LITTEN TO ADOLF HITLER: You said that no violent actions are carried out by the National Socialist Party. But didn't Goebbels come up with the slogan: 'One must pound the adversary to a pulp'?
ADOLF HITLER TO HANS LITTEN: That's not to be taken literally!

Hans Litten's cross-examination of Hitler, the Eden Dance Palace trial, 1931

Taking Hitler to Court

He was small, plump-cheeked and going bald, a skilful lawyer who had long defended the underdogs of society. Now, in May 1931, Hans Litten was preparing to take on the most formidable foe in his entire career.

In the dock before him stood Adolf Hitler, leader of the Nazi Party, who was accused of waging a systematic and brutal war against the enemies of Nazism. Hans Litten, the chief prosecutor, was determined to prove Hitler guilty.

The Eden Dance Palace trial was to prove one of the most dramatic legal showdowns in history. In the run-up to the case, Litten – who was born of Jewish parents – had grown increasingly appalled by the lawlessness of Hitler and his supporters.

Just a few months earlier, an SA Rollkommando (a small paramilitary unit) had launched a savage attack on a nightclub frequented by communists. Three people were killed and twenty badly injured in a violent brawl that had clearly been planned in advance.

The ensuing police investigation was bungled from the outset and made little headway. The incompetence of the police so infuriated Hans Litten that he took it upon himself to investigate the events of that night in November. He centred his case on four of the injured, convinced that he would be able to secure a conviction for manslaughter against their attackers. If found guilty, the perpetrators of the violence could expect to spend years behind bars.

But Litten hoped to achieve far more than a prison sentence for the men. He wanted to demonstrate that the Nazis were deliberately and systematically using terror tactics to destroy the Weimar Republic. If he could prove this, the days of the Nazi Party were certain to be numbered.

Hitler had already appeared in court the previous September. On that occasion, he had been called as witness in a case against two army officers who had joined the Nazi Party. (At the time, it was forbidden for army officers to be party members.)

Under oath, Hitler had contended that his party operated in accordance with the law. He described its paramilitary wing as an organization of 'intellectual enlightenment'.

His second appearance in court – the Eden Dance Palace trial – was to be a more bruising affair. Litten summoned Hitler to the witness stand on 8 May 1931. He began by contending that SA unit Storm 33, which had attacked the Eden Dance Palace, was a paramilitary unit. Furthermore, he alleged the attack had been undertaken with Hitler's full support.

Hitler was wary of being challenged in court by Hans Litten, for he knew that he was facing a formidable adversary. Litten had a brilliant intellect and a near-photographic memory. He also knew many languages, including English, Italian and even Sanskrit. He was to use all his intellectual resources in his attempt to destroy Hitler's credibility.

Litten repeatedly asked Hitler about the role of the Rollkommando unit. Hitler responded by denying any knowledge of its existence.

He next asked Hitler why, if he preached non-violence, did he allow Goebbels to use the slogan: 'One must pound the adversary to a pulp.'

Hitler was rattled by this and claimed that Goebbels was merely using a metaphor. What he had meant to say, said Hitler, was that the Nazis needed to 'despatch and destroy opposing organizations'.

Litten chipped away at Hitler, constantly reminding the court that Goebbels's violently anti-Semitic propaganda was endorsed by the Nazi Party. He cited Goebbels's revolutionary journal, *The Commitment to Illegality*, as an example of a party-sanctioned publication. The Nazis, he said, were a party dedicated to violence and lawlessness.

As the trial progressed, Litten steadily got the upper hand. He produced scores of examples of Nazi-sponsored brutality and flaunted it before the court. Hitler was enraged. Unable to control his anger, he shot to his feet and started screaming at Litten.

'How dare you say, Herr Attorney, that is an invitation to illegality? That is a statement without proof!'

Just at the moment when Hitler was looking extremely vulnerable, there was a most unexpected development. The pro-Nazi judge suddenly announced that Litten's interrogation had no relevance to the attack on the Eden Dance Palace. He silenced the chief prosecutor, halted the case and then brought the trial to a dramatic close. His intervention saved Hitler the ignominy of being found guilty of sponsoring violence.

Within two years of the court case, Hitler was to find himself Chancellor of Germany. He would never forget the humiliation he received at the hands of Hans Litten. Indeed, he turned an angry shade of red at the very mention of Litten's name. On one notable occasion, he shouted at Crown Prince Wilhelm of Prussia: 'Anyone who advocates for Litten goes in the concentration camp, even you.'

Litten's glittering legal career did not last long after the Eden Dance Palace trial. He had one more attempt at prosecuting the Nazis, in January 1932, but it was no more successful than the last.

He must surely have known that the writing was on the wall. On the night of the Reichstag fire, less than a month after Hitler became Chancellor, Litten was arrested and incarcerated in Spandau Prison. For the next five years he was brutally beaten, interrogated and tortured. In the summer of 1937 he was sent to Dachau concentration camp and realized that the end was near. On 5 February 1938, in the middle of the night, he took his own life.

Hitler was haunted for many years by the memory of Litten's cross-examination. Long after his death in Dachau, he forbade anyone from mentioning Litten's name in his presence.

Lone Wolf

The American marines had crawled through the tropical undergrowth in order to gather intelligence on the Japanese positions. But as they reached the clifftops on Saipan Island, they found themselves blinking in disbelief.

A lone US soldier, Guy Gabaldon, was sitting on the ground surrounded by hundreds of Japanese troops. He had not been taken captive. Rather, he had talked them all into surrendering. Now, he was preparing to lead them to safety.

Gabaldon was something of a legend amongst his comrades. A tough-nosed eighteen-year-old from one of the Spanish neighbourhoods of east Los Angeles, he had already captured dozens of Japanese soldiers.

Now, he had made the biggest haul of his wartime career. More than 800 prisoners sat before him: diehard troops that normally chose suicide over surrender. Gabaldon alone had persuaded them to lay down their arms.

It was an extraordinary act from an extraordinary individual. Toughened by a childhood in a multi-ethnic gang, Gabaldon had picked up Japanese from the family that had cared for him. His language skills were to serve him well in the battle for Saipan.

The capture of Saipan in the Mariana Islands was a vital first step towards any land invasion of Japan. It was the ideal place to establish airfields for the American B-29 Superfortress bombers.

The attack on Saipan began on 15 June 1944, and Guy Gabaldon was one of 128,000 American soldiers taking part. He was only too aware of the danger posed by the Japanese defenders; they were utterly ruthless and had vowed to fight to the death.

Gabaldon found it hard to work in a team. On his first night on the island, he ventured out alone and approached a cave in which he believed Japanese soldiers were sheltering. He shot the guards at the entrance and then yelled in Japanese: 'You're surrounded and have no choice but to surrender. Come out and you will not be killed!' A few minutes later, he had bagged his first two prisoners.

His commanding officer was furious that he had undertaken a solo mission and almost had him court-martialled. Undeterred, Gabaldon repeated the exercise on the following night. This time, he returned with fifty prisoners.

His superiors were so impressed that they allowed him the rare privilege of working as a 'lone wolf', a soldier who planned and undertook his own solo missions.

On 7 July, Gabaldon clambered up to the clifftop caves of Saipan and overheard Japanese soldiers talking about a massive offensive due to take place on the following day. He passed this information back to headquarters, enabling them to successfully halt the Japanese advance.

The day after the advance was stopped, Gabaldon returned to the cliffs and captured two Japanese guards. He persuaded them to enter the caves and talk their fellow soldiers into surrendering. It was a high-risk strategy. Gabaldon was alone and completely defenceless against such a huge number of men.

'It was either convincing them that I was a good guy or I would be a dead Marine within a few minutes,' he later said. 'If they rushed me I would probably kill two or three before they ate me alive. This was the final showdown.'

There were a tense few moments as Gabaldon awaited the return of the guards. Then, from further down the cliffs, he heard the sound of voices. Hundreds and hundreds of Japanese soldiers could be seen walking towards him.

Gabaldon was as nervous as he was excited. 'If I pull this off,' he said to himself, 'it will be the first time in World War II that a lone Marine Private captures half a Japanese regiment by himself.'

The men were extremely jittery but they decided to surrender when Gabaldon assured them they would receive medical treatment. So Gabaldon found himself with 800 prisoners. It earned him the nickname the Pied Piper of Saipan. It also earned him the Navy Cross, the Marines' highest award for valour after the Medal of Honor. 'Working alone in front of the lines,' reads the citation, 'he daringly entered enemy caves, pillboxes, buildings and jungle bush, frequently in the face of hostile fire, and succeeded in not only obtaining vital military information, but in capturing well over 1,000 enemy civilians and troops.'

His greatest moment came many years later, in 1960, when his story was turned into a Hollywood movie, *Hell to Eternity*. He had always seen his role as that of a movie star, even when fighting in Saipan. 'I must have seen too many John Wayne movies,' he said, 'because what I was doing was suicidal.'

Suicidal but highly effective. By the time his combat days came to an end, he had captured more Japanese prisoners than any other soldier. 'When I began taking prisoners it became an addiction,' he said. 'I found that I couldn't stop. I was hooked.'

Fight of the Century

It was a swelteringly hot afternoon. The mercury had risen above 110° Fahrenheit and there was not a whisper of wind. But the heat inside the boxing ring in Reno, Nevada, was nothing in comparison to the fiery atmosphere in the country at large.

Monday 4 July 1910 was to witness one of the most infamous boxing bouts in history, a bout that pitched black against white in a foolhardy attempt to demonstrate white racial supremacy.

The two men in the ring were both undisputed champions. Jack Johnson, the black-skinned son of an ex-slave, had been named World Heavyweight Champion in 1908 after successfully knocking out the Canadian fighter, Tommy Burns. His victory had caused such racial animosity among whites that boxing promoters had begun to search for a 'great white hope' to crush the black upstart.

The boxer they settled upon was the former undefeated heavyweight champion, James Jeffries. He was persuaded out of retirement to challenge Johnson.

He seemed to represent the best hope of knocking Johnson down to size. After all, he had retired undefeated and was famous for his extraordinary strength and stamina. A natural left-hander, he possessed a one-punch knockout power in his left hook.

There was one problem. He was seriously out of shape by the time the fight against Johnson was being arranged. He hadn't fought for six years and was hugely overweight. He also had little interest in the overtly racist fight, being quite content with his new life as a farmer. He was finally tempted back into the ring with the offer of a staggering $120,000 fee.

There was intense nationwide interest in the fight and racial tension increased dramatically in the days beforehand. 'No ring contest ever drew such an attendance,' proclaimed the *Los Angeles Herald*, 'and never before was so many thousands of dollars fought for or paid by the sport-loving public to see a fight.' To prevent any violence in the arena, guns were prohibited, along with the sale of alcohol.

Jeffries remained out of the limelight until the day of the fight, whereas Johnson did everything he could to court publicity. Confident he would win, he appeared for interviews and photo-shoots. He was a celebrity athlete before his time and his constant womanizing (with white women) ensured that he was a regular feature in the gossip columns.

The fight took place in front of 20,000 people. It quickly became apparent that Jeffries was unable to impose his will on the young black champion. Indeed Johnson dominated the fight and, by the fifteenth round, Jeffries had suffered enough. To the horror of the white spectators, he threw in the towel.

Johnson showed no magnanimity in victory. 'I won because I outclassed him in every department of the fighting game,' he said. 'Before I entered the ring, I was certain I would be the victor.'

The outcome triggered race riots across the United States. Johnson's victory had dashed white dreams of finding a 'great white hope' to defeat him. Many whites felt deeply humiliated by the defeat.

According to the *Los Angeles Herald*, 'race rioting broke out like prickly heat all over the country late today between whites, angry and sore because Jeffries had lost the fight at Reno, and negroes, jubilant that Johnson had won.'

Blacks were indeed jubilant, and they hailed Johnson's victory as a boon for racial advancement.

In some cities, the police joined forces with furious white citizens and tried to subdue the black revellers. There were murders, knife-fights and even running gun battles. In New York, violence spread throughout the poorer districts.

There were riots in more than twenty-five states and fifty cities. Thirteen deaths were certified and hundreds were injured, some seriously.

The ringside film *Fight of the Century* caused almost as much controversy as the fight itself. In the aftermath of Johnson's victory, there was a mass white campaign to ban the film. The would-be censors found heavyweight support in former President Theodore Roosevelt, himself an avid boxing enthusiast. He wrote an article supporting the banning of the film.

Not until 2005 did the Library of Congress decree the film to be of such importance that it should be entered on the National Film Register. Almost a century after the most infamous fight in boxing history, the clash between black and white has finally been granted its official place in history.

Part XVI

Rule-Breakers

If you obey all the rules, you miss all the fun.

Katherine Hepburn

The Unbelievable Missing Link

Charles Dawson stared in astonishment at the bone he had just unearthed. It was the fragment of an ancient human skull and it lay undisturbed in a prehistoric gravel bed near the village of Piltdown, in Sussex, England.

Dawson was convinced that he had just stumbled upon the 'missing link' between apes and humans. As such, it was a truly spectacular discovery. Ever since Charles Darwin had formulated his theory of evolution more than half a century earlier, palaeontologists had been searching for evidence of the evolutionary link. Now, Dawson had found it.

On 15 February 1912, he wrote to Arthur Woodward, keeper of geology at the British Museum, informing him that he had found a portion 'of a human skull which will rival *H. heidelbergensis* in solidity'.

The reference to *Homo heidelbergensis* was important. For decades, there had been intense competition between rival palaeontologists, one that was fuelled by nationalist pride. German scientists had only recently unearthed some significant discoveries in the Heidelberg region. French palaeontologists had also met with considerable success and dismissed their British rivals as 'pebble hunters'. Now, it seemed as if Charles Dawson had trumped them all.

Dawson returned to the gravel bed and soon found other objects as well, including more bone fragments and the tooth of a hippopotamus.

He forwarded them all to Arthur Woodward, who conducted a full scientific analysis. He was in no doubt as to the significance of Dawson's find, but expressed caution about publicizing the news. First, he wanted to join Dawson in the gravel pit in the hope of finding yet more pieces in the evolutionary jigsaw.

The two men worked at Piltdown throughout the summer of 1912. They unearthed more skull fragments, a jawbone with teeth and a variety of primitive stone tools, further evidence of Piltdown Man's ancient existence.

Dawson proved particularly adept at finding fragments of bone. Indeed it was he, not Woodward, who found all the most important finds of that summer.

Locals dubbed him the 'Wizard of Sussex', and with good reason. For more than three decades, this unremarkable solicitor with no formal training in either palaeontology or archaeology had made a series of spectacular finds.

Amongst his discoveries were teeth from a previously unknown species of mammal (which was named *Plagiaulax dawsoni* in his honour), three new species of dinosaur (including *Iguanodon dawsoni*), and a new form of fossil plant (*Selaginella dawsoni*).

The British Museum gave him the title of Honorary Collector in recognition of his discoveries and he was elected a fellow of the Geological Society.

It was not long before Dawson's finds came with increasing frequency. He unearthed several curious medieval artefacts, a unique Roman statuette made of iron and an ancient timber boat. These finds brought yet more honours: at the age of just thirty-one, and without a university degree, he was elected a fellow of the Society of Antiquaries. He was now Charles Dawson FGS, FSA.

The British Museum's Arthur Woodward returned to London in order to make a detailed analysis of all the finds that had been unearthed in the Piltdown gravel pit. He became convinced that the skull fragments and jawbone came from the same individual.

He now proceeded to make a reconstruction of the skull, which confirmed what he had believed from the outset: Dawson had indeed found the missing link between apes and humans. The finished reconstruction suggested an early human with a large brain, indicating a level of intelligence that set it clearly apart from the apes. Woodward concluded that the person had lived about 500,000 years ago and he gave it the scientific name *Eoanthropus dawsoni*, Dawson's Dawn Man.

On 18 December 1912, at a packed Geological Society meeting, Arthur Woodward announced to the world the sensational discovery of Piltdown Man. Dawson's find was reported around the globe, with the *Manchester Guardian* getting the scoop: 'The Earliest Man: Remarkable Discovery in Sussex'.

There were sceptics from the very outset. Professor Arthur Keith of the Royal College of Surgeons was unconvinced, especially after the discovery of a canine tooth in the Piltdown jawbone. The professor pointed out that the Piltdown man would not have been able to eat with the combination of teeth that had been found.

His scepticism was greeted with a barrage of criticism. It was said he was motivated by jealousy and ambition.

A further four decades were to pass before the truth about Piltdown Man was finally revealed. In 1953, a *Time* investigation comprehensively demonstrated that Dawson's discovery was a fraud, one that had been designed to deceive the world.

Piltdown Man was actually a composite of three distinct species: a medieval human skull, the 500-year-old lower jaw of an orang-utan and the fossilized teeth of a chimpanzee.

The appearance of great age had been created by staining the bones with a solution of iron and chromic acid. Experts also discovered file-marks on the teeth: someone had modified them to a shape more suited to a human diet.

The identity of the forger was without doubt Charles Dawson himself. Archaeologist Miles Russell of Bournemouth University recently conducted an investigation into his lifetime's discoveries and found that almost forty of them were fakes. He concluded that Dawson's career was 'built upon deceit, sleight of hand, fraud and deception'.

As for Charles Dawson himself, he died in 1916 at the height of his fame, celebrated around the world for his spectacular discoveries.

The World's Most Secret Address

From the outside, it looked like any other military compound. There were a few houses, a couple of huts and the occasional vehicle going in and out. Yet PO Box 1142 was very different from any other army base on American soil.

The PO Box address at Fort Hunt in Virginia was actually an intelligence centre at its most active in the aftermath of the Second World War. It was here that many captured Nazis, including leading rocket scientists and nuclear engineers, were interrogated. In total, more than 4,000 high-ranking prisoners passed through the base. Among them were the rocket scientist Wernher von Braun and the nuclear technician Heinz Schlicke. Prisoners were grilled about Nazi scientific discoveries and developments in weaponry – anything, indeed, that could be of use to the victorious Allies.

The base was in violation of the Geneva Convention but this did not unduly concern the American government. Surviving transcripts and testimonies suggest that human rights were generally respected and torture was never employed. Rather, prisoners were rewarded if they revealed sensitive information. Some prisoners were given gourmet food in order to soften them up.

One of the American interrogators was George Mandel, a twenty-year-old scientist who spoke fluent German. 'My job was to interrogate scientifically trained and experienced Germans,' he explained.

Many of the men were such experts in their field of work that Mandel had trouble understanding them.

'One of them worked on enriching uranium, and I didn't know why anybody would want to enrich uranium,' he later recalled. 'My job was to find out what he was doing and how it was being carried out, and then I reported this to the Pentagon.'

Many of the most senior Nazi scientists were brought to PO Box 1142 as part of Operation Paperclip. This was a highly secretive plan to offer employment in America to hundreds of distinguished German scientists, the aim being to deny the Soviet Union access to the skills of these experts.

Among the prisoners at PO Box 1142 was the brilliant German engineer Heinz Schlicke, who developed the infrared fuses needed to trigger an atomic warhead. His interrogator, John Gunther Dean, said that Schlicke took time to cooperate. 'The war had ended in Europe at that point . . . he was willing to help us, but his wife was in the Russian zone.'

Dean was eventually sent to Europe to find Schlicke's wife and two small children and to reunite the family in America. Schlicke ended up working in America for the remainder of his life.

In the spring of 1945, the camp received its most prestigious German prisoner, the rocket scientist Wernher von Braun. He had developed the V1 and V2 rockets that had reduced parts of London to rubble. When he realized the war was lost, he surrendered to American forces in Bavaria.

The American high command knew the importance of their catch:

Wernher von Braun was at the very top of their Black List – a list of German scientists and engineers targeted for immediate interrogation. He was flown to the United States and interrogated by officers of PO Box 1142.

Each prisoner was assigned a so-called 'morale officer': Von Braun's was a young official named Arno Mayer whose orders were to keep him happy. To this end, he supplied him with magazines and alcohol and even took him and three others on a shopping trip to Washington, DC.

Mayer recalls that the men wanted to buy lingerie for their wives, who were still in Germany.

'We told the sales person what size and so on. And the woman held up a pair of panties. The Germans were appalled. They didn't want nylon underwear,' recalls Mayer. 'They wanted woollen ones that should be long, so as to cover their legs.'

Wernher von Braun was to prove PO Box 1142's most controversial prisoner, especially when it was discovered that he had used forced labour from Mittelbau-Dora concentration camp when building his deadly V1 and V2 rockets.

He could have been tried and condemned at the Nuremberg Tribunal. Instead, the American government decided that his extraordinary brain was too useful for him to be put on trial. He was given a false employment history and his Nazi Party membership expunged from the public record. He was then given security clearance to work in the United States.

Wernher von Braun was eventually given a leading job at NASA. He would reward his adopted country by designing the Saturn V rocket that launched the crew of Apollo 11 on their successful mission to the moon.

Few people ever knew that he had previously been a prisoner at PO Box 1142. Nor did they know that he had once been Hitler's most faithful scientist.

The Man Who Stole the Mona Lisa

He could scarcely believe the ease with which he carried out the crime. On Monday 21 August 1911, an Italian eccentric named Vincenzo

Peruggia walked out of the Louvre with the *Mona Lisa* tucked under his jacket.

No one saw him steal the world's most famous painting; no one even heard him remove it from the wall. He managed to slip out of the gallery unnoticed and take the painting back to his apartment.

The Louvre was closed to the public each Monday, making it the perfect time to undertake the theft. Peruggia entered the museum dressed in white overalls and pretending to be a workman. He then made his way to the gallery where Leonardo da Vinci's famous painting was displayed and simply lifted its box frame off the wall.

None of the Louvre's employees noticed that the painting was missing. Twelve hours after it was stolen the duty caretaker reported to his boss that everything in the museum was in order.

Nobody even remarked on the painting's absence the following morning. Paintings in the Louvre were often removed from the walls, because the museum's photographers were allowed to take them to their studios without having to sign them out.

When the artist Louis Béroud went to look at the *Mona Lisa* that Tuesday morning, he found four iron hooks in the place where she normally hung. He presumed that a photographer had taken her and joked with the guard: 'When women are not with their lovers they are apt to be with their photographers.'

When the painting was still missing at 11 a.m., Béroud made enquiries as to when she would be back. Only now, more than twenty-four hours after Peruggia had removed the *Mona Lisa*, did it dawn on museum staff that she had been stolen.

No one had any idea as to the identity of the thief, nor could they fathom his motive. After all, it would be impossible to sell such a painting.

The Louvre closed for a week as investigations got under way. When the museum finally reopened, there was a massive queue waiting to see the spot where the *Mona Lisa* used to hang. Overnight, this moderately famous painting had become an international icon. Postcards of La Gioconda's face sold around the world. She was also featured on numerous cigarette cards.

The French police made frantic efforts to trace the thief, but all to no avail. Their only clue was a fingerprint on the wall.

And this was the point at which the story acquired a bizarre twist, one that was to implicate Pablo Picasso in the theft. Just a few months earlier, an eccentric bisexual Belgian named Honoré Joseph Géry Pieret had visited the offices of *Le Journal* and sold a journalist a little statuette that he had stolen from the Louvre. He bragged about having sold other stolen statuettes to an unnamed artist friend.

Now, in the aftermath of the *Mona Lisa* theft, the police were informed of Géry's crime and began investigating.

News of the investigation came as an unwelcome surprise to the young Pablo Picasso, then living in Paris. He was an acquaintance of Géry and was fully aware that the statuettes he had bought had been stolen from the Louvre. Worse still, he had used two of them as models for his famous painting *Les Demoiselles d'Avignon*.

The net soon closed in on Picasso and he was arrested by the Paris police. He remained cool under intense questioning. He denied any knowledge of Géry's crimes and said (quite truthfully) that he knew nothing of the *Mona Lisa* heist. He was eventually released and allowed to go free. The police never learned about the stolen statuettes and their Louvre enquiries had reached yet another impasse.

More than two years were to pass before the *Mona Lisa* spectacularly resurfaced. In November 1913 a Florentine antique dealer named Alfredo Geri received a cryptic letter which said: 'The stolen work of Leonardo da Vinci is in my possession. It seems to belong to Italy since its painter was an Italian.' The letter was signed 'Leonardo'.

Geri eventually got to meet 'Leonardo' and to see the *Mona Lisa*. Peruggia even allowed Geri to have the painting authenticated. It was not long before news reached the press that the *Mona Lisa* had been found.

Peruggia was arrested, tried in Florence and found guilty of what was to prove the most spectacular art heist of the twentieth century. He told the court that his sole motive for stealing the picture was to return her to Italy. She was intended as recompense for all the Italian paintings stolen by Napoleon.

The judge viewed Peruggia as a harmless fool. He received a sentence of one year and fifteen days in jail, but this was soon overturned and he was allowed to walk free.

The biggest winner in the whole saga was the Louvre itself. It now found itself with a world-famous painting to hang on its walls. Vincenzo Peruggia's extraordinary theft had turned the *Mona Lisa* from a moderately well-known painting into an internationally recognized masterpiece.

Part XVII

When Lenin Lost His Brain

Now exhibiting at No. 225 Piccadilly, near the Top of the Haymarket, from twelve 'till four o'clock, Admittance 2s. each, THE HOTTENTOT VENUS, Just arrived from the Interior of Africa, The Greatest Phoenomenon ever Exhibited in this Country, whose stay in the metropolis will be but short.

Advertisement for Sarah Baartman,
'The Hottentot Venus', *circa* 1810

When Lenin Lost His Brain

The mould is regularly wiped from his face and his body is occasionally bathed in glycerol to prevent it from rotting. But despite being on display for almost nine decades, Lenin's preserved corpse is in remarkable condition. He looks as if he has drifted into a deep sleep.

But Lenin is hiding a secret, one that is almost invisible to the naked eye. Before being embalmed, scientists sliced open his head and carefully removed his brain in order that it could be studied in microscopic detail. The Soviet regime wanted to know the exact nature of Lenin's genius.

It was an investigation that appalled Lenin's widow, Nadezhda Krupskaya. When her husband died on 21 January 1924, she begged for him to be buried in the plot next to his beloved mother. 'Do not put up buildings or monuments in his name,' she said.

But Lenin's Politburo colleagues strongly disagreed. Indeed, they wanted his corpse to become a permanent monument to the revolution. Felix Dzerzhinsky, chairman of the Lenin Funeral Committee, said: 'If science permits, Lenin's body must be preserved.'

This posed a real problem. There were many known techniques for embalming a body in the manner of the ancient Egyptians, but none that could be guaranteed to preserve Lenin's likeness.

When the distinguished Soviet pathologist Aleksei Abrikosov was asked if it was possible, he replied that 'science today has no such means'. Others disagreed. Vladimir Vorobiev, a professor of anatomy at Kharkov University, argued that 'many anatomical compounds can be preserved for decades; this means we can try and apply them to an entire body'.

The most important organ to be safeguarded was Lenin's brain. It was removed intact from his skull and placed in formaldehyde. For two years no one dared touch it. But in 1926, the German neurologist Oskar Vogt was invited to try to unlock the key to Lenin's supposed genius. Professor Vogt established the Brain Institute in Moscow, with Lenin's organ as the focus of its studies.

The body had meanwhile been placed in the capable hands of Professor Vorobiev, who was given the weighty responsibility of saving

Lenin's flesh from ruin. He was aided in his work by another expert, Boris Zbarsky: both men knew they would be executed if they failed.

Lenin's blood, bodily fluids and internal organs were removed shortly after the brain, as part of the initial embalming process. (The whereabouts of his heart remains a mystery to this day: it seems to have been lost shortly afterwards.)

Once the internal organs had been removed, the corpse was immersed for many weeks in a special solution that contained glycerol and acetate. The dark, mould-like spots that had started to appear on the body were later removed with acetic acid and hydrogen peroxide.

It was essential to keep the eye sockets from collapsing: artificial eyes were inserted into the holes as replacements for the originals. It was also important that the face looked as lifelike as possible. Lenin's eyebrows, moustache and goatee were therefore left untouched. His genitals, too, were left *in situ* (although it goes without saying that they are not on display).

While the body underwent a lengthy embalming process, the brain was given a detailed examination. Professor Vogt had long argued that there was a direct link between brain structure and intelligence. If correct in this assumption, there was no reason why he couldn't map the origins of Lenin's supposed genius.

The professor chopped the brain into four chunks and then had each chunk sliced into 7,500 microscopically thin sections. This required a custom-built brain slicer, not unlike the slicing machines used to cut Parma ham.

Some slices were stained purple and black for study under microscopes. The rest were left untouched in order that future generations might be able to study them.

Vogt and his team of Soviet scientists spent years studying the slices of brain and trying to make sense of their findings. The results of their scientific tests were eventually set down in fourteen volumes bound in green leather and embossed with a single word: LENIN.

But neither the professor's work, nor that of the scientists that followed in his wake, was ever published. It was not until 1993 that Dr Oleg Adrianov, one of the Brain Institute's most distinguished technicians, was finally allowed to publish a paper on Lenin's brain.

There was good reason why the findings could not be made public earlier. Lenin's brain did indeed hold a secret, one so shocking that the Soviet hierarchy was determined to keep it under wraps.

The secret was this: his brain was no different from that of anyone else. 'A brain is like a water melon,' said Dr Adrianov, 'ninety-five per cent of it is liquid.' Although Lenin's brain had unusually large pyramidal neurons, this had no bearing on its internal mechanism. 'Frankly,' said Dr Adrianov, 'I do not think he was a genius.'

And what of the rest of his body? For many years his corpse was under the supervision of Yuri Denisov-Nikolsky. When asked about his macabre job, he confessed to having shaking hands whenever he touched it.

'Not every expert is allowed to restore such treasured historical objects, like a Raphael or a Rembrandt. Those who do it, we tremble. I feel a great responsibility in my hands.'

Boris Yeltsin was the first senior political leader to suggest that Lenin should be buried. He said that following the collapse of the Soviet Union it was no longer appropriate to keep his corpse on show.

But neither he, nor Vladimir Putin, nor any other senior politician has been inclined to remove from display what must surely rank as one of the most macabre tourist attractions in the world.

So there he lies, marble white, wrinkled and sometimes a little mouldy. His brain, meanwhile, is being held in storage a mile or so across town, sliced into 30,000 slivers mounted on glass slides. No one has yet proposed that body and brain should be reunited.

Into the Monkey House

The Bronx Zoo in New York attracted large crowds of visitors whenever newly acquired animals were first put on display. In previous years, it was the elephants and lions that had been the crowd-pullers. Tigers, too, proved extremely popular.

But in September 1906, the zoo's new addition was altogether more alluring. Ota Benga was a pygmy from the African Congo and he had been locked up in the monkey house.

Ota Benga had been brought to New York by an American businessman-cum-missionary named Samuel Phillips Verner. Verner had travelled to the Belgian Congo in 1904 in order to acquire an assortment of African pygmies for display at the St Louis World Fair.

Verner first met Ota Benga while on an expedition deep into the equatorial rainforest. He managed to barter him for a pound of salt and a roll of cloth. Ota Benga was unwilling to leave Africa on his own and managed to persuade a few companions to join him on an expedition to North America. It was a voyage that was to change their lives.

Ota Benga proved an instant (if controversial) attraction at the world fair. He was put on display with other pygmies in the fair's anthropology tent.

Part of the attraction was his strange teeth; they had been filed to sharp points when he was a young boy, as part of a Congolese ritual. Newspapers described him as 'the only genuine African cannibal in America'.

Ota Benga returned briefly to the Congo after the fair but made a second visit to America with Verner in 1906. This time, his treatment was far more injurious. After a brief spell at the American Museum of Natural History, he was moved to Bronx Zoo.

The zoo's director, William Hornaday, was quick to realize the appeal of a 'human savage' on display. Aware that it was controversial, he sought the backing of Madison Grant, the distinguished Secretary of the New York Zoological Society.

Grant thought that it was a brilliant idea: Ota Benga was to live in the monkey house, along with a parrot and an orang-utan called Dahong. The display panel read: 'The African Pygmy, Ota Benga. Age, 23 years. Height, 4 feet 11 inches. Weight, 103 pounds. Brought from the Kasai River, Congo Free State, South Central Africa, by Dr. Samuel P. Verner. Exhibited each afternoon during September.'

In an article for the Zoological Society's bulletin, Hornaday wrote enthusiastically about the zoo's new acquisition: 'A *genuine* African Pygmy, belonging to the sub-race commonly miscalled "the dwarfs". Ota Benga is a well-developed little man, with a good head, bright eyes and a pleasing countenance. He is not hairy, and is not covered by the "downy felt" described by some explorers.'

His presence in the zoo excited controversy from the opening day. Indeed, it was to spark a violent debate about racism, evolution and evolutionary Darwinism.

The *New York Times* initially defended the decision to put him in the monkey house. 'We do not quite understand all the emotion which others are expressing in the matter,' declared their editorial. 'It is absurd to make moan over the imagined humiliation and degradation Benga is suffering. The pygmies are very low in the human scale, and the suggestion that Benga should be in a school instead of a cage ignores the high probability that school would be a place from which he could draw no advantage whatever.'

The debate intensified with every day that passed. White churchmen were dismayed by Ota Benga's presence in the monkey cage, not because it was inhumane but because they felt he was being used to promote Darwin's theory of evolution. This was something that many of them opposed.

African American churchmen were even more appalled by Ota Benga's new home. Pastor James Gordon spoke for many when he said that 'our race, we think, is depressed enough, without exhibiting one of us with the apes. We think we are worthy of being considered human beings, with souls.'

Before long, Ota Benga was released from the monkey house and allowed to wander freely around the zoo dressed in a white linen suit. But this scarcely helped his plight.

Visitors taunted him and tried to poke and prod him. According to William Hornaday, 'he procured a carving knife from the feeding room of the Monkey House and went around the Park flourishing it in a most alarming manner'.

The *New York Times* now changed its tune and joined the growing chorus of dissent about Ota Benga's treatment. The newspaper complained that his time at the zoo had only served to brutalize him. At the end of 1906, he was released from captivity and housed in an orphan asylum in New York.

Ota Benga always dreamed of returning to Africa but it was not to be. When the First World War broke out – and the Atlantic crossing became too dangerous – he despaired of ever making it back to the Congo. Depressed by his experience of life in the 'land of the free', he stole a pistol and shot himself through the heart. He was buried in an unmarked grave in New York.

The American Museum of Natural History retains a life-size cast of Ota Benga's head and shoulders. To this day it is not marked with his name or any indication that he was a human being. The label has just one word: 'pygmy'.

The Human Freak Show

She was forced to squat in front of a jeering mob, a bewildered stranger who was far from home. The crowd stared at her protruding buttocks and oversized vulva before cracking lewd and bawdy jokes.

Sarah Baartman had arrived in England a few weeks earlier, in the autumn of 1810, and had already earned herself unwitting notoriety as the 'Hottentot Venus'. Now, she was displayed (to a fee-paying audience) as a sexual deviant and an example of the inferiority of the black race.

Baartman had been brought to England from Cape Town by a British doctor named William Dunlop. He was fascinated by her large buttocks and genitalia – a common trait in the Khoisan people to whom she belonged – and realized that she had the potential to earn him lots of money. He coerced her into travelling to London with the promise that she would get very rich.

Sarah Baartman's arrival in the capital came less than three years after the abolition of the Slave Trade. She was taken to fashionable Piccadilly, where, outside Number 225, she was exposed to the city's baying crowds.

According to a contemporary account, she was paraded on a two-foot high stage 'along which she was led by her keeper and exhibited like a wild beast, being obliged to walk, stand or sit as he ordered'.

Her promoters had originally intended her to be completely naked, but this proved too risqué. Instead, she was 'dressed in a colour as nearly resembling her skin as possible'. According to *The Times*, 'the dress is contrived to exhibit the entire frame of her body, and the spectators are even invited to examine the peculiarities of her form'. The show's promoters knew what the punters were paying to see: they billed Sarah's genitals as resembling the skin that hangs from a turkey's throat.

The spectacle of an enslaved woman being put on public display courted controversy from the outset. Among the outraged was a young Jamaican named Robert Wedderburn. He knew all too well the horrors of slavery, for his mother had been the slave of a Scottish sugar plantation owner. When she had fallen pregnant, Wedderburn senior had sold her to an aristocrat friend with the proviso that the baby should be free from birth.

Robert's rough upbringing left him with a strong sense of justice. He was appalled by the spectacle of Sarah Baartman being paraded before the crowds. After courting the abolitionist African Association, he petitioned for her release.

In November 1810, the attorney general tried to discover whether 'she was exhibited by her own consent'. Two affidavits were produced which suggested that she had never agreed to be brought to England for public display.

The first affidavit revealed that she had been brought to Britain by people who referred to her as their private property. The second described the degrading conditions under which she was exhibited.

Sarah herself was also questioned. She claimed that she had not been coerced and had been promised half the profits of her travelling tour. But her testimony was flawed and was almost certainly made under coercion.

The attorney general backed the attempt to stop the freak show, but the court ruled that Sarah had entered into a contract of her own free will. The show went on.

After four years on the road, Sarah was moved to Paris where she was sold to a travelling circus. Her promoters made extra money by exhibiting her at society functions where she proved an instant hit with the guests.

At one ball she was dressed in nothing but a few feathers: Napoleon's surgeon general, Georges Cuvier, was fascinated by the sight and began a detailed study of her body.

Sarah eventually turned to alcohol and prostitution and died in 1815, possibly of syphilis. Cuvier managed to acquire her corpse, which he promptly dissected. He then pickled Sarah's genitals and brain, and put them on display, along with her skeleton.

She remained in the Musée de l'Homme until 1974, when public revulsion caused the pickled body parts to be removed. But it was not until 2002, after the intervention of Nelson Mandela, that her remains were finally returned to her native South Africa and given a decent burial.

Sarah was neither the first nor the last person to be displayed as a human freak. Seventy years later, another human specimen found himself being paraded through the streets of London. His name was Joseph Merrick, better known as the Elephant Man.

His skeleton is yet to be buried: it is still housed in the pathology collection of the Royal London Hospital.

Part XVIII
Just Bad Luck

It was just like a mountain, a wall of water
coming against us . . .
I had to swim and crawl to get back to the controls
to put the ship back on course.

Göran Persson, First Officer on the *Caledonian Star* when the
ship was hit by a 90-foot freak wave

Freak Wave

On Boxing Day 1900, the Scottish supply ship SS *Hesperus* dropped anchor close to the Flannan Isles, a windswept group of islands near Scotland's Outer Hebrides. The vessel had come to deliver essential supplies to the three lighthouse keepers who had been left on the island some three weeks earlier.

The *Hesperus*'s crew were expecting the usual welcome: two of the keepers normally rowed out to greet the arriving vessel while the third raised a flag as a sign that all was well. But on this occasion, there was no sign of any rowing boat and no raising of the flag. Captain Harvie gave a blast on the ship's siren and awaited a response. There was none.

More intrigued than alarmed, he ordered two of his crew – Joseph Moore and Second Mate McCormack – to row ashore in the ship's boat.

When the men landed at the island they shouted greetings to the keepers. There was no reply. All they heard was the echo of their own voices. As they made their way towards the lighthouse, they grew increasingly concerned. There was no sign of any life and the lighthouse's outer door was locked.

Moore had a set of keys and now proceeded to unlock the building. With trepidation he pushed the creaking door and stepped inside. Silence. He called the men's names. There was no one. James Ducat, Thomas Marshall and Donald Macarthur had mysteriously disappeared.

Moore looked around and took a mental note of everything he saw. The clock on the inner wall had stopped working. There was no fire in the grate and the three beds were empty. A meal had been left uneaten on the table. It was as if the men had been spirited away.

The three keepers had been ferried to the Flannan Isles on 7 December 1900. They had been accompanied by Robert Muirhead, the Superintendent of Lighthouses, who wanted to make a routine inspection of the building and check that the place was well supplied.

This was important, for the Flannan Isles were one of the loneliest spots on earth. They stand some twenty miles to the west of the Outer Hebrides, a place so forlorn that the rotating lighthouse crews were rarely left for more than a few weeks. Longer stays on the island had been known to drive men mad.

Once he was satisfied that all was well, Robert Muirhead had helped the three outgoing keepers onto his ship, wished the new team luck and then bade them farewell. He was the last person to see them alive.

In the week that followed Muirhead's departure, the island was kept under close telescopic observation from the Outer Hebrides. It had long been arranged that if an emergency arose, the keepers were to hoist a large flag. A boat would then be sent to the island to bring help.

It was a system that worked but imperfectly. The island was often obscured by banks of swirling sea mist and the distance from the Outer Hebrides was such that it meant accurate observation was almost impossible.

For several days following the arrival of James Ducat and his team, the island was enveloped in thick fog and the lighthouse was invisible for much of that time.

The lamp itself was easier to see, especially at night. It was glimpsed on the evening of 7 December, a sign that all was well, but then obscured by bad weather for the next four evenings. It was sighted again on 12 December. After that, it was not seen again.

Three days after the last sighting, a vessel named the SS *Archtor* passed close to the island. Captain Holman looked for the light in the night sky but saw nothing. He was concerned that something was wrong and immediately raised the alarm.

Atrocious weather prevented the SS *Hesperus* from reaching the island until Boxing Day, when Moore and McCormack finally managed to row ashore. When they found the lighthouse to be empty, they searched the rocky island for the three keepers. They were nowhere to be seen.

Moore and McCormack rowed back to the *Hesperus* in order to inform Captain Harvie of the men's mysterious disappearance. The captain, in turn, signalled the mystery to the Northern Lighthouse Board.

'A dreadful accident has happened at the Flannan,' he wrote. 'The three keepers, Ducat, Marshall and the Occasional [Macarthur] have disappeared from the island. Poor fellows must have been blown over the cliffs or drowned trying to secure a crane or something like that.'

An investigation was soon under way, led by Superintendent Muirhead. After a detailed search of both the lighthouse and island, he was able to piece together a story of what might have happened to the men. It was one that few were prepared to believe.

Muirhead felt sure that everything had been running smoothly until the afternoon of 15 December. The principal lighthouse keeper, James Ducat, had compiled weather reports until the 13th, and had also written draft entries for 14 and 15 December. These revealed that there had been a storm on 14 December, followed by a surprising calm on the next morning. After that, there were no more entries. In the aftermath of that calm, something had gone seriously, fatally wrong.

Muirhead's inspection of the island proved most revealing. He found that the lighthouse and its outbuildings had sustained considerable damage, so much so that some of these buildings had been structurally weakened. The jetty was badly warped and the iron railings had been strangely contorted, as if a giant fist had wrenched them apart. One of the storehouses, built to withstand winter storms, had been washed clean away.

When Muirhead examined the upper levels of the lighthouse, he found something so bizarre that it was almost impossible to explain. The lighthouse ropes, usually stored at ground level, had become snared on a crane that stood 70 feet above sea level.

Muirhead could only offer two hypotheses as to what might have happened and neither seemed particularly plausible. Either the three men had been blown off the cliffs – a conjecture that did nothing to explain the snared ropes – or they had been swept off the island by what Muirhead referred to as 'an extra large sea'. What he meant, but declined to say for fear of ridicule, was a gigantic freak wave.

Few people countenanced such an idea at the time of the disaster. Freak waves were believed to exist only in novels, poems and sailors' fertile imaginations. It was deemed impossible that Muirhead's 'extra large sea' could have swept the men to their deaths.

But it is now known that freak waves (not to be confused with tsunami or tidal waves) do exist and can be immensely destructive. In 2001, the expedition ship *Caledonian Star* was hit by a 90-foot wall of water that seemed to arise from nowhere. It struck the ship with such force that the bridge windows were shattered and the ship's electricity wiped out. The crews of other vessels have described similarly destructive waves. They are caused by the conjunction of high winds and strong currents that produce an underwater surge. Given the right atmospheric conditions, this can be forced upwards to create a truly violent natural phenomenon.

It will never be known for certain what happened to the unfortunate men on the Flannan Isles. But it seems likely that they were swept off their rocky home by a huge wave – at least 70 feet in height – that then sucked them into the undertow and carried them to a watery grave.

Japan's Deadly Balloon Bomb

Pastor Archie Mitchell had promised his wife, Elsie, a treat. Both of them were tired of reading newspaper articles about the war in the Far East. On Saturday 5 May 1945 Archie suggested a day of escapism, driving up into the mountains of southern Oregon and having a picnic.

Elsie was delighted by the prospect and even happier when Archie offered to bring along five children from their local church. Elsie was heavily pregnant and the idea of taking the youngsters on a special outing had particular appeal.

They set off by car in late morning and were soon winding through spectacular mountain scenery. The children were restless in the crowded car and wanted to hike across the hills. Archie suggested that Elsie lead them on foot to Leonard Creek, a well-known beauty spot, while he drove round in the car. It would enable him to start preparing the lunch.

The children were delighted and waved their goodbyes before setting off into the forest. Archie meanwhile drove to Leonard Creek and began installing the picnic.

It was while he was unpacking the sandwiches that he heard shouts from a couple of the children. Running towards him, breathless with excitement, they said they had found a strange balloon lying on the ground just a short distance away.

Archie warned them not to touch it in case it was dangerous. He promised to come and inspect the balloon just as soon as he had finished preparing the picnic.

As he was setting off to see what they had found, the ground beneath him was suddenly rocked by a tremendous explosion. A series of shockwaves ripped through the undergrowth, filling the air with dust. A plume of black smoke could be seen rising above the trees.

Archie rushed to the scene, only to find the trees shredded and charred. But worse, far worse, was the fact that twenty-six-year-old Elsie, together with the five children, Dick Patzke, fourteen, Jay Gifford, Edward Engen and Joan Patzke, all thirteen, and Sherman Shoemaker, eleven, were sprawled on the ground and covered in blood. On closer inspection – and to his absolute horror – he saw that all of them were dead.

He had no idea what had happened and could only assume that the 'strange balloon' had somehow exploded. Only later did he discover that Elsie and the children had been the victims of a balloon bomb, a devastating new weapon that the Japanese were intending to drop on North America in massive quantities.

This Japanese bomb represented a terrible new threat. Unpredictable and highly explosive, it also had the potential to disperse biological agents across the length and breadth of the country.

It was the brainchild of Major General Sueyoshi Kusaba, head of the Japanese Army's secret Number Nine Research Laboratory. The technical work was supervised by a gifted scientist by the name of Major Taiji Takada.

Their idea was strikingly simple: to use the winter jet stream to carry bomb-laden balloons from Japan to North America, where they would land and explode, causing widespread destruction. Better still, from the Japanese point of view, they would instil fear into the American population at large.

Research revealed that the jet stream could carry a large balloon at high altitude across the 5,000 miles of Pacific Ocean in about three days. But there were some technical hurdles to be overcome if the balloons were to be successful.

The most pressing problem was the fact that they were filled with hydrogen, which expanded in the warmth of the sunshine and contracted in the cool of night. To prevent this from happening, the balloon had to be fitted with special altimeters programmed to jettison ballast if the balloon descended too low. Once the prototypes had been successfully tested, the balloon project got under way in earnest.

There was enormous potential for destruction. Each balloon carried a massive incendiary bomb as well as high-explosive devices that could target cities and (in the dry heat of midsummer) forests.

In the first week of November 1944 the first wave of bombs was launched. Chief scientist Takada was there for the lift-off. 'The figure of the balloon was visible only for several minutes following its release,' he later recalled, 'until it faded away as a spot in the blue sky like a daytime star.'

The initial wave of balloons landed and exploded in no fewer than seventeen states, as far apart as Alaska, Texas, Michigan and California.

General Kusaba was hoping that 10 per cent of his balloons would reach their target destination: with more than 9,000 on the production line, this represented a significant threat to the United States.

America soon awoke to the dangers of this devastating new weapon, which struck at random and without warning. Fighter jets were scrambled to intercept the balloons but they met with little success. Japan's wonder-weapon flew extremely high and fast and fewer than twenty were shot down from the sky.

Balloons soon started landing and exploding right across America. News of their existence was kept secret: the Office of Censorship ordered newspapers not to mention the bombings lest they create widespread panic.

Japan was meanwhile reporting massive damage to American property. One article claimed as many as 10,000 casualties in a single raid.

In truth, the balloons prove less effective than the Japanese had hoped. Nor were they particularly accurate: the vast majority landed on farmland or in the sea.

Japan's scientists worked tirelessly to increase the accuracy of the bombs and they also developed biological and chemical weapons that could be attached to the balloons and dropped onto American cities.

Given time, they might well have proved successful. But all the major technological breakthroughs came too late. The war was almost at an end and Japan was itself about to be the target of a devastating new weapon. The only known fatalities of the Japanese balloon bombings were Elsie Mitchell and her picnic party of five schoolchildren.

Archie's life was ruined by what had happened: he had lost his wife, his unborn baby and his young parishioners. But his woes were not yet at an end. In 1960, while serving as a missionary in Vietnam, he was captured by the Viet Cong.

He disappeared without trace and was never seen again.

Never Go to Sea

On a sparkling winter's day in 1826, a young Englishwoman named Ann Saunders boarded a vessel that was sailing from New Brunswick in Canada to Liverpool.

She was looking forward to the Atlantic voyage: the outward journey had been a delight and the return seemed set to be the same. 'We set sail', she later wrote, 'with a favourable wind and the prospect and joyful expectations of an expeditious passage.'

There were twenty-one people on board, including Ann's close friend Mrs Kendall, the wife of the captain.

The *Francis Mary* had been at sea for almost three weeks when, on the first day of February, she was hit by a ferocious storm. 'About noon, our vessel was struck by a tremendous sea, which swept from her decks almost every moveable object.' Ann looked on helpless as one of the mariners was washed overboard. He was extremely fortunate to be plucked from the water by his comrades.

Worse was to come. As the storm increased in intensity it lashed at the timbers and pitched the vessel from peak to trough. Ann watched in terror as a monstrous wave emerged from nowhere, slamming against the side of the vessel and striking with such force that it ripped away a part of the hull.

Water gushed into the hold, flooding the storage areas and threatening to drag the ship down. The *Francis Mary* was already listing heavily when another huge wave struck the vessel and flipped her upwards through forty-five degrees. Everyone on board clung to the rigging and slowly pulled themselves up towards the forecastle, the only part of the ship that remained above the waterline.

Still she didn't sink. Indeed, she had stabilized at an erratic angle in the water, heaving up and down in the heavy swell.

Several of the crew now made a desperate attempt to descend into the waterlogged interior and rescue whatever provisions they could. At great risk to their lives they clambered below decks and managed to drag out 50 pounds of bread and biscuit, along with a few pounds of cheese. It was precious little sustenance for everyone on board, especially as they were exposed to the full fury of an Atlantic winter.

It was not long before they began to die. James Clarke was the first to succumb: he breathed his last on 12 February and his body was hurled overboard.

Next to die was John Wilson. His death coincided with the last of the biscuit rations being consumed. After a brisk debate, the crew and passengers took the momentous decision to keep themselves alive by eating him.

Ann Saunders watched stoically as Wilson's corpse was roughly dismembered and then chopped into manageable chunks. 'It was cut into slices, then washed in salt water, and after being exposed to and dried a little in the sun, was apportioned to each of the miserable survivors.'

Ann was of a genteel disposition and could not bring herself to eat human flesh. She refused to take her portion. But after twenty-four hours of further starvation she 'was compelled by hunger to follow their example'.

She noticed that the group act of cannibalism changed the dynamics of life aboard the stricken vessel. 'We eyed each other with mournful and melancholy looks,' she said. Each person had become a potential meal.

Men now began to die every day. When Sailor Moore succumbed to exposure they feasted on his liver and heart. Henry David and John Jones were the next to expire, followed by several of the cabin boys. One of them died 'raving mad, crying out lamentably'. All were dismembered and consumed by the surviving crew.

Several barrels of water had been rescued in the aftermath of the storm. These now ran dry, driving those on board to 'the melancholy distressful horrid act (to procure of their blood) of cutting the throats of their deceased companions a moment after the breath of life had left their bodies'.

Miss Saunders watched aghast as her female companion Mrs Kendall munched through the brains of one of the seamen. When the last morsel was finished, she turned to the others with dripping fingers and declared it 'the most delicious thing she ever tasted'.

The next death weighed particularly heavily on young Ann. James Frier was a youthful admirer of hers, one who had plucked up the courage to propose marriage in the terrible days that followed the storm. Ann had accepted without hesitation and promised to tie the knot as soon as they reached England.

Now, as young James slipped from unconsciousness into death, she had little choice but to eat him. She described herself as being 'so far reduced by hunger and thirst' that she was obliged 'to suck the blood as it oozed half-congealed from the wound inflicted upon his lifeless body'.

Several more of the crew expired in the days that followed Frier's death and soon there were only six people left alive. When a vessel was finally sighted on the horizon − it was the HMS *Blonde* − all six were on the verge of death.

The captain of the *Blonde* was horrified to discover that those aboard the *Francis Mary* had kept themselves alive by gorging on their crewmates. He was even more appalled to discover that the ship's ropes were festooned with thin slices of human flesh left to dry in the stiff sea breeze. Yet he took pity on the gaunt survivors and rescued them from their waterlogged vessel.

The *Blonde* finally arrived in England in April 1826 with Ann and five others. Although deeply shaken by her ordeal, Ann was relieved to have survived a voyage that had killed fifteen of her travelling companions. And she remained surprisingly philosophical about having eaten her fiancé.

'I think that I witnessed more of the heavy judgements and afflictions of this world than any other of its female inhabitants,' she said.

Part XIX

Not Quite Normal

We, Norton I, by the Grace of God Emperor of the
Thirty-three states and the multitude of Territories
of the United States of America, do hereby dissolve the
Republic of the United States.

Emperor Norton's 1860 decree dissolving the
United States government and
replacing it with an absolute monarchy

Eiffel's Rival

It was the crowning achievement of his career. Gustav Eiffel was feted in France as a national hero at the 1889 inauguration of his famous tower.

Among the few who did not appreciate his Paris skyscraper was a fervent English patriot by the name of Edward Watkin. He resented the Eiffel Tower for one simple reason: it stood more than five times higher than Britain's most celebrated monument, Nelson's Column. And that, he felt, was a deep insult to national pride.

Yet Watkin was not a man to nurse his grievances. He vowed to do everything in his power to construct a British tower that would be taller, bigger and more spectacular than anything the French could build.

Watkin had made his fortune in railways, building extensive networks in England, India and the Belgian Congo. Immensely energetic and ambitious, he was always looking for ways to increase his fortune.

He reasoned that if his planned mega-tower was built in Wembley Park, a stretch of unused wasteland in the north-west of London, then his own Metropolitan Railway could be used to transport the thousands of annual visitors that would surely flock to the site.

Watkin was convinced that he was onto a winning idea and now launched his competition to build a British tower – one that would overshadow Gustav Eiffel's monument. 'Anything Paris can do, London can do better!' was his war cry.

By the end of 1889, architects from across the world were working on designs for a tower that would be taller and more spectacular than Eiffel's. There was to be a prize of 500 guineas for the best-designed entry.

The project fired the public imagination and gained a great deal of publicity. Watkin's Metropolitan Tower Construction Company became a byword for national pride. With more than a hint of mischief, Watkin even approached Gustav Eiffel and asked if he would care to submit an entry.

Eiffel politely declined. 'If I,' he said, 'after erecting my tower on

French soil, were to erect one in England, they would not think me so good a Frenchman as I hope I am.'

It was not long before a variety of designs began to arrive on Watkin's desk: they came from Italy, Sweden and Turkey, along with many local ones.

Watkin was disappointed to discover that many of them were eccentric flights of fancy. One, named Ye Vegetarian Tower, was submitted by the London Vegetarian Society. It came complete with hanging vegetable gardens. Another, the so-called Tower of Babel, was so vast that it had a road and railway leading to the top. The most extraordinary design of all – a tower far taller than Eiffel's – was to be built entirely of glass.

As Edward Watkin leafed through the numerous entries, he realized there was only one design that stood any practical chance of being built. It was made of open metal latticework and rose to a point at the top. Standing upon four legs (the original design had six) it was in every respect an exact copy of the Eiffel Tower. The only difference was that it was 87 feet taller.

It was selected as the winning entry and building work began immediately. By 1891, the gigantic foundation holes in Wembley Park had been plugged with concrete and work began on the 3,000-ton tower itself.

Work began well. It had soon reached a height of more than 60 feet and curious Londoners began to flock to see the beginnings of what was being called Watkin's Tower.

Edward Watkin claimed it would be finished by 1894. But this proved wildly optimistic. When the surrounding park was opened to the public in that year, the tower was still only 155 feet high.

Some 100,000 people came to visit the stump. Most were extremely disappointed to see a partial replica of Eiffel's architectural triumph. Only 18,500 bothered to buy a ticket to ascend to the first (and only) level.

At the end of 1894, Edward Watkin's workmen downed their tools. The Metropolitan Tower Construction Company had run out of money and the general public no longer had any enthusiasm for a project that seemed increasingly pointless.

The tower was abandoned shortly afterwards. For the next thirteen years, Watkin's folly remained as an embarrassment on the London skyline, a rusting and derelict eyesore.

By the time it was finally blown up in 1907, Edward Watkin was dead and Britain had signed the Entente Cordiale with France. Anglo-French rivalry was set aside – for the time being.

Emperor of the United States

He reigned for more than two decades, an autocratic monarch with absolute powers over one of the most powerful countries on earth. Emperor Joshua Norton I declared himself supreme ruler of the United States in 1859: his avowed intention was to restore stability and integrity to a country he felt was falling into ruin.

Emperor Norton might easily have been dismissed as a harmless eccentric, were it not for the fact that he had a large number of supporters. Promoted by the newspapers of San Francisco, his decrees and proclamations soon became known across the entire nation.

His reign began on 17 September 1859, when he issued a proclamation to the Californian papers: 'I declare and proclaim myself emperor of these United States.' He immediately called for a public meeting of representatives of all the different states in America, signing his declaration: *Norton I, Emperor of the United States*. (He soon added *Protector of Mexico* to his title.)

The proclamation was greeted with wild enthusiasm by the people of California. They loved his conviction, his authority and his bluntly worded decrees. Norton's clever manipulation of the media rapidly turned him into a nationwide celebrity.

He achieved even greater publicity when he awarded himself autocratic powers. With a theatrical flourish, he formally abolished the House of Congress in the second week of October 1859.

'Open violations of the laws are constantly occurring,' he declared, 'caused by mobs, parties, factions and undue influence of political sects. The citizen has not that protection of person and property to which he is entitled.'

The following year, Emperor Norton called upon the army to forcibly depose the elected members of Congress, in order that he might consolidate his tenuous grip on power.

The army and congress chose to ignore Norton, but he was not disheartened. In 1862, he ordered the Protestant and Roman Catholic churches to ordain him emperor. (They also ignored him.) Seven years later, he abolished the Democratic and Republican parties. Shortly afterwards, he issued a decree forbidding religious warfare.

Norton was a familiar figure in his imperial capital of San Francisco. He wore a naval uniform with gold epaulettes and a spectacular beaver-skin hat bedecked with rosettes and peacock feathers. Twirling a cane in his hand, he liked to patrol the streets, chatting with his subjects and inspecting the state of public buildings.

He had been a penniless bankrupt in the years before proclaiming himself emperor. It was his flair for showmanship that had rescued him from ruin. Dressed in his unmistakable regalia, he was invited to dine in San Francisco's finest restaurants. In return for free food, he would reward them with an imperial seal: 'By appointment to his Imperial Majesty, Emperor Norton I of the United States'.

Restaurants fought to get such seals as they provided a significant boost to trade. The emperor was also much sought after by theatres and music halls and always had the best seat reserved for him on opening nights.

He had his occasional brush with the law, but usually got the upper hand. When he was arrested and committed to a mental asylum in 1867, there was a public outcry. It led to his immediate release and a grovelling apology from the police. Ever magnanimous, Norton granted an imperial pardon to the officers who arrested him.

By the 1870s, Norton was issuing his own currency: the banknotes became widely accepted in San Francisco. He was also granted recognition of sorts by the United States government: the 1870 census lists his occupation as 'emperor'.

His reign was to last another decade before coming to a dramatic end: in January 1880, he collapsed in the street and was pronounced dead shortly afterwards.

The *San Francisco Chronicle* announced the tragic news to the world. Under a banner headline in French, 'Le Roi est Mort', it said: 'In the darkness of a moonless night under the dripping rain, Norton I, by the grace of God, Emperor of the United States and Protector of Mexico, departed this life.'

He was buried in Woodlawn Cemetery in California and was given a headstone that still draws the eye of curious visitors: 'Norton I, Emperor of the United States and Protector of Mexico'.

The Man Who Bought His Wife

Samuel Baker had always enjoyed the thrill of the hunt: it offered excitement, adventure and the chance to spend time in the great outdoors. When he was asked to accompany Duleep Singh, the crowned ruler of the Punjab, on a hunting trip around central Europe, he jumped at the opportunity. It was a trip that would bag him a most unusual quarry.

The journey had begun conventionally enough. The two men had shot their way through large numbers of birds, bears and wolves. But their progress through the hunting grounds hit a snag in January 1859, when their wooden boat was damaged by an ice floe in the River Danube. They had little option but to take a temporary break from hunting while the craft was repaired.

The riverside town in which they found themselves was called Vidin, a provincial town in Bulgaria, then a province of the Ottoman Empire. It was a dreary place to put ashore: there were no particular sights and little to occupy the two men. The impatient maharajah was keen for some entertainment.

Samuel Baker soon found something to keep his Punjabi host amused. He learned that the Finjanjian family, the town's most important dealers in white slaves, was about to hold an auction. The matriarch of the family was selling off some of the harem girls.

Among the slaves for sale was Florenz Szasz, a beautiful teenager from Transylvania. Although young, she had already undergone more adventures than most people experience in a lifetime. Orphaned in the 1848 Hungarian Revolution when still a young girl, she had endured both adoption and abduction. She had eventually ended up in the Finjanjian family's harem.

Now, in January 1859, her life was about to take an entirely new twist. She was to be sold at auction, with her future in the hands of the highest bidder.

In the days before the auction, Florenz was prepared for the market.

She was given new clothes that accentuated her comely figure and an advertisement about her forthcoming sale was placed in local newspapers.

As a virgin, she almost certainly had a certificate of virginity signed by a certified midwife: proof of virginity greatly enhanced the value of female slaves.

Astonishingly, Florenz did not know she was being sold until the day of the auction. Only when she saw the potential buyers gathered in the opulent public salon of the Finjanjian mansion did she realize what was taking place.

Most of the slave buyers were wealthy Ottoman Turks. But as Florenz scanned the room, she saw one face that was clearly not Turkish. Samuel Baker had curly russet hair, thick sideburns and wore a wool tweed suit. He was instantly recognizable as being English. His companion was equally recognizable as being Indian.

Baker was not attending the slave sale with the intention of buying anyone: he had a moral abhorrence of slavery that was to endure throughout his life. He was attending solely because he thought it would be an entertaining diversion for the maharajah.

But he was deeply affected when the young Florenz was brought out for public display. She was beautiful, vulnerable and seemingly terrified of being sold to a Turkish master. Baker found himself shaken to the core. His own wife had died four years earlier: now, desperate to save the young girl, he placed a bid for her.

It was unfortunate that there was another would-be buyer in the room. The powerful pasha of Vidin had sent his representative to the auction and was determined to buy Florenz, even if it meant paying an inflated price.

The bidding increased incrementally with both would-be buyers determined to gain their prize. But the pasha of Vidin had a limitless budget, whereas Baker's was extremely modest. When the bidding reached seventy thousand *kuruş* – some eight hundred pounds – he had no option but to withdraw from the sale.

Angered by his failure, Baker took a personal vow to leave Vidin with Florenz in tow, even if it meant resorting to bribery. He secretly approached Ali, the black eunuch who controlled the Finjanjian harem, and struck a deal. In return for a large wad of notes, which he stuffed into Ali's hands, he was allowed to smuggle Florenz out of the compound and into his custody.

It all happened in seconds. Florenz was bundled out of an arched window at the rear of the Finjanjian mansion and helped into Samuel's waiting carriage. Bewildered by what had happened – but happy to have escaped the pasha's clutches – she now made the acquaintance of the English stranger who had tried to buy her.

She spoke at length about her turbulent childhood, unaware that she was about to embark on further adventures. For she was destined to become one of the great Victorian explorers of central Africa, accompanying Baker on his most arduous voyages into the tropical unknown. She proved an invaluable companion since she spoke fluent Arabic (which she had learned in the harem) as well as Hungarian and German.

The two of them made a deeply unconventional couple. Unmarried until 1865, they headed first to Cairo and together explored the Sudan and Abyssinia. Later from Khartoum they embarked on a dangerous voyage up the Nile.

At one point they encountered the explorer John Hanning Speke who was returning from Lake Victoria, which he had correctly identified as the source of the Nile.

In conditions of terrible hardship, Samuel and Florence (her name was by now anglicized) pressed on into uncharted territory, exploring the lake regions of Africa and discovering and naming the Murchison Falls and Lake Albert.

After a brief stint in England – where they finally married – they were off again, this time to equatorial Africa. Together they led a bloody military expedition against slave traders, a fight that must have given Florence considerable personal satisfaction. It ended in a victorious battle at Masindi, in today's Uganda.

The Bakers finally returned to England in 1874 and bought an estate in the West Country. Samuel died in 1893, a much feted explorer. Florence outlived her husband by twenty-three years but never received the recognition she deserved for her extraordinary journeys across the Dark Continent. Nor was she presented at court, as might have been expected for someone who had achieved so much.

Queen Victoria adamantly denied her a royal audience on the

grounds that her husband had been 'intimate with his wife before marriage'.

Florence finally died in 1916, by which time the world of her childhood had changed beyond all recognition. The age of harems and eunuchs was in its late twilight and even the Ottoman Empire, in which she had been sold into slavery, was on the point of permanent collapse.

Part XX
Mein Führer

To sum it all up, I must say that I regret nothing.

Adolf Eichmann, 1960

For the occupants of Hitler's private bunker the news could scarcely have been bleaker. The Soviet army was advancing so rapidly that it was now within a few hundred yards of the bunker's perimeter fence.

The nearby Schlesischer railway station had already been captured. The Tiergarten was also in Soviet hands and the tunnel in the Voss Strasse was in the process of being occupied. Soon the bunker itself would also be overrun and the Führer would be taken prisoner. Hitler knew all too well that the Third Reich was in its death throes.

In the small hours of 28–29 April 1945, he summoned a loyal official named Walter Wagner into his private conference room. Wagner's position as city administrator gave him the right to officiate at a wedding ceremony. Hitler announced that he and his long-term mistress, Eva Braun, were to be married without further ado.

The formalities were kept brief for there was no time to lose. The couple declared themselves to be of pure Aryan descent and free from hereditary disease. Then, having given their assent by simple word of mouth, they were declared to be man and wife.

The newlyweds walked out into the corridor to be congratulated by Hitler's faithful secretaries, Gerda Christian and Traudl Junge. They then sat together for several hours, drinking champagne and talking of happier times. The conversation took a rather more depressing turn as Hitler spoke of his impending suicide. National Socialism, he said, was dead. It would never be revived.

His resolve to kill himself was given fresh impetus by the shocking news that he received early in the morning of 29 April. He was told that Mussolini and his mistress, Clara Petacci, had been executed by partisans and strung up by their feet in the Piazzale Loreto in Milan.

'I will not fall into the hands of an enemy who requires a new spectacle to divert his hysterical masses!' he shouted.

In the afternoon of that same day, he had his favourite Alsatian dog Blondi destroyed with poison. His two other dogs were shot by their keeper. Hitler then distributed cyanide capsules to his secretaries for use in extremity. He expressed his regret at not giving them a better parting gift, adding that he wished his generals fighting against Stalin had been as faithful and reliable as they had been.

At two thirty in the morning, some twenty faithful servants assembled to greet Hitler as he emerged from his private quarters. He offered them his final farewells and then returned to his quarters. Everyone was sure that his suicide was imminent.

Yet he was still alive as dawn broke the following morning and he continued to receive military reports on the situation across Berlin. At 2 p.m., he even sat down to eat lunch with his two secretaries. His SS adjutant, Sturmbannführer Günsche, was meanwhile fulfilling the Führer's orders to acquire 200 litres of petrol.

When Hitler had finished eating, he emerged from his private quarters accompanied by his new wife. Another farewell ceremony took place, this time with Martin Bormann, Joseph Goebbels and others. Eva embraced Traudl Junge and said: 'Take my fur coat as a memory. I always like well-dressed women.'

Hitler then turned to address the little group for a final time. 'It is finished,' he said. 'Goodbye.'

He led Eva back into his private room. Soon afterwards, a single shot was heard.

The group who had gathered to say their farewells to Hitler lingered for a few minutes in the corridor before entering his room. Hitler himself was lying on the sofa, drenched in blood. He had shot himself through the mouth.

Eva Braun was also sprawled on the sofa. A revolver was by her side but she had not used it. She had swallowed poison instead.

Two SS men were summoned, one of them Hitler's faithful servant, Heinz Linge. The two men wrapped the Führer's body in a blanket and carried it into the courtyard.

Eva Braun's body, too, was taken outside. One of the men who helped to carry her body noted she was wearing a blue summer dress made of real silk and that her hair was artificially blonde.

The two corpses were doused in petrol and then set alight. A small group of mourners stood to attention, gave the Nazi salute and then withdrew back inside the bunker. Just beyond the bunker walls, the deep boom of the Soviet artillery lent a theatrical eeriness to the scene.

More petrol had to be poured on the corpses because they would not burn properly. Even after many hours, when most of the flesh had burned away, Hitler's blackened shinbones were still visible.

Shortly before midnight, as the Soviet troops neared the perimeter of the bunker, the two charred corpses were tipped into a bomb crater and covered with soil.

According to Russian reports, the bodies were later exhumed by the Soviet troops who captured the bunker. They were then transferred to Magdeburg in East Germany. It was in Magdeburg – it is claimed – that Hitler's body was finally destroyed by KGB officers in spring 1970.

Yet even that was not quite the end of the story. Two fragments of bone, his jawbone and skull, were preserved as grisly relics. They were last displayed in an exhibition at the Russian Federal Archives in Moscow in April 2000.

Seizing Eichmann

He was walking down the street clutching a large bouquet of flowers, a smiling family man by the name of Ricardo Klement. He was looking forward to celebrating his silver wedding anniversary that evening.

When he reached his house on Garibaldi Street in Buenos Aires, the front door was opened by his wife, Vera. Ricardo pushed the flowers into her hands and gave her a kiss. From inside came the sound of happy laughter: the children were already dressed in their party clothes.

Ricardo Klement had no idea that he was being tracked by Mossad secret agents. Nor did he know that those Israeli agents had been on his trail for more than a year.

They were convinced that Klement was not his real name. They had received a tip-off that he was actually Adolf Eichmann, the most senior Nazi still on the run. As Hitler's right-hand man, Eichmann had been responsible for organizing the mass deportation of millions of Jews to death camps such as Auschwitz and Treblinka. When the war came to an end, and the Third Reich collapsed, he had escaped capture by vanishing into thin air. For almost fifteen years he had evaded Mossad.

But in 1959, a German prosecutor named Fritz Bauer received a sensational tip-off. The daughter of one of his Argentina-based friends had been dating a lad named Eichmann (unlike his father, he had retained the old family name). Ignorant of the fact that the girl was Jewish, the young Eichmann bragged of his father's role in exterminating millions of Jews.

Fritz Bauer contacted Mossad, who immediately set to work on the operation to capture Eichmann. Absolute secrecy was paramount: if Eichmann got any hint that Mossad was on his trail, he would disappear again.

The undercover operation was led by Isser Harel, the brilliant head of Mossad. He was determined to bring Eichmann to justice. 'At all the Nuremberg trials of Nazi war criminals this man was pointed to as the head butcher,' he wrote. 'His were the hands that pulled the strings controlling manhunt and massacre.'

As Mossad began to research Eichmann's past, it transpired that he had remained incognito in Europe until 1950, when he was helped to escape to Argentina. He and his family moved several times before settling in Buenos Aires, where he was said to have changed his name to Ricardo Klement.

But Mossad's agents needed to be absolutely certain they were tracking the right man. It was the silver wedding anniversary flowers that provided them with the clinching evidence. They knew that Eichmann's twenty-fifth wedding anniversary was on 21 March 1960. When they saw 'Ricardo Klement' hand the flowers to his wife on the evening of that day, they had confirmation that Klement and Eichmann were one and the same person.

The Mossad operation to capture Eichmann coincided with Argentina celebrating 150 years of independence. This provided Isser Harel with the perfect cover to smuggle thirty special agents into the country.

Nothing was left to chance. Mossad set up a bogus travel agency in Europe to ensure that there would be no problems with visas or plane connections.

Harel was acutely aware that Mossad was violating Argentinian sovereignty by kidnapping Eichmann: secrecy was therefore of the utmost importance. By 11 May, the Mossad team was ready to swoop.

Harel knew that Eichmann usually returned home from work at around 7.40 p.m. He stationed his agents in the street shortly before this time. Two of them pretended to be repairing the engine of their car. A second Mossad vehicle was parked thirty yards behind the first one.

Two buses arrived but Eichmann was not on them. Harel was about to call off the operation when a third bus pulled up and a middle-aged man alighted. It was Eichmann.

As he neared the Mossad car, one of the Israeli operatives called 'just a moment' before jumping on him. Eichmann was terrified. 'He let out a terrible yell, like a wild beast caught in a trap.'

The other agents bundled Eichmann into the car and drove off at high speed. Eichmann was gagged and his hands and feet were tied together. He was told that he would be shot if he made a sound.

He was taken to a safe house where he was interrogated. He offered no resistance: indeed, he went out of his way to be helpful.

'Gone was the SS officer who once had hundreds of men to carry out his commands,' recalled Harel. 'Now he was frightened and nervous, at times pathetically eager to help.'

Eichmann was held for a week before he could be flown to Israel aboard an El Al flight. The Mossad agents pretended to be helping a brain-damaged patient return to Israel. They faked papers to this effect. To make the ruse more convincing, they drugged Eichmann and carried him onto the waiting plane.

Exactly eleven months after his capture, Eichmann was put on trial in Israel. He was indicted on fifteen criminal charges, including crimes against humanity, war crimes and crimes against the Jewish people. Eichmann's only defence was that he was following orders.

It was not enough to save him. He was convicted on all counts and sentenced to death. He was hanged on the last day of May 1962, in an Israeli prison.

The Celebrity Executioner

It was Friday the 13th and there were thirteen prisoners, all of them awaiting execution: ten men and three women who had sent tens of thousands of concentration camp victims to their deaths. Now, it was their turn to die.

There was never any doubt as to who would undertake the executions. Albert Pierrepont was Britain's most experienced hangman. He had first been given the job of executioner in 1932, following in the footsteps of his father and uncle. He proved so reliable and efficient that he was promoted to Chief Executioner in 1941. He turned his trade into an art, becoming an expert at double executions, hanging two men at the same time. Now, in December 1945, his services were required to carry out the numerous executions that followed the Nazi war crime trials. The most sensational of these was the hanging of the so-called 'Beasts of Belsen'.

The 'beasts' included Irma Grese, a twenty-one-year-old blonde dairy maid who had joined the SS and got herself transferred to Belsen, where she earned infamy for lashing her Jewish prisoners to death with her riding whip as they were on their way to the gas chambers.

Also convicted was Juana Bormann, who had treated her prisoners with horrific violence, setting her Alsatian dog onto the weak and sick. 'First she egged the dog on and it pulled at the woman [victim's] clothes,' said one witness at her trial. 'Then she was not satisfied with that and made the dog go for her throat.' She, like Irma Grese, was found guilty and sentenced to hang.

The Belsen executions were to be rather different from Pierrepont's previous hangings. He usually worked with an assistant, but on this occasion he was put in charge of the entire process. It was a job that required meticulous planning. 'I had to supervise the weighings and measuring of the condemned thirteen in order to work out my drops.'

When he first arrived at Bückeburg prison, where the criminals were being held, he was appalled to see that thirteen graves were already being dug for the condemned prisoners. He felt this was unseemly. 'I complained about it to a prison official but was told that nothing could be done to stop it.'

His next duty was to meet the men and women he was due to hang. 'I walked down the corridor and the thirteen Belsen faces were pressed close to the bars.' He was taken aback. 'Never in my experience have I seen a more pitiable crowd of condemned prisoners.'

Pierrepont had executed scores of people over the previous decade but he had never hanged thirteen in one day, nor had he hanged anyone quite so evil as these prisoners. He expressed a particular interest in meeting Irma Grese.

'She walked out of her cell and came towards us laughing,' he wrote. 'She seemed as bonny a girl as one could ever wish to meet.'

When he asked her age, she paused and gave a weak smile. Pierrepoint also found himself smiling, 'as if we realized the conventional embarrassment of a woman revealing her age'.

The first of the criminals to be weighed and measured was Josef Kramer, who had killed thousands of victims. He was extremely sullen and answered Pierrepoint's questions with gruff reticence.

The next prisoner, Dr Fritz Klein, had killed 300 victims at a time: he had also killed individual inmates using hypodermic syringes. Pierrepoint found him full of energy and not a bit contrite. '[He] came walking briskly down the corridor and efficiently complied with the formalities.'

Once all the prisoners had been weighed, Pierrepoint had to work out the length of rope that would be needed to kill them. If the drop was too long, it would tear their heads off. If it was too short, it might not break their necks.

Pierrepoint arose at 6 a.m. on Friday 13 December 1945, the day of the executions. He decided to hang the women first, beginning with Irma Grese. She proved a model of calmness, walking slowly to the trap and standing on the white chalk mark.

'As I placed the white cap over her head, she said in her languid voice: "Schnell."' The trapdoor crashed from under her feet and her body twisted as the rope broke her neck. Pierrepoint's first prisoner was dead.

He hanged the two other women before pausing for a much-needed cup of tea. Then he set to work on the men, adjusting the scaffold so that he could kill them in pairs.

First to go were Josef Kramer and Fritz Klein. They were bound together and then roped by their necks. 'I adjusted the ropes and flew to the lever,' recalled Pierrepoint. Twenty-five seconds later, both were dead.

And so it continued. It was dark by the time all the prisoners had been despatched. Pierrepoint was exhausted and in need of more conventional entertainment: he thoroughly enjoyed himself at the mess party that night.

He was proud to have hanged the 'Beasts of Belsen': it had all gone like clockwork. He would subsequently be called to execute a further 190 Nazi war criminals, including Bruno Tesch, inventor of the gas Zyklon B.

Pierrepoint was a model of efficiency and liked to boast that he could get his clients from their cells to the gallows – and hang them – in under a minute.

He was eventually retired due to failing eyesight at the age of seventy-two. Home Office officials cancelled his contract when they learned that he almost sent his assistant through the trapdoor by mistake.

Part XXI

Get Me Out of Here!

I saw that a boiling red river was coming from another part of the hill and cutting off the escape of the people who were running from their houses. The whole side of the mountain seemed to open and boil down on the screaming people.

Account of Havivra Da Ifrile, one of three known survivors of the 1906 eruption of Mount Pelée

Trapped on an Iceberg

Wilfred Grenfell had been in many dangerous situations, but none had been quite as precarious as his current one. He was adrift on a floating island of ice and being swept out towards the wild Atlantic Ocean.

The snow-covered coastline of Newfoundland lay far behind him; indeed it had faded to a distant smudge. Ahead lay only danger and death. Grenfell could already hear the sickening slush of sea-ice being ground to pulp by the waves. He knew it was only a matter of time before his own little island of ice would give way beneath him.

Grenfell had taken a huge risk in attempting to cross the ice-bound Newfoundland bay, but he was on a mission of the utmost urgency. He was required at the local hospital, where a young lad lay seriously ill with poisonous gangrene in his leg. The leg needed to be treated – and possibly amputated – if he was to have any chance of survival. In the wilds of rural Newfoundland, Grenfell alone could perform the operation.

The safest and most reliable route to the hospital was along the rough coast path. But it was an arduous journey, for it traversed rocky inlets and snow-bound ravines. Far quicker, though considerably more dangerous, was to cross the sea-ice.

Grenfell's journey on Easter Sunday 1908 began well enough. He had the right equipment for crossing the ice, with a change of clothes, snowshoes, rifle and oilskins. He also had a team of six dogs who were to pull his *komatic* or heavy sledge.

But as he pushed out into the frozen bay he suddenly grew alarmed. The heavy swell was breaking the ice into blocks that were held together by wafer-thin skins. Some of these skins had melted, turning the blocks into floating islands known locally as ice-pans.

With considerable effort Grenfell managed to make it to a stable island of ice. From here, it was a further four miles across slushy ice to the rocky headland. He set off undaunted and was close to the landing point when disaster struck. He suddenly found himself crossing 'sish' – a slush-like porridge of ice. The ice-pans had completely disappeared.

One moment he was afloat; the next, he was sinking. 'There was not a moment to lose. I tore off my oilskins, threw myself on my hands and shouted to my team to go ahead for the shore.'

But the dogs were as frightened as he was and they also began to sink in the slush, along with the sledge. Soon they were flailing in icy water 'like flies in treacle'.

After swimming through the icy water, Grenfell managed to reach a lone ice-pan. With considerable difficulty, he pulled himself onto the ice and then managed to save his dogs as well. But the wind was now whipping off the land and dragging Grenfell's ice-pan relentlessly out to sea.

He was bitterly cold and had lost all his equipment. 'I stood with next to nothing on, the wind going through me and every stitch soaked in ice water.' His only comfort was the fact that he would meet with a mercifully quick death, for the sea temperature was close to freezing and the waves were mounting in height.

'Immense pans of Arctic ice, surging to and fro on the heavy rolling seas, were thundering into the cliffs like medieval battering rams.'

Grenfell was a born survivor and now used every technique he had been taught. He cut off his moccasins and split them open in order to make a makeshift jacket.

Still freezing, he realized that his only course was to start killing the dogs. He made a slipknot from leather, pulled it over the neck of one of the animals to stop it from biting him and then stabbed it through the heart. He proceeded to hack off the skin and wrap the bloody pelt over his shoulders. He then killed two more dogs and used their skins to keep warm.

By now it was growing dark: he realized that he must have been adrift for many hours. He hadn't eaten for the entire day but managed to keep his hunger at bay by chewing a band of rubber.

Sheer willpower kept him alive through the icy night, with the wind whipping across the ice and causing frostbite in his feet. When the sun finally rose, he tied together the thigh-bones of his slaughtered dogs and slipped his shirt over the end, making a rudimentary flag. It was his last hope of being sighted.

He was by now in a sorry state: 'my poor, gruesome pan was bobbing up and down, stained with blood and littered with carcasses and debris'.

He was unaware that he had been sighted shortly after dawn. A man on the cliffs had seen him drifting out to sea and raised the alarm. Now, rescue was on its way. Four men were rowing with tremendous effort through the slush, aware that their village comrade could not keep himself alive for much longer.

Grenfell didn't see them coming, for he was by now badly afflicted with snow blindness. The first thing he knew about his rescue was the cries of the men's voices.

'As the man in the bow leaped from the boat onto my ice raft and grasped both my hands in his, not a word was uttered.' Grenfell knew that he had had a very lucky escape. 'We all love life,' he wrote in the account of his adventure. 'I was glad to be back once more with a new lease of it before me.'

Grenfell was also able to bring a new lease of life to the sickly boy who was awaiting him. He went straight to the hospital and successfully operated on his gangrenous leg. The boy went on to make a full recovery.

Volcano of Death

It was as if someone had switched off the sun. At exactly 8.02 a.m. on 8 May 1902, the Caribbean town of Saint-Pierre was rocked by a cataclysmic explosion. The sky above Martinique was plunged into instant darkness and the volcano, Mount Pelée, could be heard to roar like a beast.

When the sky lightened for a moment, the inhabitants turned their gaze to the volcano. They were horrified by what they saw. A vast wall of molten rock was roaring towards them, gathering momentum as it cascaded down the steep slopes above the town. In its wake was an avalanche of superheated gas and dust. The temperature of the flow was in excess of 1,000°C and was vaporizing everything in its path.

Among the 30,000 terrified inhabitants was Léon Compère-Léandre, a local shoemaker. He had been outside when the volcano spectacularly erupted. 'I felt a terrible wind blowing, the earth began to tremble, and the sky suddenly became dark,' he later wrote. 'I turned to go into the house, with great difficulty climbed the three or four steps that separated me from my room, and felt my arms and legs burning, also my body.'

As he collapsed in agony, four other people burst into the room, 'crying and writhing with pain'. It was clear that they had suffered massive internal injuries from the noxious volcanic gases filling the air, even before the main avalanche arrived.

One of the victims was the young daughter of the Delavaud family, whose father had already sought refuge in Léon's house. She was in a terrible state and died almost immediately. The others struggled to their feet, coughing violently as they fled back outside in the hope of finding some avenue of escape.

Léon went into another room, 'where I found the father Delavaud, still clothed and lying on the bed, dead. He was purple and inflated, but the clothing was intact.'

By now Léon was desperate, 'crazed and almost overcome'. Unable to move, he lay on a bed, 'inert and awaiting death'.

The people still outside in the streets were doomed, for there was no hope of outrunning the advancing avalanche. But there were to be a few witnesses to the ensuing disaster – people on boats at the time of the eruption. They watched in appalled fascination as the torrent of toxic rock slammed into the outskirts of the town, flattening everything in its path.

Seconds later, it engulfed the centre of Saint-Pierre. 'The town vanished before our eyes,' said one.

Virtually everyone in Saint-Pierre was killed in seconds, either gassed by the noxious fumes or incinerated by the solid wall of heat. But there were to be a couple of miracle survivors on that bleak morning in 1902.

One hour after the avalanche had struck the town, Léon Compère-Léandre suddenly awoke. He had lost consciousness at the moment the debris reached Saint-Pierre and was in a daze as to what had happened.

He picked his way out of his shattered house and found a scene of absolute desolation. The town of his childhood was a charred and smoking ruin with scarcely a single building left standing. He stumbled over the hot cinders, walking for miles until he eventually emerged from the zone of destruction and reached a village where he told astonished locals the story of his survival.

How he managed to escape the burning avalanche remains a mystery. The cloud of toxic gas, boiling dust and molten rock had left him completely unscathed.

But Léon was not the only survivor of that terrible spring day in 1902. One other man emerged alive from the inferno and he was able to recount exactly how he had cheated death on that grim morning.

Louis-Auguste Cyparis had been incarcerated in the city's prison on the day before the eruption, having been involved in a violent pub brawl. He was locked into an underground cell with windowless stone-built walls. The only ventilation came from a grating in the metal door that faced away from the volcano.

Cyparis heard the violent explosion and immediately realized that Mount Pelée had erupted. The sunlight that he could glimpse through the grating vanished in an instant.

Seconds later, scorching air and burning ash began filtering into his cell, causing him severe burns. He urinated on his clothes and stuffed them into the ventilation hole in order to protect himself. He knew that if the ash kept falling, he would soon be trapped in an underground tomb.

A rescue operation began within hours of the eruption. The warship *Suchet* reached the burning town at 12.30 p.m. But the wreckage of Saint-Pierre was still pumping out such ferocious heat that the vessel could not dock until 3 p.m., when the captain finally managed to get ashore.

He was staggered by what he found. Not a building, nor even a tree, was left standing. Everything was charred beyond recognition. The entire population of 30,000 was dead.

Except for one. Cyparis was still trapped in his lonely tomb and he would remain there for fully four days until a team of rescuers heard his forlorn cries. He was dug from the compacted ash and helped to safety by his astonished rescuers. He eventually recovered from his burns, was pardoned for his crime and would earn a celebrity of sorts as a performer with Barnum & Bailey's circus.

The only other survivor of that terrible morning was a young girl named Haviva Da Ifrile. Her escape was even more bizarre than the other two. She was found adrift in a boat, unconscious but alive. She had no recollection of how she got there.

The Female Robinson Crusoe

In the third week of August 1923 the good ship *Donaldson* arrived at the desolate shores of Wrangel Island, far to the north of Siberia. The crew were bringing supplies to five colonists left here two years earlier and were expecting to find them all in good health. Instead, they found just one of those colonists, a half-starved young woman named Ada Blackjack. She was gaunt and sick, but alive. And she had an incredible story to tell.

Two years earlier, Ada Blackjack had volunteered to take part in one of the strangest missions in the history of colonization. She and four others were to test the feasibility of living on ice-bound Wrangel Island.

The 1921 colonial experiment was the brainchild of Arctic explorer Vilhjalmur Stefansson. One of his key goals was to claim the land for Canada. Another was to prove that this bleak land was habitable. Stefansson entertained hopes of establishing an extreme tourism company that would offer adventure tours of this remote outpost.

Four of Stefansson's team were men: three Americans named Lorne Knight, Milton Galle and Fred Maurer, and a Canadian called Allan Crawford. They had impressive academic credentials but rather less experience of surviving in extreme Arctic conditions.

The fifth colonist was a young Inuit woman named Ada Blackjack. Ada's husband had died some years earlier leaving her destitute. She also had a child with chronic tuberculosis, an illness that required costly treatment. She decided to join the expedition for a year, lured by the promise of a good salary. She was officially employed as the team's seamstress.

Just twenty-five years of age, Ada was an odd choice to accompany the mission. She knew nothing about hunting or trapping and had never before lived off the land. She didn't even know how to build an igloo.

The rest of the team expressed deep misgivings when they learned that she had been selected to join them. They said she would be a hindrance to the others and was too frail to survive the harsh conditions. But their concerns were overruled by Vilhjalmur Stefansson.

Ada Blackjack was officially employed as the fifth member of the team.

On 16 September 1921, the five colonists were left on barren Wrangel Island. Stefansson, who declined to accompany the expedition, believed the island to be so well stocked with wildlife that he left the colonists with enough food for just six months. He promised to send a supply ship in the following summer: in the meantime, the five would have to fend for themselves.

The mission got off to a flying start. The colonists built a large snow house and had great success in hunting the local wildlife. They managed to kill ten polar bears, thirty seals and many geese and duck. They were confident that they could survive until the ship's return.

But the promised vessel failed to materialize and the five settlers realized they faced a long and arduous autumn. They soon ran short of tea, coffee and sugar. They then ate the last of their flour and beans. As the November gale whipped in a ferocious Arctic winter, the wild game disappeared and the five found themselves critically short of food. Worse still, Lorne Knight developed a serious illness.

On 28 January 1923, Crawford, Galle and Maurer decided to attempt to traverse the frozen Chukchi Sea in order to reach the Siberian mainland. They wanted to alert people to the fact they were in desperate need of help.

The three of them were never seen again and their fate remains a mystery. Either they fell through the ice and drowned in the freezing seawater or they froze to death in an Arctic blizzard.

Lorne Knight had meanwhile taken a turn for the worse. He was now suffering from acute scurvy and could scarcely move his joints. He was nursed by Ada until April, when his body gave up the ghost. Ada now found herself utterly alone in this ice-bound wilderness.

She had no idea how to hunt and had never even fired the rifle that had been left behind. But she soon worked out how to use it and managed to kill seals, foxes and ducks. She then stewed the meat to make it more palatable.

She managed to prevent the fire from going out, even though fuel was scarce, and kept insanity at bay by reading the Bible. But as another summer slipped into autumn, she grew increasingly weak. She knew that her own death was now inevitable.

She had given up hope of ever being rescued when she sighted a vessel on the horizon. It was the *Donaldson*, which arrived at Wrangel Island on 23 August. The crew were astonished to stumble across Ada Blackjack and even more surprised to learn that three of her male comrades were missing and the fourth was dead.

When her story reached the outside world, the newspapers labelled her the 'female Robinson Crusoe'. Her survival, they said, was nothing short of a miracle. She had received no training in survival techniques, yet had kept herself alive for twenty-three months.

Ada did not take kindly to the media circus and shunned the publicity. She wanted nothing more than to be reunited with her son, using the expedition salary to take him to Seattle in order to cure his tuberculosis.

But the fact that she had a sickly child – who was eventually cured – brought a new dimension to the story. Ada became an unwitting celebrity, heralded as a heroic survivor in books and magazines. 'Her physical stomach wasn't a bit more adapted to seal oil and blubber than theirs [the men's],' wrote one. 'But in Ada's heart there was a fire that isn't easily blown out.'

Ada never went back to Wrangel Island, but she did return to the Arctic and eventually made it her home. The freezing climate seems to have suited her, for she finally died at the ripe old age of eighty-five.

Part XXII

Oh! What a Lovely War

ashdladiin dóó ba'ąą náhást'éidi mííl tsosts'idi neeznádiin
dízdįįhastą́ą́

The number 59,746 in Navajo, the highly complex Native
American language used for American battlefield
communications during the Second World War

The Last Post

American conscript Henry Gunther was appalled when he arrived at the battlefields of northern France in the winter of 1917. The mud-filled trenches were bleaker than he was expecting and the atmosphere of decay hung heavy in the air.

Gunther had been drafted into the 313th Regiment, known as Baltimore's Own, just a few weeks earlier. He was a supply sergeant, responsible for the clothing of his regiment.

Now, staring across a landscape of shattered buildings and trees, he felt profoundly depressed. He had no desire to fight in a war that was thousands of miles from his native land. It was a world away from the book-keeping job he had at the Bank of Baltimore. Homesick and depressed, he wrote to a friend complaining of the 'miserable conditions' in which he found himself. He told that friend to do whatever he could to dodge the draft.

It was unfortunate for Gunther that his letter was read by an army censor. The censor was appalled by such defeatist sentiments and reported Gunther to his superior. There was never any doubt that he would be punished for his lack of patriotism, but the chosen punishment was to leave him with a deep psychological scar. He was demoted from sergeant to private, bringing shame on both himself and his family.

'He brooded a great deal over his reduction in rank and became obsessed with a determination to make good before his officers and fellow soldiers,' so wrote James M. Cain, a war reporter for the *Baltimore Sun*. 'He was worried because he thought himself suspected of being a German sympathizer. The regiment went into action a few days after he was reduced [in rank] and from the start he displayed the most unusual willingness to expose himself to all sorts of risks.'

The question uppermost in Gunther's mind was how he could best 'make good' his perceived lack of patriotism. The war was rapidly drawing to a close and there were already rumours that the German army was on the point of surrendering. As dawn broke on 11 November 1918, Gunther knew that he needed to do something in the very near future.

In common with most soldiers on that chill morning, Gunther had no idea that the armistice had already been signed. At 5.20 a.m., British, French and German officials had met in a railway carriage to the north of Paris and brought the First World War to an end. Now, all they needed to do was transmit the news to the troops on the ground.

This was not easy. Many battalions were using old and inadequate communications and many more were completely cut off from their command centres. The generals realized that it would take time to notify all the troops. They decreed that the peace would not come into effect until 11 a.m.

Henry Gunther and his pals learned of the approaching armistice at 10.30 a.m. Their wisest course of action would have been to lie low for the next half an hour until it was officially declared. Instead, they continued their march towards Chaumont-devant-Damvillers, a village near Metz, arriving at the outskirts as it approached eleven o'clock.

As they made their way along the country road, they found their path blocked by two enemy machine-gun posts. The Germans were under orders to open fire, but they deliberately shot into the air so as not to claim any more lives.

Gunther's comrades were touched by the action of the Germans, who were clearly aware of the impending armistice. But Gunther himself saw things rather differently. Realizing that he had just a couple of minutes to make a heroic impact, he expressed his outrage at the fact that they had fired their guns. Against the orders of his sergeant (and close friend) Ernest Powell, he made a dramatic charge through the thick fog towards the German machine guns.

According to reporter James M. Cain, 'he was fired by a desire to demonstrate, even at the last minute, that he was courageous and all-American'.

The German soldiers were horrified when they saw their position being charged by a lone soldier. 'They waved at him and called out, in such broken English as they could, to go back, that the war was over. He paid no heed to them, however, and kept on firing a shot or two as he went.'

When the Germans saw that he was determined to keep up his forlorn charge, they had no option but to turn their machine gun on him. Gunther fell in action at 10.59 a.m. and is officially recognized as the last soldier to be killed in the First World War.

'Almost as he fell', noted his divisional record, 'the gunfire died away and an appalling silence prevailed.'

The army would eventually restore him to the rank of sergeant and also award him two posthumous medals for gallantry. Henry Gunther emerged from the war as both its last victim and its final hero.

To Hell and Back

Audie Murphy was short, skinny and underage, hardly suitable material for a fighting soldier in the Second World War. The American army certainly thought him inadequate when he tried to enroll for service in December 1941. They rejected him not only on the grounds of his youth – he was just sixteen and a half – but also because of his slight frame.

Murphy made a second attempt to enlist in the following year. He was once again rejected, not just by the regular army but also by the Marine Corps, the Airborne and the navy.

After much persistence, he finally succeeded in getting himself enrolled in the army and was sent for training in Texas. He proved unsuitable in every respect, vindicating the army's previous decisions to reject him. During one training session he fainted from exhaustion. His company commander was so alarmed that he tried to move him to an army cookery school.

But Murphy was determined to prove the doubters wrong and he was to do so in style. The first inkling of his bravery came in September 1943, when his scouting party was ambushed by German machine guns on the Italian front. Murphy returned fire and killed all five Germans. His unexpected heroism earned him promotion to sergeant.

He fought in further battles in Italy and France and began to display a reckless determination to win at all costs. He was at his most efficient leading small groups of men into attack against an overwhelmingly superior enemy.

After participating in Operation Dragoon in southern France, he and his men were transferred to Alsace, where fighting between the Allies and crack German soldiers was at its most intense.

His platoon came under heavy fire while crossing a vineyard. Murphy managed single-handedly to seize one of the enemy machine guns and then turned it on the Germans, killing or wounding them. His action was extraordinarily brave and won him the Distinguished Service Cross.

Shortly afterwards, his best friend was killed by a group of Germans who were pretending to surrender. Murphy was so disgusted by their underhand trick that he charged them, killing six, wounding two and taking eleven of them prisoner.

During seven weeks of tough fighting, Murphy's division suffered 4,500 casualties. Murphy himself was always in the thick of it. He received two silver stars for heroic action, was promoted to second lieutenant and elevated to platoon leader. Although he had proved himself one of the bravest soldiers fighting in Alsace, his moment of glory still lay before him.

In January 1945, he and his men were moved to the woods near Holtzwihr. This territory was strategically vital to the Allied advance and had only recently been captured. It was no less crucial to the Germans, who were determined to recover their ground.

Murphy's unusual leadership skills had by now so impressed his superiors that they made him a company commander. His orders were to block any German advance.

On 26 January, his men went into action against the enemy. It was bitterly cold – minus 10°C – with an arctic wind and two feet of snow on the ground. The men fought with tenacious courage but a ferocious firefight steadily reduced them to an effective fighting force of just 19 men out of their original 128.

Murphy realized that the remnants of his company couldn't hold out any longer and ordered them to retreat into the forest. But he had no intention of following their retreat. He clambered onto a burned-out tank destroyer and used his lone position to direct American artillery fire coming from the rear.

'I loved that artillery,' he later recalled. 'I could see Kraut soldiers disappear in clouds of smoke and snow, hear them scream and shout, yet they came on and on as though nothing would stop them.'

The Germans slowly advanced, despite the bombing, and were soon within fifty yards of Murphy's hiding place. When battalion headquarters asked him to inform them of the enemy's position, Murphy replied: 'If you just hold the phone a minute, I'll let you talk to one of the bastards.'

He continued to spray the advancing troops with bullets, killing some fifty German soldiers in one sustained burst of fire. At one point he spied a group of soldiers hiding in a nearby ditch. 'I pressed the trigger and slowly traversed the barrel – the bodies slumped in a stack position.'

Murphy only stopped fighting when his line of communication to headquarters was cut by enemy artillery. Although badly injured he continued to lead his men for the next two days until the area around Holtzwihr and the Colmar Canal was finally cleared of Germans. It was an exceptional feat of war and all the more remarkable given the fact that he had been twice rejected by the army on the grounds that he was too feeble to fight.

On 2 June 1945, Murphy was presented with the Medal of Honor, America's highest award. It was the peak of his military career, one that ended with thirty-two additional medals, ribbons, citations and badges.

Murphy would later become a Hollywood star, acting in the film of his own experiences, *To Hell and Back*. But his life was cut tragically short when he died in a plane crash in 1971. He was just forty-six.

When asked what motivated him to fight single-handed against a company of German infantry, he replied: 'They were killing my friends.'

Let's Talk Gibberish

Japanese code-breaker Seizo Arisue had every reason to feel satisfied with himself. He and his team had met with great success in cracking the secret transmissions of the American high command. Many of these deciphered intercepts concerned the deployment of troops, giving the Japanese a significant advantage on the battlefield.

But in the spring of 1945, Seizo Arisue found himself completely perplexed by the new code being used by the American army. He spent many hours attempting to decipher it, but all to no avail.

Ahkehdiglini was one of the words. *Tsahahdzoh* was another. And so it continued for several pages. Arisue could only conclude that it had been written in gibberish.

The messages were indeed indecipherable, just as the Americans intended. They were sending them in Navajo, a highly complex Native American language that very few people in the world were able to speak.

The idea of using the Navajo language for battlefield communications was first suggested by Philip Johnston, the son of an American missionary. He was one of the few non-Navajos in the world who spoke the language fluently.

Johnston knew that Native American languages had been successfully used for battlefield communications in the First World War. He also knew that Navajo would present the Japanese code-breakers with a formidable challenge. Its tortuous syntax and numerous dialects rendered it unintelligible to anyone who had not been exposed to it for years.

The US army first tried out Johnston's ingenious idea in the spring of 1942. It proved so foolproof that they began drafting more Navajo speakers into the army's ranks. They became known as the code-talkers and they were to play a crucial role in the war in the Far East.

Among them was Samuel Tso, a twenty-three-year-old Navajo speaker who directed communications for the United States Marine Corps during the battle for Iwo Jima. He and his team of six code-talkers transmitted hundreds of strategically vital commands during the month-long battle.

The commands were relayed as a string of seemingly unrelated Navajo words that bore no obvious relation to battlefield terms. This was because words like 'machine gun' and 'battleship' didn't exist in Navajo.

To overcome this problem of vocabulary, Tso's team used designated Navajo words to describe military hardware. 'Whale' was used to describe a battleship, 'iron-fish' to describe a submarine and 'humming-bird' to describe a fighter plane.

But the code was a great deal more sophisticated than that. One of the basic principles involved was that specific Navajo words were chosen to represent individual letters of the Roman alphabet. To represent the letter 'a', for example, Tso could use any of the following: *wollachee* (ant), *belasana* (apple) or *tsenill* (axe). These words had one key element in common: when translated into English, they all started with the letter 'a'.

Tso and his team sent and received dozens of commands each day. When they received a coded message, their first task was to translate the Navajo words into English. They would then use the first letter of each word to spell out the message. And this is why it proved so impossible for the Japanese to crack. Any code-breaker attempting to read the cipher had to know the meaning of the Navajo word in English. Since there was no Navajo dictionary, they found themselves up against an impossible task.

Tso's team transmitted information on tactics, troop movements and other battlefield communications. They were highly skilled and extremely accurate. As the US Marines fought their way up the heavily defended beaches of Iwo Jima, the code-talkers more than proved their worth.

Major Howard Connor, 5th Marine Division signal officer, was adamant that Tso's men had led the Marines to victory: 'Were it not for the Navajos, the Marines would never have taken Iwo Jima.'

The Japanese code-breakers worked around the clock in their quest to crack the Navajo code, but never succeeded in deciphering a single message.

Philip Johnston's idea of using Navajo had proved to be an inspired one. The use of this indecipherable language had saved tens of thousands of lives.

Part XXIII
Dial M for Murder

It was kept in a chamber and was a great fowl somewhat
bigger than the largest Turkey cock, and so legged and
footed, but stouter and thicker and of more erect shape,
coloured before like the breast of a young cock pheasant.

Sir Hamon L'Estrange is shown a live dodo in London, 1638,
within twenty-five years the dodo was extinct

Good Ship Zong

Captain Luke Collingwood was used to grim voyages across the Atlantic, but this one had been worse than most.

Dysentery, diarrhoea and smallpox had already claimed the lives of seven of the crew aboard the *Zong*. The slave cargo had suffered a far higher mortality rate. More than sixty had died since leaving the shores of Africa.

As Captain Collingwood searched in vain for the coast of Jamaica, he grew increasingly alarmed. He knew that the ship's insurers would not cover the cost of his lost human cargo. Since each slave was worth about £30, he stood to lose a fortune.

On 29 November 1781, he was struck by a macabre idea, one that could turn loss into profit. At a meeting with the *Zong*'s officers, he suggested that they throw the slaves overboard. There was a sinister logic to his reasoning. If his slaves died of illness, their insurance value was lost. But if they were thrown overboard in order to preserve the ship's scant supply of water (and thereby save the lives of others), an insurance claim would be valid under a legal principle known as the 'general average'. It allowed the captain of a ship to sacrifice some of his 'passengers' in order to save others.

The First Mate of the *Zong*, James Kelsall, was appalled by the captain's proposal. He said it was cold-blooded murder. But Collingwood disagreed, insisting that it would be 'less cruel to throw the sick wretches into the sea than to suffer them to linger out a few days, under the disorder with which they were afflicted'.

After much persuasion, Kelsall changed his mind and reluctantly agreed with the captain and other officers. The weakest slaves were to be pitched overboard that very day.

Collingwood went below decks to select his first 'parcel' of victims. He decided to concentrate on the women and children, probably because he knew that they would put up less of a struggle. A total of fifty-four were hurled off the ship and could be seen flailing in the sea before eventually weakening and drowning.

Two days later, on 1 December, Collingwood elected to throw out another 'parcel': this time, his forty-two victims were all men. They drowned so quickly, and with such little effort on the part of the captain and his crew, that Collingwood decided to pitch even more slaves overboard. He was intent on getting the largest possible sum of money from the ship's insurers. He ordered another thirty-six to be thrown into the ocean.

But this third batch of victims were made of stronger stuff and vehemently refused to go to their deaths without a struggle. Collingwood's men were forced to chain them by the ankle and weigh their feet with balls of iron so they would sink immediately.

'The arms of twenty-six were fettered with irons and the savage crew proceeded with the diabolical work, casting them down to join their comrades of the former days,' so reads a contemporary account of the massacre.

Ten of the slaves were so terrified by their fate that they leaped overboard before the captain had the chance to have them chained.

Three weeks after the last murders, the *Zong* finally reached Jamaica with 208 slaves still aboard. They sold for an average price of £36 each, earning Collingwood a substantial profit even before he made his insurance claim. But he did not have long to enjoy his money: he died within three days of making landfall.

His death might have been the end of a sordid and macabre tale, but there was to be an extraordinary postscript, one that caused a sensation in Georgian England.

The ship's owners expressed their full support for what the late Captain Collingwood had done and filed an insurance claim for the 132 slaves that had been thrown overboard. They hoped to recuperate nearly £4,000 in jettisoned 'cargo'.

Thus began a court case that was marked by callousness, cynicism and sheer human greed. The jury were in agreement with the owners and insisted that the insurers pay up the money for the drowned slaves. But the insurers appealed against the decision and asked for the case to be retried. This time, it was to be heard before the Lord Chief Justice, Lord Mansfield.

Those who hoped for a more enlightened approach from Lord Mansfield were quickly disappointed. 'The case of slaves', he said, 'was the same as if horses had been thrown overboard. The question was,

whether there was not an absolute necessity for throwing them overboard to save the rest.'

A hitherto unknown fact was now brought before the court. The
ship's owners had argued that the slaves were killed because there was
not enough water on board. But this was not true. When the ship
arrived at Jamaica, it still had more than 420 imperial gallons of stored
water.

This ought to have proved the turning point: Collingwood and his
crew were clearly guilty of cold-blooded murder. Yet the new evidence
was deemed to be of no consequence and the *Zong*'s owners ultimately
won the day. The insurers were forced to pay up for the 'cargo' that
had been dumped at sea.

The English abolitionist Granville Sharp was appalled by the verdict
and tried to bring forward a case of murder. This was brushed aside
by Lord Mansfield.

'What is this claim that human people have been thrown overboard?'
he said. 'This is a case of chattels or goods. Blacks are goods and
property; it is madness to accuse these well-serving honourable men
of murder.'

The Suspicions of Inspector Dew

In the early hours of 1 February 1910, the inhabitants of Hilldrop
Crescent in north London were shaken from their sleep by a muffled
scream. It was followed by a short silence and then an anguished plea
for mercy. A few seconds later there was a loud report that sounded
like a gunshot.

The commotion came from number 39, home to Dr Hawley Crippen
and his wife, Cora. It was obvious to everyone that something deeply
disturbing was taking place inside the house. But no one thought to
intervene and on the following morning, when everyone left their
houses for work, they chose not to mention the noises in the night.

Dr Crippen greeted his neighbours as usual and found himself
warmly greeted in return. He then took himself off to the Music Hall
Ladies Guild where his wife, who used the stage name Belle, was
honorary treasurer.

He handed the guild a letter, purportedly written by Belle, in which she tendered her resignation. The letter explained how she had to make an urgent voyage to America in order to visit a near relative who was gravely ill.

This news caused surprise but no suspicion. Belle was American, like her husband, and there was no reason to suppose that either of them were telling anything but the truth.

A few weeks after Belle's supposed departure, a new woman moved into Dr Crippen's home. Her name was Miss Ethel Le Neve, a demure and attractive secretary. Aged twenty-seven, she was twenty years younger than him.

Ethel caused quite a stir when she attended the Music Hall Ladies Ball later that month. Not only did she accompany Dr Crippen as his apparent partner, but she was also noticed to be wearing one of Belle's brooches.

Belle's music-hall friends were by now deeply suspicious of what might have happened to their old friend. They went so far as to make enquiries in America as to her possible whereabouts. But it was to no avail. There were no records of Belle having returned to her homeland.

They were now so concerned that they contacted Scotland Yard to inform them of her disappearance. The case was assigned to Chief Inspector Walter Dew, whose first port of call was Dr Crippen's office in New Oxford Street.

Crippen proved a master of composure. He told the inspector that Belle had run off with a lover, a boxer named Brice Miller, and that he had been too humiliated to admit the truth to his friends.

Inspector Dew swallowed every word. He asked for permission to search the house in Hilldrop Crescent, but only as a formality, and found nothing to awaken his suspicions. As far as he was concerned, the doctor was in the clear.

Crippen was deeply shaken by the enquiries from Scotland Yard. He was concerned that Inspector Dew would find holes in his story and question him again. This was something he wanted to avoid at all costs.

He took the dramatic decision to flee the country with Ethel in tow. He explained to her that they would be happier, and safer, in America. They would also be away from Scotland Yard.

When Inspector Dew attempted to make contact with the doctor about some minor discrepancies in his account – and learned that he and his secretary had left England – he ordered a more thorough search of the house. This time, events took a more serious turn.

On 13 July, police found a decaying human body in the cellar. It was headless, limbless and in a gruesome state of decomposition. The rotting remains were found to contain traces of hyoscine. Detectives next discovered that that Dr Crippen had purchased just such a poison days before his wife's supposed departure.

Two days after the exhumation of the body, Scotland Yard issued a warrant for Dr Crippen's arrest.

But Crippen and Ethel were by now on their way to Canada, having boarded the SS *Montrose* sailing from Antwerp. They registered themselves as father and son – Ethel looked remarkably boyish – and might have deceived everyone on board had it not been for their indiscreet behaviour.

Just hours after setting sail, the ship's captain, Henry Kendall, noticed 'father' and 'son' behaving in an intimate fashion behind the lifeboats. Alarmed by their behaviour – and deeply suspicious – he checked the 'wanted' descriptions in the newspapers. He realized that they answered to the description of Crippen and his lover.

Kendall wired his suspicions to Scotland Yard, whose officers acted immediately. Inspector Dew was able to board the SS *Laurentic*, which was on the point of setting sail across the Atlantic, and found himself in a desperate chase to overtake the *Montrose* before it reached Canada.

At around 9 p.m. on the morning of 31 July, in thick St Lawrence fog, the inspector boarded the *Montrose*, purporting to be one of several 'pilots' helping to steer the ship to its berth.

Sighting Dr Crippen, he removed his pilot's hat and shook the doctor by the hand. Crippen froze: he immediately recognized Dew and realized the game was up. 'Thank God it's all over' were his only words as he allowed himself to be handcuffed.

Dr Crippen and Ethel Le Neve were immediately charged with 'murder and mutilation' and sent back to England in order to be tried by London's Central Criminal Court.

Crippen protested his innocence, but to no avail. He was found guilty of wilful murder and hanged in prison in November 1910.

Ethel Le Neve was acquitted of any wrongdoing and subsequently fled to America, sailing on the day that Crippen was hanged. And that seemed to be the end of a brutal and tragic story.

But there was to be a surprising postscript, one that has turned the case on its head. Recent mitochondrial DNA evidence suggests that Crippen may have been innocent after all. Working from a sample of blood held at the Royal London Hospital Archives, a team of American forensic scientists have compared Belle's DNA with samples taken from one of her surviving relatives.

The results are startling and highlight two key facts: first, the body in the cellar was not Belle. Secondly, it was not even female.

According to Dr David Foran, head of forensic science at Michigan State University, 'that body cannot be Cora [Belle] Crippen, we're certain of that'.

If he is correct, and no one is doubting the results of his tests, then Crippen may be innocent of the crime for which he was hanged.

Two weeks before his execution he wrote: 'I am innocent and some day evidence will be found to prove it.'

The recent DNA analysis may yet clear his name.

Dead as a Dodo

They had endured nine long days adrift in a longboat with only their own urine to drink. They were half-crazed by dehydration, hunger and the relentless tropical sun.

But now, as Dutch seadog Volkert Evertszoon and his fellow mariners were washed ashore at a remote islet, they rubbed their eyes in disbelief. The place was home to scores of flightless birds. They waddled along the beach in a most undignified fashion and showed no fear when confronted by the newly arrived men. 'They were larger than geese but not able to fly,' wrote Evertszoon. 'Instead of wings they had small flaps.'

Evertszoon and his comrades could scarcely believe their luck. They had watched their crippled vessel *Arnhem* sink beneath the waves, convinced that they would die a lingering death in their longboat. But here on the Ile d'Ambre, off the east coast of Mauritius, there was enough food to keep them alive for months.

They were to be the last eyewitnesses of the hapless dodo, a bird on the verge of extinction. Indeed, it was almost certainly their empty bellies that led to the dodo's final demise in the spring of 1662.

Ever since the bird had first been sighted in Mauritius in the 1590s, it had been ruthlessly hunted for food. The introduction of pigs had further depleted their number. Indeed the only reason why the bird had survived on Ile d'Ambre – but nowhere else in Mauritius – is that it was the last remaining islet without any pigs.

The dodo did not make for an appetizing feast: it was widely known as the 'loathsome bird' on account of its disgusting taste. But it was extremely easy to catch and the sailors who hunted it were often so hungry that anything was better than the putrid salt-pork they had on board.

One ship's commander declared that dodos were at their most palatable if cooked slowly and over a low heat. 'Their belly and breast are of a pleasant flavour and easily masticated,' wrote Wybrand van Warwijck in 1598.

Such culinary delights were far from the minds of Volkert Evertszoon and his men when they stepped ashore on Ile d'Ambre. Their needs were simple – food – and they were delighted to find that the native dodos were so tame.

'They were not shy at all,' wrote Evertszoon, 'because they very likely were not used to see men pursuing them, and which became us exceedingly well, having neither barrel nor ammunition to shoot them.'

The birds seemed intrigued by the unwashed mariners who had intruded on their realm. 'They stared at us and remained quiet where they stood, not knowing whether they had wings to fly away or legs to run off, and suffering us to approach them as close as we pleased.'

The slaughter began within hours of landing. Evertszoon and his men drove a flock of the birds into one place 'in such a manner that we could catch them with our hands'. No sooner had they caught one lot than another flock 'came running as fast as they could to its assistance, and by which they were caught and made prisoners also'.

A diet of dodo meat was neither appetizing nor balanced, but it kept the men alive for the three months until they were rescued by the English ship *Truro*.

Evertszoon did not record whether he and his men killed all the dodos on the islet. But it is highly probable that they did, for there were no further sightings in the years that followed. When the Dutch hunter Isaac Lamotius recorded seeing dodos in 1688, he was referring to a different bird. By the time he was writing, the flightless red rail had been given the same Dutch name: *dodaers*.

Unless new evidence comes to light, it seems likely that Evertszoon and his men ate the hapless dodo into extinction.

Part XXIV
The Great Escape

Laden with the weight of human blood and believed
to have banqueted on human flesh . . .

Hobart Town Gazette's opinion of escaped convict
(and self-confessed cannibal) Alexander Pearce

A Sting in the Tale

Walter Harris had a nose for a good story and this one seemed better than most. As Morocco correspondent for *The Times*, he knew that violent battles and skirmishes always made entertaining copy.

On a blistering afternoon in June 1903, he was brought news of a bloody onslaught taking place near the town of Zinat. Not wishing to miss out on the action, he climbed onto his horse and headed towards the fighting.

As he approached Zinat, the air was filled with an ominous silence. 'The whole country was absolutely deserted,' he wrote. 'Not a single person, not a head of cattle, was to be seen.'

He was riding across the empty plain when a single volley rang out. Sensing danger, he spurred his horse and rode away from the spot where the gun had been fired.

But as he entered a deep gully, he saw he had fallen into an ambush. 'From every side sprung out tribesmen and in a second or two I was a prisoner, surrounded by thirty or forty men.'

It did not take long for Harris to discover the identity of his captor. It was the dreaded Mulai Ahmed er Raisuli, the most powerful bandit in northern Morocco.

Raisuli ruled his fiefdom with appalling brutality. His favourite punishment was burning out his captives' eyes with heated copper coins. 'By nature he was, and is, cruel,' wrote Harris, 'and the profession he had adopted' – that of bandit – 'gave him unlimited scope to exhibit his cruelty.'

The Englishman's life was in great danger. Raisuli and his bandit tribesmen were convinced that Harris was a supporter of the Moroccan sultan, whose troops had only recently regained much ground in the area.

Raisuli had often argued that capturing Christians was entirely legitimate. He also maintained that torturing them or even killing them were not crimes, 'because they were commissioned by Allah'.

He led Harris to an underground cell and locked him inside. The room was dark and stank of putrid flesh. It took time for Harris's eyes to get accustomed to the gloom, but when they did he was in for a terrible shock.

'The first object that attracted my eyes was a body lying in the middle of the room. It was the corpse of a man and formed a ghastly spectacle. Stripped of all clothing and shockingly mutilated, the head had been roughly hacked off and the floor all round was swimming in blood.'

Harris had a great deal of experience of life in Morocco and had also written at length about Raisuli. He tried to keep calm and to assess the situation with a clear head. He reckoned that he was worth more to Raisuli alive, as a hostage who could be used as a bargaining chip.

But he became increasingly concerned when he was led outside in order to witness an even more gruesome cadaver than the one sharing his cell.

'A ghastly sight,' he later wrote. 'The summer's heat had already caused the corpse to discolour and swell. An apple had been stuck in the man's mouth and both his eyes had been gouged out.'

He was informed that the same treatment awaited him if he tried to play any tricks.

The British Minister, Sir Arthur Nicolson, learned of Harris's capture and tentatively opened negotiations with Raisuli. The bandit had a number of demands, the most important of which was the release of his fifty-six blood relatives. These were being held alongside hundreds of other bandits in the sultan's prisons in Tangier and Larache. The sultan would have executed them long ago, if only he had known which of them were related to Raisuli.

After much wrangling a deal of sorts was struck. Twelve prisoners would be released in exchange for Harris's freedom. But Raisuli proved a slippery captor and kept raising the number, aware that he was holding an extremely valuable Christian hostage.

Harris was caught in an impossible predicament. Yet he held a few cards and he was determined to play them with skill. He persuaded Raisuli to tell him the names of all fifty-six relatives whom he wanted released. He promised to send this list to Tangier in order that Nicolson could exert his influence to win their freedom. Raisuli did exactly as Harris requested, unaware that he had fallen headlong into a trap.

'You propose to kill me,' said Harris to the bandit chief. 'Possibly you will do so, but you have kindly given me a list of all your relations who are in the Moorish prison. This list is now in Tangier. You will have the satisfaction of killing me, but remember this – on fifty-six consecutive days one of your sons or brothers or nephews will be executed, one each morning.'

Shortly afterwards Harris was released by a furious Raisuli. *The Times* correspondent delighted in his trick and took great relish in describing it in his memoirs.

'It was a splendid bluff,' he wrote, 'and I felt the greatest delight in using it.' Not only had he saved his own life, but he had also made a mockery of Raisuli and his tribesmen. 'They swore and cursed and threatened, but to no avail.'

Not for the first time – nor the last – Walter Harris had got the upper hand.

And Then There Were None

There were eight of them at the outset, convicts making their escape from a penal colony in Van Diemen's Land, today's Tasmania. Their leader was Alexander Pearce, a pockmarked Irishman with a hot head and a reputation for violence. He, in common with his fellow convicts, had been incarcerated in the dreaded Macquarie Harbour penal settlement on Tasmania's remote west coast.

In September 1822, Pearce was working in a labour gang and made his escape by stealing a boat. Seven others jumped into the boat and made their getaway with him.

They were a motley band of thieves, highwaymen and common criminals: Matthew Travers, Alexander Dalton, Robert Greenhill, John Mather, William Kennerly, Thomas Bodenham and Edward 'Little' Brown.

The men rowed unnoticed to the far side of the bay and then sank their stolen boat before making their way into the dense forest. Their goal was the settlement of Hobart at the mouth of the Derwent, where they hoped to steal a ship and sail for England.

They were unaware that to reach Hobart meant traversing some of the most rugged and inhospitable terrain in Australia. The weather only added to their woes. The rain tipped down relentlessly, soaking them to the bone. As the chill wind whipped at their scant clothing, some of them began to complain that they were unable to keep up.

One of the men, William Kennerly, made a cruel but telling jest about their lack of food. 'I am so weak', he said, 'that I could eat a piece of man.' It soon transpired that he was not joking. He suggested that they should kill the weakest of their company and eat him.

Not everyone agreed. Even though they were hardened criminals, several spoke out against cold-blooded murder. But Robert Greenhill sided with Kennerly. Deranged by hunger, he singled out Alexander Dalton and decided to act immediately, picking up his axe and smashing it into Dalton's skull. He was killed instantly.

Greenhill's comrade-in-arms Matthew Travers willingly joined the bloodletting. 'With a knife [he] also came and cut his throat . . . we tore out his insides and cut off his head.' The remaining seven men divided Dalton into equal portions and ate him.

Even so, the meal proved poor sustenance and did little to help them regain their strength. Two of the men soon fell behind the others and were lost. Both would eventually be recaptured by local guards: both would die soon after.

The remaining five escapees crossed the many rivers by dragging each other over with a long pole. The procedure consumed so much energy that they decided another man had to die. This time it was Thomas Bodenham's turn. Greenhill split his skull with an axe and the remaining four men ate him until there was nothing left.

They had been on the run for nearly a month when John Mather fell seriously ill with dysentery. Aware that he was next for the axe, he begged to be allowed to pray before they killed him. He then 'laid down his head and Greenhill took the axe and killed him'.

Shortly after Mather had been eaten, Matthew Travers was bitten by a snake. As he weakened, he, too, was axed to death.

Now, there were only Pearce and Greenhill left. Greenhill had the sole axe, which he zealously guarded. Neither man dared to sleep, for fear that he would be killed by the other.

After several days of playing a deadly game of cat and mouse, both men were exhausted. Against his better judgement, Greenhill fell asleep.

Pearce seized the opportunity. 'I run up [sic], and took the axe from under his head, and struck him with it and killed him.' He hacked off Greenhill's arm and thigh and took them with him.

Pearce continued through the wilderness for several days until he reached a clearing that was being farmed by a shepherd. The shepherd took pity on Pearce and offered him shelter. Once he was restored to health, Pearce fell in with a couple of criminal bushrangers and lived with them for two months before all three men were tracked down and captured. By this time, Pearce had been on the run for four months, of which almost half had been spent in the wild.

Pearce was placed under lock and key in Hobart, where he made a full and frank confession to the Reverend Robert Knopwood, the town's chaplain and magistrate. Knopwood didn't believe Pearce's account of cannibalism – it was too horrific – and had him sent him back to Macquarie Harbour.

Within a few months Pearce once again made his escape, this time taking with him a young lad named Thomas Cox.

Cox's freedom was to prove short-lived. Pearce killed him within a few days and was in the process of eating him when he was once again captured. This time his tales of cannibalism were found to be true, for poor Cox's mutilated remains were discovered nearby.

Pearce was hanged in July 1824. Shortly before he died he was heard to say: 'Man's flesh is delicious. It tastes far better than pork or fish.'

After his death, his body was given to a surgeon and dissected. His skull was eventually presented to the Academy of Natural Sciences in Philadelphia where it was given pride of place in a glass showcase.

It remains there to this day.

Edwin Darling's Nightmare

Lieutenant Colonel Edwin Darling was confident that he ran the most secure prisoner-of-war camp in Britain.

Camp 198 near Bridgend in South Wales, known locally as Island Farm, was surrounded by a high-wire fence and equipped with search-lights and guard dogs. At night, sentries made frequent patrols around the site.

There was good reason for the security. By the spring of 1945, the camp housed more than 2,000 German POWs. These included several elite SS commanders and half a dozen Luftwaffe fighter pilots. When these hardened Nazis had been brought to the camp, they arrived in defiant mood, singing 'we are marching to England'.

Darling knew that any successful escape would be a propaganda disaster. The last thing he wanted was a German equivalent of the Allied breakout from Stalag Luft III. The men involved in that escape had been feted as heroes and their courage would later be immortalized in the Hollywood movie *The Great Escape*.

On the evening of 10 March 1945, Darling retired to bed unaware of anything untoward in the offing. The evening roll call had brought no unwelcome surprises and the prisoners had returned to their dormitories without trouble.

The only clue that something was wrong came later that night, when Darling's sleep was interrupted by the sound of prisoners singing loudly. But this was not unusual, for the inmates of Camp 198 often sang until late into the night.

Their rousing choruses were for a purpose. For many months, they had been secretly digging a huge underground tunnel that led from Hut 9 to the outside world. By the second week of March, it was complete and scores of prisoners were hoping to make their escape.

The 70-foot tunnel was a consummate work of German engineering. It descended deep into the clay subsoil before rising towards a small opening in a newly ploughed field on the far side of the perimeter fence. The prisoners had excavated it using knives and cooking utensils stolen from the camp kitchens.

The soil was disposed of in novel fashion. The POWs had managed to construct a fake wall at the end of Hut 9, using old tiles and bricks. They then pushed the excavated soil through a false air vent and into the cavity behind the wall.

The tunnel's roof was supported with wood stolen from oak benches in the canteen and the floor was lined with old clothes to ensure that escapees would not get dirty. There was even electric lighting, which could be used as a warning system whenever a guard was approaching.

Most extraordinary of all was the tunnel's air supply. Dozens of milk tins had been linked together to form a tube and air was forced through this tube by means of a four-bladed fan.

The night of the great escape was meticulously planned. Each prisoner was given an allotted time to pass through the tunnel and many of the men were equipped with maps of the local area. Some planned to steal cars and drive to Cardiff in the hope of smuggling themselves aboard ships heading to the continent. Others, emboldened by their training as pilots, hoped to steal planes and fly back to Germany.

It was shortly before midnight when the great escape began. Among the escapees was an SS officer named Karl Ludwig and his colleague Heinz Herzler. They slipped through the tunnel and successfully emerged into the field beyond the perimeter fence. They then followed their fellow escapees into the surrounding woodland.

As they crept along the road towards Cardiff, they encountered a drunken man returning home. They hid themselves in a hedge and waited for him to pass.

It was an unfortunate hiding place. The man staggered over to where Karl Ludwig was crouched in the undergrowth and answered a call of nature, unaware that he was urinating on an SS officer.

Most escapees had chosen to flee from the camp in small groups. One band of four men made their getaway in a stolen car. Others went on foot, trying to reach nearby railway stations before dawn.

Back at Camp 198, Lieutenant Colonel Darling slept on through the night, ignorant of what was taking place. It was not until 2.15 a.m., four hours after the first batch of prisoners had escaped, that the camp guards heard strange noises and realized something was wrong. They immediately woke Darling and then raised the alarm. A roll call of prisoners revealed that almost ninety had gone missing.

By daybreak a massive nationwide manhunt was under way. According to the *Daily Express*, 'spotter planes flew over the Vale of Glamorgan while troops, Home Guard and police, all armed with tommy guns, searched the woods, fields and ditches'.

Though well trained, the German prisoners were at a huge disadvantage. They were highly conspicuous and poorly equipped. Karl Ludwig and Heinz Herzler redoubled their efforts to reach Cardiff after their unfortunate incident in the hedge, but it was not long before they were sighted by a local policeman named Philip Baverstock. He promptly arrested them.

Other prisoners were even less successful: most were captured within a few miles of the camp and it was not long before all of them were soon back in their huts.

At least that was the official version of the story. But how many really escaped? And how many were recaptured?

Unofficial accounts suggest that 84 prisoners got out of the camp, eight more than the Allied POWs who escaped from Stalag Luft III. But because fourteen were quickly recaptured, officials claimed (for propaganda purposes) that only 70 Germans escaped.

When the issue was raised in Parliament, the Minister of War, Arthur Henderson, assured the country that the actual number was 67. There was good reason for him being economical with the truth. Several days after the breakout, three suspicious-looking Germans – escaped prisoners – were spotted near Canterbury in Kent. They managed to evade capture and were never seen again.

What happened to them remains a mystery. The most likely explanation is that they stole a boat and tried to make it back to Germany. Whether or not they were successful remains unclear.

But their empty beds at Camp 198 must have been a thorn in the side of Edwin Darling and a constant reminder that he had presided over one of the greatest prison breakouts of the Second World War.

Part XXV
When Churchill Slaughtered Sheep

I don't know what we'll fight them with. We shall have to
slosh them with bottles, empty of course.

Winston Churchill's quip to a colleague,
made just seconds after delivering his famous speech:
'We shall fight them on the beaches'

When Churchill Slaughtered Sheep

On a blustery July morning in 1943, a strange kerfuffle could be seen taking place on the shores of Gruinard Bay on the west coast of Scotland. A group of men, some in army uniform, were attempting to herd dozens of sheep into a landing craft. After much effort, the sheep were finally loaded and the little boat set sail for low-lying Gruinard Island.

The island lay approximately half a mile offshore: it was bleak, windswept and extremely remote. It was also uninhabited, one of the principal reasons why it had been selected for an experiment so secret that not even the local crofters were allowed to know what was taking place.

Alice MacIver, a young girl at the time, found all the commotion terribly exciting: 'There was lots of activity. It was great fun, when you remember this is a very quiet place. We just thought it was some military exercise.'

But it was not a military exercise, nor were the men soldiers. They were scientists – brilliant ones – and they had travelled to Scotland from Porton laboratories in Wiltshire. Some, like Paul Fildes, worked for the Biological Department. Others were employed by the Chemical Defence Experimental Station. All of them knew they were playing for very high stakes: the tests to be conducted on Gruinard Island, known as X Base, had the potential to change the course of the Second World War.

Winston Churchill himself had led the discussions about using biological weapons against Nazi Germany. He had debated the subject with his chiefs of staff and come up with the germ of an idea. This idea was codenamed (with characteristically black humour) 'Operation Vegetarian'. Churchill wanted to know if it was possible to contaminate the German countryside with so many anthrax spores that huge numbers of livestock and people would be instantly killed.

'It was a nasty business,' recalls local Scottish historian Donald Macintyre, then a young lad serving in the RAF. 'But nobody would have dreamt of making a protest. It was wartime and people wanted to show their patriotism and do their part.'

Paul Fildes and his team of biological scientists shipped eighty sheep to Gruinard Island in preparation for the tests. They also took a cameraman, whose task was to record everything that happened during those few days in July.

Once on the island, the sheep were herded into individual container crates and covered in fabric jackets. This was to ensure that they would contract the anthrax from inhalation, rather than from spores on their fleeces.

The anthrax chosen for the experiment was Vollum 14578, a highly virulent strain whose efficacy had already been demonstrated in laboratories. The principal method of dissemination was to fire the anthrax by mortar.

Fildes and his men took the extraordinary decision to remain on the island while the trials were taking place. Although they were wearing cloth overalls, rubber gloves and gas masks, they were nevertheless exposing themselves to unprecedented risk.

Once the equipment was set up and the cylinders of anthrax in position, the order was given to fire the mortar. In a matter of seconds, the charge was detonated and a highly toxic cloud began travelling on the stiff sea breeze towards the crated sheep.

At first, they showed no sign of having been infected. Fildes and his team were surprised to watch the sheep chewing on the stubbly grass, seemingly unaffected by the vast quantities of anthrax that had been blown in their direction. But on the third day after the experiment they suddenly began to die, keeling over as if they had been struck by paralysis. Within hours of the first death, almost the entire flock had succumbed to the anthrax. Only those at the extreme fringes of the field – and therefore exposed to limited doses – survived the experiment.

Fildes and his men were stunned by the efficacy of Vollum 14578. They realized that a mass detonation of anthrax over Germany would cause death on an unprecedented scale. But they were also alarmed by their inability to decontaminate Gruinard Island in the aftermath of the experiment. Once the anthrax spores had settled on the land, they proved impossible to remove. Even their contaminated clothes had to be burned, since washing them did not remove the spores.

An additional scare came when an unexpected storm swept one of the sheep carcasses over to the mainland. It instantly infected other livestock, leading to a secret cull of sheep and a swift payment of compensation to the local farmer.

Donald Macintyre was bemused by the speed with which the compensation was paid. 'It's not often that you put in a complaint and get paid straightaway.'

The virulence of the anthrax was to prove both its strength and its weakness. Churchill was alarmed by the way it spread so uncontrollably and the project was temporarily put on hold.

But by the spring of 1944, anthrax was back on the agenda. After a series of meetings with his military advisers, Churchill approved an order for an initial stockpile of 500,000 anthrax bombs. He stressed that he would only give the order for a biological strike on Germany in retaliation for a similar attack on Britain. 'If our enemies should indulge in this form of warfare,' he said, 'the only deterrent would be our power to retaliate.'

The Inter-Service Sub-Committee on Biological Warfare noted that the initial anthrax order 'was based on an appreciation that the number would be sufficient for retaliatory attacks on six large enemy cities'. But after prolonged deliberation, they dramatically increased the quantity of anthrax.

'It has now been concluded that it may be necessary to arrange provision of eight times this number of bombs in order to achieve results on the scale originally envisaged.'

The production of the initial order took time – far longer than the experts had expected. 'The plant for manufacturing the filling of the bombs [with anthrax] should be in operation by the end of the year [1944]. We could not, therefore, engage in this form of warfare on any effective scale before the spring of 1945.'

By the time the first bombs were ready, a secret report to a Cabinet Defence Committee revealed that even deadlier anthrax weapons were being trialled. These had the potential to reduce Germany to an uninhabitable wasteland.

'Judging by its effect on monkeys,' reads the report, '[it] might kill half the population of a city of the size of Stuttgart in one heavy bomber raid and render the site of the city uninhabitable for many years to come. It is clear, therefore, that biological warfare is potentially a most deadly weapon and, if it is ever used in warfare, may have revolutionary effects.'

But the end of the war was now in sight and a new deadly weapon, the atomic bomb, was in development. Anthrax was no longer required and the biological weapons project was quietly shelved.

As for Gruinard Island, it was so badly contaminated that it was proclaimed off-limits. Locals were warned not to set foot on the island and 'Keep Out' signs were erected all around the foreshore. The island was to remain out of bounds until 1990, when the removal of the topsoil and spraying of the island with formaldehyde solution finally rendered it safe.

There is still no one living on the island. These days, the only inhabitants are a flock of sheep who munch on the grass, blissfully unaware of the deadly spores that until recently infected their island home.

The Black Sheep

It was almost midnight and most of the office lights had been switched off. The secretaries and clerical assistants had long since left and headed back to their homes in the suburbs of Moscow.

Leon Trotsky remained in his office alone, although he was no longer concentrating on his work as head of the Red Army. His thoughts were focused entirely on the woman seated opposite him. Her huge eyes and high cheekbones were typically Slavic, yet there was nothing Russian about Clare Sheridan. She was half English, half American; a talented sculptor who had come to Moscow in order to undertake a number of important commissions.

Her trip, undertaken in the autumn of 1920, attracted the immediate attention of MI5. Russia was a hostile power and the British government was actively discouraging travel to the country. There were many in the security service who feared that Clare Sheridan sympathized with the new Communist government.

But there was another, altogether more compelling reason for MI5 officers to be concerned. Sheridan was the first cousin of Winston Churchill. (Her mother, Clarita Jerome, was the sister of Churchill's mother, Jeanette Jerome.) As such, her trip had the potential to be extremely damaging. Churchill was the country's most vociferous advocate of military intervention against Russia and he had made countless speeches about his loathing for the Bolsheviks.

'Of all the tyrannies,' he said, 'the Bolshevist tyranny is the worst, the most destructive and the most degrading.'

Clare Sheridan had done nothing to hide her trip to Moscow, but she had neglected to tell anyone that she had been commissioned to sculpt some of the leading figures in the revolutionary government, including Lenin, Trotsky, Dzerzhinsky and Kamenev.

Trotsky had initially resisted sitting for a cousin of the hated Winston Churchill, but he quickly changed his tune when he met Sheridan. As she measured his features with her callipers, he flashed his eyes at her and murmured in a seductive tone: 'You're caressing me with tools of steel.'

Sheridan paid her visits to Trotsky's office in the evenings, when the ministry building was deserted. Trotsky soon found himself completely under her spell. 'When your teeth are clenched and you are fighting with your work, you're still a woman,' he told her.

She had a struggle to persuade Trotsky to remove his pince-nez, but she eventually succeeded. 'It seemed akin to physical pain taking them off,' she later wrote. 'They have become part of him and the loss of them completely changes his individuality.'

It was clear to both artist and sitter that there was a chemistry between them and Trotsky was only following his instincts when, at the end of one of their late-night sittings, he agreed to undress and show her his 'splendid neck and chest'.

Clare Sheridan had long believed in free love and was quite open in expressing her views. Moscow was soon alive with rumours that she and Trotsky were having an affair.

There were also rumours that Sheridan was having a simultaneous affair with Lev Kamenev, a senior member of the Politburo. The two of them had first met while Kamenev was on a Soviet trade mission to London in the summer of 1920. He had spoiled her with expensive restaurant lunches, to the extreme annoyance of Mrs Kamenev.

'We don't live chic like that in Moscow,' was the icy greeting she gave her husband on his return to Russia. She gave an even frostier reception to Clare Sheridan, telling her that England had turned her husband into one of the hated bourgeoisie.

It is not known whether or not Clare Sheridan consummated her affair with Trotsky. If she did, it was to prove a brief liaison. She stayed just a few weeks in Moscow before returning to England. By now MI5 agents were fully on her case, tapping her phone, intercepting her mail and monitoring all her movements.

Their intelligence file on her behaviour is full of accusations of treachery. 'She has conducted herself in a disloyal manner in various foreign countries, adopting a consistently anti-British attitude.'

Every development brought new embarrassment for Churchill. In 1922, MI5 discovered that Sheridan was in contact with Indian nationalists in Lausanne and was receiving private letters via the Russian diplomatic bag.

When she undertook a trip to Italy, British agents followed in her wake, noting that she 'not only openly aired her views in favour of Bolshevism, but tried to convince some of the guests of its advantages, especially in connection with free love'.

She was certainly a practitioner of the latter. When staying in Istanbul, she took as her lover a certain Ismet Bey, a known political agitator who was vociferous in seeking the overthrow of British rule in India.

Churchill might have forgiven his cousin these indiscretions, but in 1923 she surpassed them all. As an MI5 informant observed, 'she appears to have been recently all over Germany, and was present at Munich at one of Hitler's meetings. She was very much impressed with the extraordinary enthusiasm that Hitler aroused among an audience of 10,000 people with an extraordinarily blood-thirsty speech.'

She tried to put her 'free love' ideas into practice in Germany, but met with no success. 'She found the German was nothing like so responsive to her personal charms as was the Russian, a fact she deplored.'

In 1925, telephone tapping revealed that she had passed details of her conversations with Churchill, then Chancellor of the Exchequer, to Norman Ewer, the foreign editor of the *Daily Herald* and a known Soviet agent. When, later that year, Sheridan moved to Algiers, MI5 concluded that she was in the pay of the Soviets.

WHEN CHURCHILL SLAUGHTERED SHEEP

'In view of the facts regarding her financial position [we] are strongly of the opinion that Clare is in the pay of the Russians and that she has been sent to North Africa to get in touch with the local situation and to act either as a reporting agent or possibly as a forwarding agent.'

Eventually, the head of MI5, Vernon Kell, visited Churchill and told him about the dossier of evidence they had gathered against his cousin. Churchill said to Kell that 'he was prepared to believe anything'. He also said he was 'prepared to take any action' that MI5 thought necessary.

Clare Sheridan's dalliance with Trotsky, Kamenev, Nazism and free love was a source of continual embarrassment for Churchill, yet he never completely broke relations with his wayward cousin. Indeed, by the outset of the Second World War, he had forgiven her for her past misdeeds and even allowed her to sculpt his bust.

MI5 were not quite so forgiving. They kept a close eye on the black sheep of the Churchill clan and continued to intercept her letters for years to come.

Winston's Bombshell

Private Boctroff and his Red Army comrades had grown used to British planes flying over their positions in northern Russia. Ever since Allied forces had landed in Archangel in the summer of 1918, aerial raids had been an almost daily occurrence.

But at around lunchtime on 29 August, the raid above Plesetzkaya was to prove rather more devastating than previous ones. As the plane passed overhead, it dropped dozens of exploding metal canisters. Private Boctroff watched in alarm as the strange-looking canisters fell to the ground. They exploded as they neared the treeline, emitting clouds of green gas.

Private Boctroff ran for safety and managed to avoid the worst of the gas cloud, yet his nose nevertheless began to stream with blood and he felt so giddy that he could hardly stand. His comrades were less fortunate. Twenty-five of them choked to death, while a further twenty lapsed into unconsciousness.

The chemical attack on Bolshevik-controlled northern Russia was undertaken on the orders of Winston Churchill. As Secretary of State for War he had argued for military action against the Bolsheviks, much to the annoyance of the prime minister, David Lloyd George. 'He has Bolshevism on the brain,' said Lloyd George after one conversation with Churchill, '[and] he is mad for operations in Russia.'

In the aftermath of the First World War there was little appetite for putting troops on the ground. Churchill was forced to look for a more creative solution when dealing with Lenin's Bolsheviks. He was an enthusiastic proponent of biological warfare and knew that scientists at the governmental laboratories at Porton in Wiltshire had recently developed a devastating new weapon.

The top secret 'M Device' was an exploding shell containing a highly toxic gas called diphenylaminechloroarsine. The man in charge of designing the shell, Major General Charles Foulkes, called it 'the most effective chemical weapon ever devised'.

Trials at Porton suggested that it had an instant effect on all who inhaled it. Uncontrollable vomiting, coughing up blood and crippling fatigue were the most common symptoms.

The head of chemical warfare production, Sir Keith Price, was convinced its use would lead to the rapid collapse of the Bolshevik regime. 'If you got home only once with the Gas you would find no more Bolshies this side of Vologda.'

The Cabinet was deeply hostile to the use of chemical weapons, but Churchill argued his corner with customary vigour. He told his colleagues that they should also consider using the M Device against the rebellious tribes of northern India.

'I am strongly in favour of using poisoned gas against uncivilized tribes,' he declared, and criticized his colleagues for their 'squeamishness'. In one notable memo, he declared that 'the objections of the India Office to the use of gas against natives are unreasonable. Gas is a more merciful weapon than the high explosive shell, and compels an enemy to accept a decision with less loss of life than any other agency of war.'

He ended his memo on a note of ill-placed black humour: 'Why is it not fair for a British artilleryman to fire a shell which makes the said native sneeze?' he asked. 'It is really too silly.'

Some 50,000 M Devices were shipped to Archangel in the summer of 1919 and aerial attacks began soon after. The village of Emtsa, 120 miles to the south of Archangel, was one of the first to be targeted. Fifty-three M Devices were dropped around midday and a further sixty-two in the evening. The Bolshevik soldiers on the ground could be seen fleeing in panic as the thick green cloud of toxic gas drifted towards them.

British scientists were keen to study the effects of the gas. To this end, a small team was sent to Russia in order to examine the victims of the chemical attacks. Private Boctroff was one of those interviewed in the wake of the attack on Plesetzkaya Station. Although he was caught in the outermost fringe of the gas cloud, he was described (in the scientists' notes) as being 'affected with giddiness in head'. He had also 'bled from nose and coughed with blood, [his] eyes watered and [he had] difficulty in breathing'.

Private Boctroff told the scientists that many of his comrades had been stationed much closer to the spot where the M Device had landed. '[They] were overpowered in the cloud and died there; the others staggered about for a short time and then fell down and died.'

Other witnesses described their gassed comrades as 'lying practically helpless on the ground and the usual symptoms of bleeding from the nose and mouth'.

The chemical attacks continued throughout the month of September, with aerial strikes on the Bolshevik-held villages of Chunova, Vikhtova, Pocha, Chorga, Tavoigor and Zapolki. Some of these attacks used large quantities of M Devices: no fewer than 183 canisters were dropped on Vikhtova.

Once the gas had dissipated, British and White Russian troops (equipped with gas masks) would push forward and kill any remaining Bolshevik soldiers.

The use of chemical weapons caused widespread demoralization on the battlefield, yet they proved less effective than Churchill had hoped. They did not lead to the collapse of the Red Army, as he had predicted, nor did they lead to any lasting victories by the Allied and White Russian forces. The weather was primarily to blame. Toxic gas proved ineffectual in the damp conditions of an early Russian autumn.

By September, British forces were preparing to withdraw from

Archangel and the chemical attacks were permanently brought to a close. According to a report written for the War Office, a total of 2,718 M Devices had been dropped on Bolshevik positions, while 47,282 remained unused.

It was too dangerous to ship these remaining devices back to England. In mid-September, the decision was taken to dump them in the White Sea. A military tug took them to a position some thirty miles north of the Dvina estuary and they were tipped overboard.

They remain on the seabed to this day in forty fathoms of water.

Part XXVI

A Question of Mistaken Identity

I congratulate you upon no longer being the Chevalier d'Eon,
but rather Mademoiselle d'Eon.

The Comte de Vergennes, French Minister of Foreign Affairs,
congratulates his old friend on becoming legally accepted as a
woman

The Double Life of Chevalier d'Eon

The corpse that lay on the mortuary slab was clothed in a full-length dress and a mass of hair was spilling across the marble. It was in a pristine state and there was no outward reason to suspect anything untoward.

But the attendant surgeon, Thomas Copeland, knew that appearances could be deceptive. He was about to examine the cadaver of an illustrious French aristocrat, one whose gender had long been the subject of gossip and speculation.

The speculation had been fuelled by the outlandish behaviour of the deceased. For decades, Chevalier d'Eon had lived a double life, switching gender and clothes with undisguised relish. One day, he would claim to be a full-blooded male, the next he would appear at court in a long flowing dress.

Legally, the chevalier had been declared a woman and most people believed that d'Eon was indeed a member of 'the fairer sex'. But the truth was to prove rather more complex.

Charles-Geneviève-Louis-Auguste-André-Timothée d'Eon de Beaumont had been born in Burgundy in 1728 and baptized as a baby boy. For the first eighteen years of his life, he had lived as a man and displayed no outward signs of any issues with his gender.

But in 1756, while undertaking an espionage mission to the Russian court, Chevalier d'Eon began dressing as a woman. He proved so successful in living under his alter ego that he became, for a brief period, a maid of honour to the Russian empress, Elizabeth.

On returning to France, he changed back into male clothing and served as a dragoon guard, fighting in the latter stages of the Seven Years War.

In the spring of 1763, he travelled to London in order to serve as a plenipotentiary minister. He was still dressed in conventional male clothing, but rumours about his cross-dressing – and even his gender – began to circulate throughout the capital.

D'Eon encouraged the rumours and seemed to relish the attention they brought him. He gave ambiguous replies to questions about his sex, only fuelling speculation that he was in fact a woman disguised as a man.

Further evidence came when his close friend, Pierre de Beaumarchais, let slip that 'this crazy woman is insanely in love with me'.

Chevalier d'Eon became the talk of the town and the more scurrilous news-sheets were filled with stories about his gender. London's gamblers began staking huge sums on the issue and before long they had bet a staggering £200,000. As the gambling racket threatened to spiral out of control, Chief Justice Lord Mansfield was forced to intervene. He declared – controversially – that English law believed d'Eon to be a woman.

The chevalier's return to France had long been prevented by his role in a French courtly scandal. But in 1774 the old king died and the newly crowned Louis XVI decided to allow d'Eon back to Paris. This involved complicated negotiations, for the chevalier was in possession of information that had the potential to embarrass the king.

A deal was eventually struck and a legal contract duly signed. This contract contained a most unusual clause. D'Eon agreed to all of the king's terms, but only on the understanding that he would henceforth be recognized, both legally and socially, as a woman.

On 21 November 1777, the forty-nine-year-old d'Eon was formally presented to Louis XVI and Marie Antoinette at Versailles, having previously undergone a four-hour toilette at the hands of the queen's dressmaker.

D'Eon would later write in his memoirs of how he managed to shed his rough skin and learn to walk like a lady. But in spite of the extensive toilette, few of the courtiers at Versailles were impressed. 'She had nothing of our sex but the petticoats and the curls, which suited her horribly,' was the opinion of Vicomtesse de Fars.

The Chevalier d'Eon, now legally female, eventually moved back to London where she was reintroduced to Horace Walpole. Walpole was unconvinced by the apparent change in gender. 'Her hands and arms seem not to have participated of the change of sexes, but are fitter to carry a chair than a fan.' James Boswell agreed, saying that 'she appeared as a man in woman's clothes'.

The chevalier had always delighted in scandal and now began writing a salacious memoir, including a great deal of tattle about his private parts: 'I was born with a caul,' he explained, 'and my sex was hidden *in nubibus*.' What this meant was that the testicles, if there were any, had not descended.

Later in the book, he quotes his father telling his mother: 'The doctor hopes that nature [the baby's sex] will soon be developed and that it will be a good boy by the grace of God, or a good girl by the virtue of the Blessed Virgin.' This lack of certainty about his gender, claimed d'Eon, was why he had been christened with both male and female names, Charles and Geneviève.

The latter stages of the chevalier's life were difficult. Partially paralysed, bedridden and living in London as an old spinster, she shared lodgings with a widow named Mrs Cole, who was to remain with d'Eon until the very end. When the erstwhile chevalier finally died in the spring of 1810, Mrs Cole remained convinced that her lodger was a woman.

London society was rather more sceptical and the autopsy became a cause célèbre. It was of particular interest to the capital's gamblers, who had staked so much money on the issue.

The responsibility for revealing the truth fell to the distinguished surgeon Thomas Copeland and a team of twenty-six colleagues. They were charged with conducting the autopsy and revealing to the world whether d'Eon was a man, a woman or a hermaphrodite.

Gingerly and with unusual care, Copeland began to strip the chevalier's body, first removing the flowing dress and then taking off the silken stockings. Finally, he reached the undergarment and began to cut through the material with his surgeon's knife. As the clothing fell away from the corpse, there was a collective gasp from around the mortuary slab.

'I hereby certify that I have inspected and dissected the body of the Chevalier d'Eon,' wrote Surgeon Copeland in his official report of the autopsy, 'and have found the male organs in every respect perfectly formed.'

In order to be absolutely certain, he proceeded to remove the male organ and perform 'a complete inspection and dissection of the sexual parts'. He also made a thorough investigation of the nipples and breasts. These, too, were undeniably male.

Chevalier d'Eon had been a man all along, albeit one who had played a highly convincing game of sexual masquerade.

How to Catch a Spy

She stood alone on the execution ground, her dove-grey suit under-scored by a low-cut blouse. She refused to be tied to a stake and she had also declined to be blindfolded. If death was to be her fate, then she wished to look her twelve executioners in the eye.

Mata Hari had been found guilty of espionage in one of the most celebrated trials of the twentieth century. She had been convicted of passing highly sensitive documents to the enemy, her crimes exposed by France's renowned Deuxième Bureau.

But not everything was quite as it seemed in the strange case of Mata Hari. Some of her supporters were already claiming that she was being executed not for espionage, but for her scandalous behaviour in the heady days before the First World War.

In her heyday Mata Hari had been a sensation, celebrated across Europe for dancing publicly in the nude. She had brought an oriental exoticism to the outré clubs and cabarets of belle époque Paris.

The young Margaretha Geertruida Zelle, as she was then known, had arrived in Paris in 1903. She was in a desperate state, escaping from an unhappy marriage to an alcoholic and promiscuous Dutch army captain named Rudolf MacLeod. He had been a violent husband, whipping his beautiful bride with the cat-o'-nine-tails.

'I cannot live with a man who is so despicable,' wrote Zelle in a letter to her father. 'I prefer to die before he touches me again.'

She left the captain soon after discovering he had transmitted his syphilis to their two children. In revenge for leaving him, MacLeod ensured that his ex-wife was left penniless. Her only hope of financial survival was to exploit her sexuality.

Margaretha moved to Paris were she soon found employment in a circus. Shortly afterwards she changed her name to Mata Hari ('Eye of the Day' in Indonesian) and became an exotic dancer.

Her most famous act saw her steadily remove all her clothes until she was wearing just a bejewelled bra and a few golden beads on her arms. Her bra was the only item of clothing she rarely took off: she had small breasts and didn't like to reveal them in public.

The critics were left spellbound by the eroticism of her dancing. 'Feline, trembling in a thousand rhythms, exotic yet deeply austere, slender and supple like a sacred serpent,' wrote one.

The money poured in as she was courted by Parisian high society. 'Tonight I dance with Count A and tomorrow with Duke B,' she once remarked. 'If I don't have to dance, I make a trip with Marquis C. I avoid serious liaisons. I satisfy all my caprices.'

In the spring of 1914, the Berlin Metropole offered her a lucrative contract, one she was more than willing to accept. She was seemingly unaware that the world was on a fast track to war, one that threatened to engulf her.

Within days of arriving in Germany, her money and her valuable fur coats were seized and she was left penniless and adrift. Unsure what to do, she returned briefly to her native Holland.

It was while in Holland that she received a visit from the German consul, Karl Kroemer. He told her he was recruiting spies and offered her 20,000 francs and the code name H21 if she would spy for the Germans.

She took the cash as compensation for the money and coats that had been seized in Germany. But she always maintained that she never had any intention of spying. Instead, she used the money to return to Paris where she resumed her glamorous life, dancing for the many wealthy officers in the city.

Unknown to her, she was being tracked by two secret policemen who suspected that she might be involved in espionage. They opened her letters and collected information about her love life, including, embarrassingly, her nocturnal liaisons with one of their senior colleagues. But there was no evidence of spying.

This mattered little to Captain Georges Ladoux, the head of French military intelligence. His Deuxième Bureau had come in for a great deal of criticism over the previous few years for failing to produce results. Ladoux knew that exposing Mata Hari as a spy would be a sensational coup, one that would redound upon him.

Although he had scarcely a shred of evidence, he publicly accused her of passing secrets to the enemy and had her arrested on 13 February 1917. It was reported that she was completely naked when the officers came to arrest her. This was almost certainly Ladoux's doing. She was in fact dressed in a lace-trimmed dressing gown.

The case against her was flimsy and unconvincing. The prosecution failed to prove that she had passed a single document to the Germans. Mata Hari continued to protest her innocence. 'My international connections are due to my work as a dancer, nothing else,' she said. 'Because I really did not spy, it is terrible that I cannot defend myself.'

Her defence attorney was the brilliant international lawyer Edouard Clunet, yet he faced impossible odds. He was not even allowed to cross-examine the prosecution's witnesses.

The prosecutor would later admit that 'there was not enough evidence to flog a cat'. But Captain Ladoux was determined to find her guilty and he ensured that the presiding magistrate, Pierre Bouchardon, was on message.

'I had but one thought,' said Bouchardon on meeting Mata Hari for the first time, 'to unmask her.'

At dawn on 15 October 1917, Mata Hari was woken in her prison cell and told that she had been found guilty of espionage and was to be executed that morning. Ladoux was delighted by the result of the trial: he had proved that his Deuxième Bureau could get results. In condemning Mata Hari to death, he had also silenced his critics.

Mata Hari protested her innocence to the very end, but she must have known that there was no hope of overturning the death penalty. She did not flinch as the twelve soldiers, dressed in their khaki uniforms and red hats, raised their rifles in her direction. She waved to the two nuns who had accompanied her to the execution ground and blew a kiss to the priest.

Seconds later, the shots rang out and she crumpled to the ground, dying in an instant. She was forty-one years of age.

One of the non-commissioned officers attending the execution walked over to her corpse and fired a bullet into her brain at point-blank range.

It was a quite unnecessary *coup de grâce* against someone who was almost certainly innocent.

The Last Secret of the Cold War

The corpse was in a grim state of decomposition. The head and hands were missing and the torso, though still wrapped in a frogman's suit, was badly mutilated. There were few clues as to the identity of the body.

It had been pulled from the sea near Chichester in the summer of 1957 and taken to a local mortuary, where forensic experts set to work trying to discover who it was. In doing so, they were to find themselves investigating one of the greatest mysteries of the Cold War. The only certainty to emerge about the headless corpse was that everyone wanted to keep its identity under wraps, including MI5, the KGB and the British government.

The Chichester forensic team reasoned that there was an obvious candidate for the corpse. More than a year earlier, on 19 April 1956, a man named Lionel Crabb had gone diving in Portsmouth harbour. He was never seen again.

In the immediate aftermath of his disappearance, it was presumed that he had drowned and been washed out to sea. But it was not long before the story soon took a more mysterious turn. There were unsubstantiated claims that Crabb had been diving close to a Soviet cruiser at anchor in Portsmouth harbour.

The *Ordzhonikidze* had indeed been in Portsmouth at the time of Crabb's dive: it had brought the Soviet leader Nikita Khrushchev on a diplomatic visit to Britain.

The ship's presence in British waters presented military intelligence with a unique opportunity to study the capability of Soviet weaponry. MI6 was particularly interested in discovering more about the newly designed propeller that had been installed on the cruiser.

Crabb's mysterious disappearance became a story of national interest and questions were raised in Parliament as to why he was diving so close to Khrushchev's vessel. But the answers, such as they were, only served to deepen the mystery.

On 29 April, ten days after his dive, the Admiralty admitted that Crabb had been taking part in secret trials of underwater weaponry. This provoked an immediate response from the visiting Soviet delegation, which released a statement claiming that the *Ordzhonikidze*'s crew had spotted a diver close to the cruiser on the very day that Crabb had vanished.

In the absence of any hard facts, the British press reported rumours that Crabb had been captured by Khrushchev's crew. Journalists claimed the Soviets were intending to take him to Moscow for interrogation.

The prime minister, Anthony Eden, poured oil onto the fire by declaring that it was not in the public interest to disclose any more information about the disappearance of Lionel Crabb.

The story might have ended as an unsolved mystery, had it not been for the mystery corpse found floating in the waters of Chichester harbour on 9 June 1957. Was it Lionel Crabb? And if so, why was he headless?

Crabb's ex-wife was unable to identify the corpse, nor was his girlfriend, Pat Rose. The only other person who had known Crabb well enough to attempt an identification was Sydney Knowles, his sometime diving partner. Knowles was taken to the mortuary in the hope that he might be able to solve the mystery.

Much of the upper torso was eaten away, but the lower half was reasonably well preserved, providing Knowles with a very real chance of discovering whether the corpse was that of his friend. He knew that Crabb had a deep scar just below his left knee and immediately looked to see if it was there. It was not.

Knowles ought to have told the police that the corpse on the slab was not that of Lionel Crabb. Instead, he did the very opposite. He positively identified it as belonging to his old friend.

He would later confess to the *Mail on Sunday* that the secret service had ordered him to identify the corpse as being that of Crabb. He also let slip that Crabb had been working for MI6 but was intending to defect to the USSR. His diving mission, said Knowles, had been set up by MI5 in order that he could be murdered.

Sydney Knowles's version of events brought the speculation to an end, at least for a while. But it was subsequently challenged by an unlikely source. In a BBC interview in 2007, a Soviet frogman named Eduard Koltsov claimed that Crabb had been spotted trying to place a limpet mine on the hull of the *Ordzhonikidze*.

The captain of the *Ordzhonikidze* sent Koltsov into the water to investigate. 'I saw the silhouette of a diver in a light frogman suit who was fiddling with something at the starboard, next to the ship's ammunition. I swam closer and saw that he was fixing a mine.'

During his interview, Koltsov made the sensational claim that he had attacked Crabb underwater and slit his throat. He said that he left the corpse in the water and that it was slowly washed out to sea.

Crabb's surviving family remains unconvinced by the various different versions of how he met his end. 'The government [has] told lie after lie,' said one. 'No government has ever come out with the truth.'

Even Prime Minister Eden was apparently unaware of what had been taking place. He later said that 'what was done was done without the authority or knowledge of Her Majesty's government'.

The most plausible explanation for Crabb's disappearance is that he was killed while trying to place a listening device on the hull of the Soviet ship. But this is no more than supposition. To this day, the disappearance of Lionel Crabb remains one of the last great secrets of the Cold War.

Part XXVII

Kings, Queens and Madmen

Why is Buckingham Palace the cheapest piece
of property in England?
It was bought for a crown and is kept up by a sovereign.

A popular Victorian joke

Getting Clinical: The Madness of King George

No one at court was sure what to do. The king was ranting like a lunatic, telling his courtiers that London was underwater and that he could see Hanover through Sir William Herschel's telescope.

He lavished honours on the lowliest servant, composed fantasy despatches to foreign courts and punctuated his speech with weird phrases such as 'What? What?' and 'Hey! Hey!'.

It was the autumn of 1788 and the madness of King George III, which had begun as a 'pretty smart bilious attack', had taken a turn for the worse. The king was agitated, sweating profusely and overcome with convulsions. Worse still, he rambled endlessly. On one occasion he spoke for nineteen hours without a break, his discourse punctuated with crude sexual innuendos.

It was clear to everyone that the king was profoundly sick, but no one was quite sure what was causing his malady. His physician, Sir George Baker, nine times president of the College of Physicians, had never seen anything quite like it.

For more than two centuries, medical historians have tried to unravel the nature of the king's illness. But only in recent decades have scientists been able to advance plausible theories as to what might have been wrong.

In the 1970s, two psychiatrists – Ida Macalpine and her son Richard Hunter – studied the king's medical records and found a hitherto neglected symptom. His urine was stained a darkish blue-red colour. The psychiatrists believed that this was an unmistakable sign of a rare blood disorder called porphyria.

In its most severe form, porphyria can be devastating. It causes severe abdominal pain, cramps, and powerful bodily seizures not unlike epileptic fits. It is frequently misdiagnosed. Even nowadays, sufferers are often held to be mentally ill.

But if the king was suffering from porphyria, it was of a peculiar kind. His attacks were unusually severe: so severe, indeed, that he had to be physically restrained.

Such attacks are rare and men of the king's age hardly ever suffer from such an acute form of the illness. Even more unusual was the fact that the king didn't display any symptoms until he was into his fifties.

One possible explanation for the severity of the attacks came in 2003, when a new piece of evidence was discovered in the vaults of a London museum. An envelope was found containing a few strands of human hair. The words written on the front caused great excitement: 'Hair of His Late Majesty, King George 3rd'.

Among the scientists involved in the ensuing research was Professor Martin Warren of the University of Kent. He was convinced that a detailed analysis of the king's hair would enable him to solve the mystery of the illness.

The strand of hair was tested at a specialist laboratory in Oxfordshire and it gave results that no one was expecting. It was heavily laden with arsenic, containing more than three hundred times the toxic level.

Professor Warren already knew that porphyria attacks could be triggered by a number of different substances, including alcohol. Now he suspected that arsenic could also be a trigger.

He contacted Professor Tim Cox, one of the leading experts on porphyria, and learned that arsenic could indeed cause the illness. When the two men subsequently searched through the king's medical records, they found that he had used arsenic as both a skin cream and a wig powder.

This evidence seemed to add credence to the porphyria theory, but it has recently been cast into doubt by researchers at the University of London. They have taken a more detailed look at the king's medical records and found a very different explanation for the blue-red urine. They discovered that he was being prescribed medicine made from gentian, a plant whose deep blue flowers have been known to change the colour of urine.

The researchers also studied thousands of King George III's handwritten letters. They were startled by what they found. Whenever he was undergoing one of his bouts of illness, his sentences were a great deal longer than when he was well. A single sentence often contained as many as eight verbs and 400 words and the king frequently repeated himself, using vocabulary that was as creative as it was colourful.

Such symptoms are most often found in patients suffering from extreme versions of bipolar disorder. Bipolar patients also display the same behavioural traits as those of the king, with euphoria and severe depression interspersed with moments of lucidity. Was this the explanation for the king's supposed madness?

By the end of his life, the king was living in a fantasy world, in which the dead were alive and the alive were dead. Deaf, blind and insane, his rambling monologues grew ever more fantastical. On 20 January 1820, he chattered incessantly for fifty-eight hours. Nine days later, he was close to the end. 'Do not open my lips but when I open my mouth,' he said clearly and eloquently in his dying breath.

They were strangely rational words for someone who had spoken complete gibberish for the final months of his life. And they provide further evidence that 'mad King George' was suffering from neither porphyria nor madness, but from an extreme and debilitating form of bipolar disorder.

How to Meet the Queen in Bed

On the night of 8 July 1982, Queen Elizabeth II slipped into her nightdress and climbed into bed, safe in the knowledge that she lived in one of the most secure buildings in the world.

Her bedroom was guarded by an armed policeman, there were alarms in most of the rooms and the extensive Buckingham Palace gardens were surrounded by a fourteen-foot wall topped with spikes and barbed wire. It was inconceivable that such elaborate security could be breached.

But not everyone shared that view. Just a few weeks earlier, a Londoner named Michael Fagan had brought his children to see the outside of the queen's palace and had been surprised by how few security guards were on duty. He began to wonder if it would be possible to get inside the place.

The idea rapidly developed into an obsession. Shortly after taking his children to see the palace, he returned alone and at night. He climbed over the perimeter wall (with barbed wire and spikes), shinned up a drainpipe and got into the building through an unlocked window.

The window belonged to the bedroom of housemaid Sarah Carter. She was sitting on her bed at about 11 p.m. when she was disturbed by a strange noise outside. 'Turning towards the window, I saw some fingers on the outside of the frame,' she later recalled. 'They were a few inches up from the sill itself. I saw the fleeting glimpse of a man's face.' She was absolutely terrified and jumped out of bed. 'Then I ran out of the room into the corridor, shutting the door behind me.'

She left in the nick of time. Scarcely had she closed the door than Fagan pulled himself through the window and slid down onto the bedroom floor. He had made it inside Buckingham Palace.

Once inside, he decided to explore the place. He wandered down corridors looking at the nameplates on the doors and noting who slept in which bedroom. 'Princess Anne was in one room and Captain Mark Phillips in another. I decided not to disturb them.'

When he saw a door marked 'Prince Philip', he could not resist turning the handle. But the bedroom was empty. And then he realized why: 'They were out seeing President Reagan.'

Fagan made his way down to the post-room and poked his head around the door. There was a bottle of Californian wine on one of the shelves. Since he felt like a drink, he opened it and drank half the bottle.

Housemaid Sarah Carter had raised the alarm in the intervening time and the hunt was on to find the intruder. But fortunately for Fagan, no one thought to search the post-room where he was glugging Prince Charles's wine. When he eventually decided to leave the palace, he did so undetected.

A month after his first visit, Fagan decided to break into Buckingham Palace again. This time, he was determined to meet the Queen.

At around 6 a.m. on 9 July 1982 he scaled the perimeter wall and jumped down into the gardens of the palace. When he looked towards the building, he noticed an open window on the west side. He clambered inside and found himself in a locked room that housed King George V's stamp collection.

Unable to enter the rest of the palace, he climbed back outside and pulled himself up a drainpipe that led to the office of the man responsible for the Queen's security. He had by now triggered two alarms, but the police assumed the system was malfunctioning and they turned it off – twice.

Fagan walked along one of the upper floor corridors admiring the paintings. At one point he picked up a glass ashtray and accidentally broke it, cutting his hand. He also passed a palace housekeeper who said 'good morning' to him. A few minutes later, he found himself outside the queen's bedroom.

Her room should have been under guard, but the night shift of the policeman on duty had just ended and the footman replacing him had not yet arrived (he was walking the Queen's corgis). Astonishingly, Fagan was able to enter the bedroom undetected.

When Fagan pulled open the bedroom curtain on her four-poster bed the Queen awoke with a start. He sat down on her eiderdown and admired her Liberty print nightdress.

The Queen was terrified. 'What are you doing here?' she said to Fagan in a voice he later described as being 'like the finest cut-glass you can imagine'.

The night alarm bell was immediately pressed by the Queen, but there was still no guard outside her room. She then used her bedside telephone to tell the palace receptionist to send police to her bedroom urgently. The receptionist phoned the police lodge and her call was logged at 7.18 a.m. But no help was forthcoming.

Some six minutes later the Queen made another phone call. She had managed to keep Fagan at bay, but was by now growing desperate. The noise of her phone calls eventually attracted the attentions of a maid who was working in an adjoining room. She now entered the Queen's bedroom and was appalled to see a stranger sitting on Her Majesty's bed. She and the Queen managed to usher Fagan into a nearby pantry on the pretext of giving him a cigarette.

They were now joined by a footman, Paul Whybrew, who offered Fagan a glass of The Famous Grouse in an effort to defuse the situation. 'I tried to keep him calm and he said he was all right. I noticed his breath smelled of alcohol.'

The two of them were still drinking whisky when policeman Cedric Robert arrived and led Fagan away. He offered no resistance and seemed to accept that his arrest was inevitable. He was later taken to court to be tried.

Fagan's crime was deemed to be a civil rather than a criminal offence and he was therefore not charged with trespass. Instead, he was convicted of theft from his first visit (the half bottle of wine) and committed to psychiatric care. He spent some months in an asylum before being released in January 1983.

Fagan has never been able to explain why he was so obsessed about breaking into Buckingham Palace, although he thinks it might have been caused by an excess of home-made magic mushroom soup. 'I forgot you are only supposed to take a little handful. I was high on mushrooms for a long, long time.'

But Fagan's mother insists that her son broke into Buckingham Palace because of the Queen's reputation for being such a good listener. 'I can imagine him just wanting to talk and say hello and discuss his problems,' she said.

The Man With a Deadly Secret

Everyone knew John Freeman and they knew him for all the right reasons. He was one of Melbourne's model citizens, a respectable churchwarden who had married an impoverished widow with two young children. He was the sort of neighbour who was totally dependable.

What no one knew was that Freeman's real name was Edward Oxford and that he had been shipped to Australia on account of his criminal past. Twenty-seven years earlier, he had attempted – and very nearly succeeded – in assassinating Queen Victoria.

His attempt on the young queen's life had gripped the nation when it first became public. What made it so fascinating was the fact that it was born out of a bizarre fantasy that had spun wildly out of control.

The young Edward Oxford was an unemployed drifter with an unhealthy interest in guns. He had first conceived of shooting the queen in the spring of 1840, when he saw her taking one of her evening carriage drives. He noticed that she and Prince Albert travelled in an open phaeton and were rarely accompanied by more than two outriders. He thought how easy it would be to shoot her.

What began as an idle fantasy rapidly became an obsession, one that preyed on his mind. He was particularly excited to learn that the queen was four months pregnant with her first child. If he succeeded in killing her, then he would also kill her heir.

The queen certainly presented an easy target for someone as proficient in shooting as Oxford. Some months earlier he had lost his job as a waiter: ever since, he had spent his time at the shooting galleries in the Strand and Leicester Square.

A week before the assassination attempt, Oxford took himself to a shop in Lambeth owned by a former school friend named Gray. He bought fifty copper percussion caps and asked Gray where he could buy bullets and gunpowder. His old friend sold him powder and told him where he could get ammunition. Oxford soon had everything he needed.

At around 4 p.m. on 10 June, he took up position on a footpath close to Constitution Hill. After a long wait, he heard the sound of horses' hooves. It was the queen and her husband, Prince Albert. As expected, they were riding without guards.

As their phaeton passed his hiding place, Oxford stepped from the shadows and fired both his pistols in rapid succession. It was not immediately clear if the queen had been hit, for the horses reared up at the noise of the shots and then took off at high speed down Constitution Hill, carrying the queen's carriage away from danger.

Horrified onlookers dragged Oxford to the ground and pulled the weapons from his hands. He made no effort to struggle nor to hide his attempt on the queen's life. 'It was I, it was me that did it,' he said, somewhat incoherently.

He was arrested that same evening and charged with treason. Once in custody, he asked the police if the queen was injured. He was informed that she was unharmed.

The police found him unusually compliant when they interrogated him. Indeed he was happy to confess to his crime and willingly gave them his home address so that they could search the place. They found a locked casket containing a sword and scabbard, two pistol-bags, powder, a bullet mould, five lead balls and some of the percussion caps.

They also found details of an underground military society called Young England, complete with a list of officers serving in this clandestine organization. Each member was said to be armed with a brace of pistols, a sword, rifle and dagger. The police even unearthed correspondence between Oxford and his fellow members.

But once they investigated Young England more closely, it was found to exist only in Oxford's fertile imagination. The society, its members and its rules were a complete fabrication.

Oxford's Old Bailey trial was postponed for almost a month as police undertook a thorough investigation of his motives. They also searched the crime scene, but were unable to find the bullets that Oxford said he had fired. Now, he dramatically changed his story, saying that the guns had contained only gunpowder.

When the trial finally opened amidst huge publicity, Oxford seemed strangely detached. Witness after witness testified that he came from a long line of alcoholics with a tendency towards mental instability.

The jury eventually acquitted him on grounds of insanity. The queen was furious, but there was nothing she could do. Her only satisfaction was seeing him sentenced to be detained 'until Her Majesty's pleasure be known'.

Oxford spent the next twenty-four years in the lunatic asylum of Bethlem in south London. He proved a model prisoner: courteous, friendly and obliging. He taught himself French, German and Italian, along with Spanish, Greek and Latin. He also spent his time drawing, reading and playing the violin, and was later employed as a painter and decorator within the asylum. No one could quite believe that this was the same man who had tried to kill the queen.

In 1864, he was transferred to Broadmoor, by which time it was clear he was a danger to no one. He was finally released in 1867, on the condition that he should leave for one of the Empire's overseas colonies and never return. He was given a new alias, John Freeman, and duly shipped to Melbourne where he married a local widow. He became a regular churchgoer and wrote newspaper articles highlighting the state of the city slums.

His wife remained in total ignorance of his criminal past: she went to her grave unaware that her husband had once been the most notorious criminal in Great Britain.

Part XXVIII
Papal Bull

For those destined to dominate others, the ordinary rules
of life are turned upside down and duty acquires an entirely
new meaning.

Pope Alexander VI, who sired more children
than any other pontiff

Accident by Design

Shortly after dawn on 9 September 1598, anguished screams could be heard coming from La Rocca castle, the country residence of Count Francesco Cenci. The screams were so loud that they woke Plautilla, one of the castle housekeepers, even though she was at her home in the nearby village.

Plautilla dashed outside in her nightclothes and ran towards the castle 'with one slipper on and one slipper off'. As she looked up at the towering facade, she glimpsed a distracted Beatrice standing at one of the windows.

She shouted up, '*Signora*, what is the matter?' But Beatrice remained 'strangely silent', in marked contrast to her stepmother Lucrezia, who could still be heard screaming inside the castle.

Plautilla immediately realized that there had been a terrible accident. One of the castle's wooden balconies, suspended forty feet above the ground, was splintered and broken.

'*Signor Francesco è morto*,' cried some of the villagers who had joined her at the base of the castle. Count Francesco was indeed dead. His corpse was spotted lying in a patch of waste ground.

It took considerable effort to reach his body, for the ground was inaccessible and strewn with rocks. When the villagers finally arrived at the corpse, they found it in a terrible state. The count had clearly landed heavily, for his head was completely caked in congealed blood.

Count Francesco's death was a sensation, for he was a well-known figure in the local area. Aristocratic and debauched, he was widely rumoured to have committed incest with his twenty-two-year-old daughter, Beatrice. He also stood accused of forcing her to perform numerous other perversions, such as massaging his testicles. In his defence, he claimed it was the only thing that brought relief from the mites that infested his skin.

The count's behaviour had proved so scandalous that it had earned him a spell in prison in Rome. But his network of powerful connections had secured him an early release.

He had only been back at home for a few hours when he fell to his death. To many, it seemed deeply suspicious that he should have died so soon after returning to La Rocca.

Local priests were summoned to prepare the body for burial. They carried the corpse to the castle pool where the dried blood was scrubbed off. Only now did the full extent of his wounds become apparent. There were three deep gashes in the side of his face, one of which had destroyed his right eye. It looked as if a metal stake had been driven through his brain. 'I turned my eyes aside so I didn't have to look,' said one of the onlookers. 'It frightened me.'

The priests immediately realized that the fall alone could not have caused such mutilation. The wounds looked as if they had been made with a 'cutting tool like a hatchet' or stake of 'pointed iron'.

The Neapolitan authorities opened an official investigation almost immediately. From the very outset, it focused on Lucrezia (the count's second wife), Beatrice and her brother, along with two possible accomplices. But the investigation soon ran into problems. One of the accused accomplices, a hitman by the name of Marzio Catalano, was tortured so severely during his interrogation at Tordinona prison that he died.

Another alleged accomplice, Olimpio Calvetti, was killed by an assassin while hiding in the Abruzzi hills. Only later did it transpire that he had been Beatrice's secret lover.

The investigators did a thorough job in exposing the systematic violence meted out by Count Francesco, who was said to have whipped Beatrice on numerous occasions.

They also produced a detailed dossier that set out exactly how the count had been killed. They contended that Beatrice and Lucrezia had decided to murder Count Francesco on his first night at home. He had been drugged with a sleeping draught prepared by Lucrezia, in order to allow the two hitmen to enter his bedroom while he was unconscious.

But the draught – claimed the investigators – had not worked. The count had woken up, requiring one of the men to pin him down with considerable force. This accounted for the livid purple bruise on the wrist of the corpse.

While he was being pinned to the bed, the second hitman had driven an iron spike deep into his skull. He had then been tipped over the balcony in order to fake an accidental death. It was noted that the damage to the balcony was recent: it was also noted that the gap was too small for the count to have fallen through without being pushed.

In the ensuing trial, the judges were quite clear as to who was guilty. The two deceased hitmen were named as the murderers, along with Lucrezia, Beatrice and the count's eldest son, Giacomo.

The three of them were sentenced to be executed by the Sant'Angelo bridge on the banks of the River Tiber. Giacomo was lynched and dragged through the streets and his flesh was burned with red-hot pincers. His skull was then smashed with a hammer.

Lucrezia and Beatrice were forced to watch this gruesome spectacle before being despatched with a sword. Prattling onlookers later said that Lucrezia had difficulty positioning herself on the block on account of the size of her breasts.

The only member of the immediate family to escape execution was Beatrice's twelve-year-old brother, Bernardino. He was sentenced to life as a galley slave.

One person alone emerged a winner. Pope Clement VIII, who had declared himself strongly in favour of the executions, confiscated all of the family's properties.

As there was no longer any heir, he awarded them to himself.

The Banquet of Chestnuts

Midnight was fast approaching and the city had fallen silent. It was the hour at which most of Rome's priests were at their prayers. But in the Palazzo Apostolico, the official residence of the pope, a rather different scene was unfolding. Fifty naked courtesans were engaged in an orgy. They were cavorting with the pope's entourage and openly performing sexual acts.

It was 30 October 1501, a night that would go down as one of the most salacious in papal history. The so-called Banquet of Chestnuts had been arranged for Pope Alexander VI by his son, Cardinal Cesare Borgia. It was an evening of such alleged debauchery that Catholic scholars have spent a great deal of time and effort attempting to prove that it never happened.

But are their denials credible? The most detailed description of the banquet was written by the pope's master of ceremonies, Johannes Burchard. He was author of the *Liber Notarum*, an official record of all the most significant papal ceremonies, including embassies, official visits and private functions. Among the functions recorded in the *Liber Notarum* is an account of the Banquet of Chestnuts.

Burchard was an Alsatian-born priest whose intellectual brilliance saw him serve under five successive popes. His *Liber Notarum* is a deeply serious work, with lengthy descriptions of the various papal ceremonies interspersed with explanations of church music and choral polyphony.

According to Burchard, the infamous banquet took place inside the Palazzo Apostolico, a vast building of more than a thousand rooms. Pope Alexander VI was said to have been in the best possible mood. The food had been more sumptuous than at previous feasts and the wine had flowed with liberal abundance. Even the fifty dancing girls had performed with unusual aplomb.

It was already late by the time the last dishes had been consumed, but no one was in any mood to go to their beds. The servants cleared the tables and then led the fifty dancing prostitutes out of the room and into an antechamber, where they disrobed. When they re-emerged in the banqueting hall, where the pope was still enjoying his wine, they were completely naked.

According to Burchard, the evening rapidly descended into a sexually charged floor show. 'After dinner, the candelabra with the burning candles were taken from the tables and placed on the floor, and chestnuts were strewn around, which the naked courtesans picked up, creeping on hands and knees between the chandeliers, while the Pope, Cesare, and his sister Lucrezia looked on.'

Inevitably, after the consumption of so much alcohol, the soirée soon turned into an orgy. 'Prizes were announced for those who could perform the act most often with the courtesans.' These prizes included fine shoes and tunics made of silk.

Later writers would further embellish the story, reporting that the pope himself distributed rewards for the cardinals and priests who had ejaculated the most times, 'for the pope greatly admired virility and measured a man's machismo by his ejaculative capacity'.

Catholic commentators have long argued that the entire story is a fabrication. The pope's most vociferous champion, the Right Reverend Monsignor Peter de Roo, was so outraged by the tales of sexual debauchery that he devoted years of his life to disproving them.

'We continued our search after facts and proofs from country to country,' he wrote in his encyclopaedic *Material for a History of Pope Alexander VI, His Relatives and His Time.* '[We] spared neither labour nor money in order to investigate who was Alexander VI, of what he had been accused and, especially, what he had done.'

Peter de Roo admitted to being puzzled by the fact that the usually dependable Johannes Burchard had included such a salacious story in his *Liber Notarum.* 'How could he suddenly descend from his accustomed decent ways to the lowest work of a filthy writer?'

After much research, he concluded that Burchard had nothing to do with the offending passage: in his opinion, the pope's enemies had interpolated it at a later date. But he also conceded that Pope Alexander VI's son, the outlandish Cesare, could plausibly have been involved in a 'scene truly bestial'.

The stumbling block for apologists like Peter de Roo is the fact that Alexander VI was one of the most notorious Renaissance popes. His surname Borgia became a byword for scandal, corruption and immorality.

His first mistress was Vannozza dei Cattanei, an Italian noblewoman with whom he had a long affair. Their romance began some two years after he was ordained cardinal of Albano, a commune close to Rome.

They had four children, Giovanni, Cesare, Lucrezia and Gioffre, all of whom were lavished with money and honours. Pope Alexander was particularly fond of Cesare and Lucrezia, who were said to be present at the Banquet of Chestnuts.

Alexander eventually tired of Vannozza and transferred his affections to the young Giulia Farnese, one of the great beauties of Rome. She was described as having 'dark colouring, black eyes, round face and a particular ardour'.

Giulia was already married to the wealthy aristocrat Orsino Orsini but Pope Alexander had her moved into a palace that adjoined the papal residence. It made it easier for him to make clandestine visits.

He tried to keep their relationship secret, but gossip and rumours soon spread through Rome. Giulia became known as the 'Pope's Whore' or the 'Bride of Christ'. She bore a child, Laura, but it is not known whether the father was Orsino or the pope himself.

Pope Alexander VI had been elected amidst allegations of bribery and the misuse of funds was to become a hallmark of his papacy. When the Florentine friar Girolamo Savonarola denounced him for his sinful living, Pope Alexander was said to have burst out laughing.

Pope Alexander sought to aggrandize the Borgia family during his papacy and proved extremely successful, marrying his sons and daughter into the leading families of the nobility.

He finally died in 1503 at the advanced age of seventy-two. His body lay in state, as was customary, but it rapidly started to decompose in the stifling August heat. According to the Italian theologian Raffaello Maffei, 'it was a revolting scene to look at that deformed, blackened corpse, prodigiously swelled, and exhaling an infectious smell; his lips and nose were covered with brown drivel, his mouth was opened very wide, therefore no fanatic or devotee dared to kiss his feet or hands, as custom would have required.'

The exact truth about the Banquet of Chestnuts may never be known. The only certainties are that Johannes Burchard was an unusually fastidious chronicler and that Pope Alexander VI was infamous for his illegitimate children.

Even if he did not actively participate in the orgy, he still holds the dubious record of siring more children than any other pope.

Part XXIX

Up and Away

I see my comrades of the Matterhorn slipping on their backs, their arms outstretched, one after the other, in perfect order at equal distances.

Victorian climber Edward Whymper describes how he is haunted by a recurring nightmare

Into Thin Air

It was the day on which conspiracy theorists seemed finally vindicated. For years, they had been claiming that some paranormal force was at work in the ocean to the east of Miami. They had even given it a name, the Bermuda Triangle, an area of the globe where ships and planes disappeared without trace.

Now, on 5 December 1945, they were to find themselves with their most spectacular evidence to date. Five military aeroplanes, TBM Avengers, were reported to have disappeared into thin air. Neither they nor their crews were ever seen again.

The planes had set off at shortly after 2 p.m. on a training mission that would take them far out over the Gulf of Florida. The planes were fully fuelled and in good condition. Leader of Flight 19 was Lieutenant Charles Taylor, an experienced pilot. There was no reason to expect anything other than a routine exercise.

By 3.40 p.m., the planes had been in the air for some ninety minutes and the training mission was almost complete. But just as they turned for home, something went terribly wrong. A ground-based flight instructor named Robert Cox was tuning his radio when he picked up a strange message transmitted between the planes of Flight 19.

One of the trainee pilots, Edward Powers, could be heard saying in a puzzled tone: 'I don't know where we are. We must have got lost after that last turn.'

This was followed by a more mysterious message. 'Everything looks strange, even the ocean,' said one of the voices. Another pilot could be heard saying: 'It looks like we're entering white water. We're completely lost.'

A final, crackling message was picked up much later, at about 6.20 p.m. After that, there was radio silence.

The loss of the planes was made all the more baffling by the fact that they were under the command of a pilot with more than 2,500 hours of flying experience.

As the disappearance occurred in the Bermuda Triangle it only fuelled the sense that some mysterious force was at work. But surviving evidence, such as it is, points to a more prosaic explanation.

The Bermuda Triangle may well have played a part in this. The 'triangle' covers an area of ocean where the well-known phenomenon of compass variation is particularly powerful. Pilots need to compensate for the needle pointing to geographic rather than magnetic north. It is known that prior to setting off from Fort Lauderdale, Lieutenant Taylor had complained that his on-board compass was faulty, yet no one had thought to repair it.

No less significant was the ominous build-up of storm clouds on the horizon. Although it was sunny when the planes took off, the weather began to deteriorate throughout the course of the afternoon.

Another factor that would later come to the attention of investigators was the fact that this was Taylor's maiden flight from Fort Lauderdale. Although he had clocked up many flying hours, he had previously been based in Miami and was unfamiliar with the Fort Lauderdale topography.

The five planes of Flight 19 lost contact with the control tower soon after taking off, but the ground-based radio operators were able to eavesdrop on their conversations. It soon became clear that Taylor was hopelessly lost. 'I am sure I'm in the [Florida] Keys,' he said to the other pilots, 'but I don't know how far down and I don't know how to get to Fort Lauderdale.'

Taylor's words give the first hint that Flight 19 was set on a course for disaster. It was later determined that he was probably looking down on the Bahamas, not the Florida Keys. Unaware that he had strayed wildly off course, he now took the decision to swing his planes north-east, reasoning that this would bring him back to Florida. In fact, by setting off in such a direction, he was leading his planes far out into the Atlantic.

The last message picked up by Taylor hints at the impending doom: 'All planes close up tight. When the first plane drops below ten gallons, we all go down together.'

The pilots almost certainly ditched into the ocean in the hope that they could keep the planes floating on the surface until rescue ships arrived. But Avengers are notoriously difficult to land on water and even harder to keep afloat. In the mountainous seas in which they landed, they would have sunk like rocks.

Conspiracy theorists have long disputed such a rational version of events. In the absence of any hard facts, they have made wild claims that the planes were shot down by the US Air Force (for no obvious reason) or that the entire fleet was somehow captured and abducted by UFOs.

Such beliefs were given added credence when a Mariner search plane, scrambled on the same evening as the planes went missing, also disappeared without trace, along with the thirteen men on board. Investigators later concluded that it had blown up in a terrible mid-air explosion.

In the aftermath of the disaster, the coastguard and navy combed 700,000 square kilometres of sea but found no wreckage, nor even any sign of oil on the surface of the ocean. The final report by the Navy Board of Investigation, which ran to more than 500 pages, was inconclusive. Investigators said that they were 'not even able to make a good guess'.

Over the years, the remains of a number of Avengers have been located on the ocean floor and one of them has even been raised from the seabed. But this plane, like all the others, was later found to have crashed during a training exercise at the time of the Second World War. Their tail numbers clearly show that they were not connected with Flight 19.

Until such time as the five missing Avengers are found, conspiracy theorists will continue to claim that Flight 19 is the most spectacular example to date of abduction by UFOs.

Mountain of Death

It was the crowning moment of his career. British mountaineer Edward Whymper stood on the peak of the Matterhorn, the first climber ever to have scaled this treacherous Alpine mountain. 14 July 1865 was a day he would remember for the rest of his life.

'The slope eased off,' he later wrote. 'At 1.40 p.m., the world was at our feet and the Matterhorn was conquered.'

Whymper's satisfaction was due, in no small part, to the fact that he had beaten his rival, the Italian mountaineer Jean-Antoine Carrel. The first thing he did on reaching the summit was to make a careful check of the snow. 'Hurrah!' he later wrote. 'Not a footstep could be seen.'

He might have been wiser to eschew the victory celebrations and focus his mind on the descent. For mountains as high as the Matterhorn often prove deadlier on the way down than on the way up.

The race to the top of the Matterhorn had begun with a ruptured friendship and a betrayal of trust. Whymper had been hoping to scale the peak with Carrel, his long-term climbing partner. Carrel had initially agreed, but had changed his mind shortly afterwards. He told Whymper that he already had a climbing engagement with 'a family of distinction'.

This 'family' was a team of Italian mountaineers who had vowed that an Italian should be the first to scale the Matterhorn. In the space of a few days Whymper and Carrel went from being close friends to bitter rivals.

Whymper could not climb alone: without Carrel, it looked as if his expedition was doomed. He was about to abandon his attempt when he learned that several other alpinists in Zermatt were hoping to scale the mountain. These included three Englishmen: Lord Francis Douglas, Douglas Hadow and Charles Hudson.

A French climber named Michel Croz was also keen to attempt the summit, along with two experienced local guides, a father-and-son team both named Peter Taugwalder.

Whymper hired all six men and announced they would begin their climb on the very next day. There was no time to be lost if they were to beat Carrel's Italian team.

They set off from Zermatt at dawn on the morning of 13 July and made rapid progress, reaching the Schwarzsee, a mountain lake, in less than three hours. By mid-morning they were at the base of the peak and heading up the east face.

They successfully crossed one of the most dangerous ridges and found a good position to bivouac for their lunch. Their speedy progress continued throughout the late afternoon and they reached a height of 11,089 feet (3,380 metres). They now decided to rest for the night and make their attempt on the summit the following morning.

Whymper ordered an early start, setting off at dawn and climbing without ropes. The men soon reached a height of 13,123 feet (4,000 metres), but found the eastern face of the mountain so challenging that they decided to change their route to the summit, heading up the north face instead. It was a longer but easier climb.

The seven men struggled up the rock face until they were close to the peak. When Whymper saw that only 200 feet of easy snow remained, he and Croz unhooked themselves and scrambled to the top.

Whymper's jubilation at being the first to scale the Matterhorn was further increased when he peered over the edge and saw figures far below. Carrel's party were still struggling up one of the other ridges, some 650 feet (200 metres) beneath the summit.

Carrel and his men were devastated when they realized that the English-led team had beaten them. They immediately abandoned their attempt and set off back down the mountain.

Whymper's men celebrated on the summit before starting their descent. Michel Croz led the way, followed by Hadow, Hudson and Douglas, with the two Taugwalders and Whymper bringing up the rear. Although elated at having earned themselves a place in the history books, they were also suffering from extreme fatigue. In such a state, and at such an altitude, things could go awry.

As they clambered down, roped together, Hadow suddenly slipped. He crashed into Croz, who was knocked clean off his feet. The weight of the two of them dragged down Hudson and Douglas. Within seconds, all four climbers were sliding down a near-vertical slope.

Whymper and the Taugwalders were some distance away, although they were attached to the same rope. Hearing the screams of the men, they clasped at nearby rocks to avoid being pulled down.

The rope tightened, tugged at them violently and then suddenly snapped in two. The three of them were left clinging to the mountain while their comrades were sent hurtling over the rocky cliff.

Whymper was horrified. 'For two or three seconds, we saw our unfortunate companions sliding downwards on their backs, and spreading out their hands endeavouring to save themselves; they then disappeared one by one and fell from precipice to precipice onto the Matterhorn glacier below, a distance of nearly 4,000 feet in height.' As the four men fell spectacularly to their deaths, Croz was heard to scream: 'Impossible!'

Not until the following day did Whymper and his guides reach Zermatt, where they were to find themselves embroiled in controversy. They stood accused of having deliberately cut the rope in order to save themselves. Some people even said they should stand trial for murder.

An indignant Whymper sought to defend himself against the various charges. 'A single slip, or a single false step, has been the sole cause of this frightful calamity,' he wrote to the Italian Alpine Club, while in a letter to *The Times* he said that 'from the moment the rope broke, it was impossible to help them'.

Queen Victoria was so appalled by the reports in the press that she considered banning all British nationals from climbing in the Alps.

Three of the bodies were recovered from the Matterhorn glacier on the day after the disaster, but the corpse of Lord Francis Douglas was never found. It remains on the Matterhorn to this day, a frozen human memorial to Edward Whymper's Pyrrhic victory.

The Man Who Fell to Earth

He stood at the edge of heaven. Joe Kittinger's helium balloon had carried him to more than nineteen miles above the earth. Now, he was about to do what no human had ever done before – free-fall to earth at the speed of sound.

It was part of an extreme American experiment on ejecting at high altitude.

Kittinger knew all too well that the experiment carried extraordinary risks. He had undertaken his first free-fall jump nine months earlier, at the end of 1959, and it had almost killed him. He began spinning wildly out of control, more than 120 revolutions a minute, and rapidly lost consciousness. His life was saved only when his parachute opened automatically at 10,000 feet.

Now, he was going to repeat the experiment, only this time from a far greater height. His specially constructed helium capsule would lift him to an altitude of 101,706 feet (31,000 metres), or more than nineteen miles above planet earth. Then he would step out into the void and fall to earth. No one knew if he would survive.

At such an altitude, the temperature would be minus 100°C. Equally alarming was the insufferable air pressure and mix of noxious gases. If his protective suit burst, his blood would instantly boil.

Kittinger was not doing it for kicks. The United States Air Force had become increasingly concerned about the safety of pilots forced to eject at high altitude. Tests had shown that the body went into a fatal spin when jumping from a plane. Now scientists had created a stabilizer device designed to hold the body in one position as it fell to earth. Kittinger was to test this device.

At 5.29 a.m. on 16 August 1960, his helium balloon lifted off from an abandoned airstrip in New Mexico. It rose rapidly – 1,200 feet (366 metres) a minute – until it was just a tiny blip in the sky. Although it ascended at speed, it took a long time to reach nineteen miles above the earth.

Kittinger was wearing a specially designed protective suit that contained a high-tech layer of inflating fabric intended to save him from instant death. It failed him before he even reached 40,000 feet. The glove on his right hand didn't inflate, a malfunction that could easily have killed him.

He knew that the control centre would abort the flight if he told them what had happened. 'I took a calculated risk', he later said, 'that I might lose the use of my right hand. It quickly swelled up, and I did lose use for the duration of the flight. But the rest of the pressure suit worked.'

After ascending rapidly for 1 hour and 31 minutes, Kittinger reached his maximum altitude. The balloon was not quite in the right position so he allowed it to drift for twelve miles until he was over the landing target area.

This gave him time to experience life in this twilight zone.

'You can see about four hundred miles in every direction,' he said. 'The most fascinating thing is that it's just black overhead – the transition from normal blue to black is very stark. You can't see stars because there's a lot of glare from the sun, so your pupils are too small.'

He was struck by how beautiful planet earth looked from up there. 'But I was also struck by how hostile it is: more than one hundred degrees below zero [and] no air. If my protection suit failed, I would be dead in a few seconds.'

Kittinger went through a pre-planned safety checklist. Then he disconnected the balloon's power supply, cutting all communication with earth. He was on his own, drifting in a hostile world.

'When everything was done, I stood up, turned around to the door, took one final look out and said a silent prayer: "Lord, take care of me now." Then I just jumped over the side.' He was on his way back to earth, falling through emptiness at unbelievable speed.

'I rolled over and looked up and there was the balloon just roaring into space. [Then] I realized that the balloon wasn't roaring into space; I was going down at a fantastic rate.'

He was soon travelling at an extraordinary velocity, falling to earth at the speed of sound, more than 600 miles an hour (990 kilometres per hour). The world appeared an alluring and welcoming sight. Joe had a camera strapped to his body that captured every moment: it revealed planet earth growing nearer and larger with every second.

For 4 minutes and 36 seconds, Kittinger fell through the limitless void, attaining a maximum speed of 614 miles per hour. When he reached 17,500 feet (5,334 metres) above sea level, he opened his main parachute which dramatically slowed his breakneck fall. It took a further nine minutes before he landed safely in the New Mexico desert. As the ground crew rushed over to greet him, he had just a few brief words for them: 'I'm very glad to be back with you all.'

Since making his historic jump, Kittinger's feat has been repeated twice. First in 2012 by Felix Baumgartner, who set a new altitude record of 22.6 miles (119,429 feet/ 36,402 metres); then again in October 2014 by Alan Eustace who jumped from a height of 21.7 miles (114,576 feet/ 34,923 metres) and reached a peak speed of 821 miles per hour.

But Kittinger's pioneering jump, made half a century earlier, was the most dangerous of the three. In gambling his life and using equipment that was both primitive and faulty, he fully earned himself the title of the man who fell to earth.

Part XXX

Beauty and the Beast

His structure, his caution in never changing his clothes or carrying out any natural function in the presence of anyone, the sound of his voice, his beardless chin, and several other indications had given rise to this suspicion.

After months at sea, Louis Antoine de Bougainville begins to question whether the expedition's botanist, Jean Baré, might be a woman

Wild Child

It was a bizarre human experiment, one that was welcomed by the great philosophers of Enlightenment Paris. They had spent years debating the question of what distinguishes man from beast. Was it nature? Or nurture?

Just when it seemed they would never find the answer, they were presented with a unique opportunity. In the summer of 1798, three huntsmen were riding through the forests of Aveyron in southern France, when they spotted a most bizarre creature.

In a clearing, just yards from where they had stopped, a naked and grunting child was grubbing up roots in the forest. The men watched in amazement as he stuffed raw acorns into his mouth.

The huntsmen managed to ensnare the boy and take him captive. They named him Victor and transported him to nearby lodgings in the hope of finding out how he came to be living alone in the forest.

Victor escaped their clutches within days and the huntsmen were unable to recapture him, even though he was sighted on a number of occasions. 'He wandered about during the severity of a most rigorous winter,' wrote one, 'clad only in a tattered shirt.'

His return to the wild might have been the end of the story, but Victor re-emerged from the forest in the following January. He was seized by the local townspeople and held under lock and key in a succession of different lodgings. In each place he stayed, he was 'equally wild, impatient of restraint and capricious in his temper, continually endeavouring to get away'.

Eventually a clergyman named Pierre Joseph Bonnaterre took Victor under his wing in order that he could study the lad more closely. One morning it began to snow and Bonnaterre was amazed by the child's reaction. 'He uttered a cry of joy, leaped from his bed, ran to the window and at length escaped half dressed into the garden.' Bonnaterre watched in incredulity as Victor 'rolled himself in the snow and, taking it up by handfuls, devoured it with incredible avidity'.

Bonnaterre took the child to Paris, where he introduced him to some of the city's leading savants. They believed that Victor's wild upbringing might hold the clue to answering existential questions about what distinguishes men from animals.

Bonnaterre was unable to care for Victor in the French capital and had him placed in the care of Jean Marc Gaspard Itard, a young medical student. Itard decided to make a scientific experiment of this apparently feral child. His goal was to civilize him and teach him to speak.

Itard was both fascinated and revolted by Victor. 'He was a disgusting, slovenly boy, affected with spasmodic and frequently convulsive motions, like some of the animals in the menagerie, biting and scratching those who contradicted him.'

Many of Paris's intellectuals argued that Victor was a wild beast who could never be educated. But Itard was determined to prove them wrong and he now set to work, instigating a programme that was designed to reintroduce Victor to the civilized world. He hoped to give him a social life, awaken his senses and teach him to speak.

Each of these objectives was to prove unattainable, possibly because of the length of time that Victor had spent in the wild. His eyes remained without expression and he was completely insensitive to noise. Strangely, he was unable to distinguish between a painting and an object in relief. 'In a word,' wrote Itard, 'his whole existence was a life purely animal.'

On one occasion, Victor was handed a dead canary. He showed no sorrow for the bird. Rather, 'he stripped off its feathers [and] tore it open with his hands'. Itard had to intervene to stop the lad from eating it.

Itard persevered with his experiment to civilize Victor, devoting years of his life to studying his feral behaviour. Victor eventually learned the meaning of actions and developed a primitive form of communication. But he only ever learned to say two words: '*lait*' and '*Dieu*'. Itard concluded that the wild child of Aveyron was 'the mental and psychological equivalent of a born deaf-mute'.

In recent years, scientists have restudied Itard's medical notes and come to a rather different conclusion. They believe that Victor was suffering from a form of extreme autism. They also think it unlikely that he was a genuine feral child, for no infant could survive in the wild without support. Victor was almost certainly nurtured until he was five or six years of age and then abandoned in the forest when it was discovered he was suffering from serious mental diffi-culties.

As for Victor himself, he must have been bewildered by all the attention he received. He eventually died in 1828, after three decades of detailed examination, at the house of Itard's kindly housekeeper.

His real name, identity and background remain a mystery to this day.

A Question of Sex

It was highly unusual for two men to share a cabin, but there was good reason for the arrangement. Philippe Commerson and Jean Baré were botanists aboard the *Etoile* accompanying Louis Antoine de Bougainville's 1766 circumnavigation of the globe. They needed their own quarters because they were travelling with so much specialized equipment.

It was not long before the crew began making crude jibes about the two men, with most of the innuendos focusing on the close rela-tionship between master and assistant.

Jean Baré confronted the rumours head on. He told the *Etoile*'s surgeon, François Vivez, that he was sleeping in Commerson's cabin because he needed 'to be within reach to assist him'. Commerson was suffering from acute seasickness and it was only natural for his assist-ant-cum-valet to be on hand.

The gossip persisted and soon reached the ears of the ship's captain, François Chenard de la Giraudais. He summoned Baré for questioning and demanded to know if anything untoward was taking place.

Baré reluctantly confessed a secret, one designed to put an end to the rumours. He informed Giraudais that he 'in fact belonged to the one from which the Mighty Overlord selects the guardians of his seraglio'. In other words, he was a eunuch.

This was a cause of some surprise to Giraudais, but it also satisfied his curiosity. He could see no reason why the two men should not be allowed to continue sharing a cabin.

That might have been the end of the affair, had it not been for the *Etoile*'s arrival at Tahiti in the third week of March 1767. The ship dropped anchor and the crew prepared to welcome some native Tahitians aboard.

Among them was a man named Aotourou, who noticed Jean Baré standing on deck and immediately identified him as a woman. Baré was visibly embarrassed and dashed into his cabin, leaving Aotourou to explain that he had not meant to cause offence. He said that it was common for certain men to dress as women in Tahiti. They were known as *mahu* and held a respected place in society. Aotourou had innocently assumed that Baré was some sort of reverse *mahu*, a female disguised as a man.

Commander Bougainville had hitherto been unaware of the gossip about the two botanists, for he was aboard the flagship *Boudeuse*. Now, learning of what Aotourou had said, he summoned Baré to his vessel and asked if he was a woman.

Baré admitted that this was indeed the case: that her real name was Jeanne. She declined to tell Bougainville that she was Commerson's lover, but she did confess to having disguised herself as a man shortly before coming aboard.

This was a serious state of affairs: a royal ordinance made it strictly illegal for women to sail on expedition ships. Transgression of the law carried severe punishment.

The revelation came as no surprise to François Vivez, the expedition's surgeon. He had been the first to raise suspicions about Baré. 'Everything indicated in him a feminine man,' he wrote, 'small of stature, short and plump, wide-hipped, a prominent chest, a small round head, a freckled complexion, a gentle and clear voice, a marked dexterity and a gentleness of movement that could only belong to that gender.'

Now that Baré's gender was revealed, she stood in severe danger of sexual molestation at the hands of the crew. 'She had to seek an asylum in the ordinary quarters in a hammock under the quarterdeck with the other servants,' wrote Vivez. He added that she always carried 'two loaded pistols by way of precaution'.

Events were to take a darker turn when the ships arrived at New Ireland (part of Papua New Guinea). Baré was lured ashore by her erstwhile shipmates who stole her gun and gang-raped her.

After leaving New Ireland, the two ships sailed for six weeks without acquiring any victuals. The lack of food posed particular difficulties for Baré, who discovered she was pregnant. It was impossible to know whether Commerson, or one of the rapists, was the father of her child.

In November 1768 the *Etoile* and *Boudeuse* reached the island of Mauritius and remained there for a month, allowing the crews time to rebuild their strength. When the ships finally left for France, Commerson and Baré elected to stay on the island.

Jeanne Baré was safely delivered of a baby on Mauritius and it was put into the care of a certain Monsieur Bezac. Its eventual fate remains unknown.

Philippe Commerson died in 1773. Jeanne Baré married in the following year and left Mauritius soon afterwards, landing in France in the winter of 1774. It was the end of an historic voyage. In setting foot in France, she had become the first woman to circumnavigate the globe.

There was no immediate recognition of her achievement. Indeed almost a decade was to pass before the king accepted that she was 'an extraordinary woman'. She was forgiven her 'infraction' and rewarded with a lifelong pension of 200 livres a year.

The Beast that Came from Nowhere

François Antoine was an expert marksman who had spent half a life-time shooting badgers, foxes and wolves. But he had never come across such a huge wolf as the one he killed in the third week of September 1765. It was more than two metres in length and weighed a staggering 60 kilograms. The scars on its body were said to be the result of numerous attacks it had made on shepherds and farmers.

The inhabitants of the local region, the Gévaudan in southern France, were hugely relieved to learn that Antoine had killed the wolf. They hoped it would mark the end of a terrible ordeal that had afflicted their area for the better part of a year.

The attacks had begun on a bright June day in 1764 when a young shepherdess returned to her farm in a bedraggled state. Her dress and undergarments were badly torn and she was so frightened that she could scarcely speak.

When asked to explain what had happened, all she could recall was that a ferocious creature – some sort of wild beast – had savagely attacked her. She had only escaped death when her herd of oxen had driven the animal away.

Local villagers dismissed her story as a girlish fantasy. They conjectured that she had been attacked by a wolf, one that was perhaps rabid and therefore deranged.

But the shepherdess stuck to her story and it soon became clear that she was telling the truth. Just a couple of weeks later, on 30 June, a fourteen-year-old girl named Jeanne Boulet was found mauled to death. Her wounds suggested that some sort of ferocious animal had sprung on her without warning.

A fortnight after Jeanne Boulet's death, a second girl was dragged down and killed. This attack was followed by many others, all of them fatal.

On 6 October, a young man from the village of Pouget became the first to fight off the beast with his bare hands. He returned home with appalling wounds. His scalp was slashed open and he had sustained terrible chest injuries. When questioned about what had happened, all he could remember was that he had been ambushed while walking through an orchard.

News of the attacks eventually reached the ears of King Louis XV. He despatched two professional hunters to the Gévaudan with orders to track down and kill the animal.

The hunters arrived in the area with eight specially trained bloodhounds. They spent the next four months killing wolves, but never once caught sight of the beast itself. They eventually conceded defeat and their place was taken by François Antoine, the king's Lieutenant of the Hunt.

He was quick to claim success, shooting a huge wolf in the third week of September 1765. In a report for the king, he declared that he 'never saw such a big wolf that could be compared to this one. This is why we estimate it could be the fearsome beast that caused so much damage.'

Local villagers were deeply grateful, for it seemed as if their miseries were at long last at an end. For the next two months, there were no more attacks. But at the beginning of December 1765, the supposedly dead beast once again emerged from the forest and savaged two young children. This was followed by a spate of attacks on farmers and shepherds working in the fields.

In June 1767, after a large pilgrimage to Notre-Dame-des-Tours, one of the lords of Gévaudan organized a huge hunt involving hundreds of people. Among the hunters was Jean Chastel, a sixty-year-old man who was famed as a skilled marksman.

He had positioned himself at a place called Sogne d'Auvers near the village of Saugues, and was reciting his rosary when he became aware of an enormous creature lumbering towards him.

With commendable calmness, he shouldered his gun and fired, scoring a direct hit. The beast was momentarily paralysed by the force of the bullet. Seconds later, it was knocked off its feet by Chastel's hunting dogs. The dogs proceeded to attack the wounded animal until it was dead.

Local dignitaries converged on Sogne d'Auvers in order to inspect the mauled beast. It was clear to everyone that it was not a wolf. It was far too large and had features that had never been seen on any other animal. When the men opened its stomach, they found it contained human remains. Mystified as to what sort of animal it was, they declared it to be a monster of unknown origin.

Chastel hoped to take the creature to Versailles so that the royal experts could examine it. But the corpse putrefied in the stinking heat of summer and had to be buried. It was never officially identified.

Mystery surrounds the nature of the beast to this day. Some say it could only have been a giant wolf: others, more fancifully, cite its attacks as evidence of the survival of a type of mesonychid or prehistoric carnivorous dog.

One thing is sure: Jean Chastel's bullet put an end to the beast's attacks. After three years of terror, the farmers of the Gévaudan were free from nature's most terrifying serial killer.

Part XXXI

Captives and Slaves

This execrable commerce . . .

Thomas Jefferson's opinion of the slave trade in the draft
version of the Declaration of Independence: Jefferson owned
about two hundred slaves

The Last Stand

The soldiers were crowded onto the beaches of Dunkirk and desperate to get away. They had been told that Hitler's SS regiments were advancing towards the coast at an alarming rate. What they did not know was that a small group of their heroic compatriots had brought that advance to an abrupt halt.

It was 26 May 1940: Private Bert Evans and one hundred of his comrades had vowed to block the advancing German army as it marched towards the coast. They knew that the longer they kept the enemy at bay, the more Allied soldiers would be plucked from Dunkirk's beaches.

The men decided to make their stand at Wormhoudt, a small village just a few miles from the English Channel. Their commander's orders were clear: 'The division stands and fights.' He told them to hide in local farmhouses and await the Germans.

When the Wehrmacht finally arrived, the fighting was furious and deadly. Hundreds of shells rained down on the British defenders, many of them exploding in mid-air and wounding them with shrapnel. Nineteen-year-old Private Evans and his comrades from the Royal Warwickshire Regiment knew they were fighting against impossible odds.

After two days of near-constant gunfire, an SS regiment – the Leibstandarte Adolf Hitler – joined the attack. Their heavy weaponry turned the tide of battle. By early afternoon on 28 May, the Warwickshires were completely overrun.

'I was captured with a group of "D" company soldiers,' Evans said. 'We knew we were up against Hitler's elite. But we could never have expected the treatment they would mete out.'

Along with eighty surviving comrades, Evans was marched out of the village and taken to a remote cowshed outside the village of Esquelbecq. The men naively hoped they would be treated according to the rules of the Geneva Convention. But as they were forced into the cowshed, they began to fear for their lives.

'We were jammed inside,' said Evans. 'They pushed more and more in. No one could breathe. Our wounded were falling and we were falling over them.'

The British prisoners begged their captors for water. Captain Lynn-Allen, the most senior officer, banged on the door and shouted: 'For the love of God, there's no more room in here.'

A German officer outside laughed scornfully and said: 'Where you're going, there will be a lot of room.'

Private Evans shared his cigarette with his friend Charlie, who said: 'This is it, Bert. We're finished.'

Seconds after he spoke, all hell broke loose. One of the SS men pulled a stick grenade from his pack and lobbed it into the barn. It exploded instantly, killing many of the prisoners and maiming the rest with shrapnel and splintered wood.

A second grenade was followed by a third, turning the interior of the barn into a slaughterhouse. But there were still some men alive, so the SS men began pulling them outside in batches of five and shooting them.

Evans's right arm had been almost severed by the three blasts and he was in deep shock. But Captain Lynn-Allen was unharmed and determined to make his escape, taking Evans with him. The two of them pushed their way through a small hole at the rear of the barn and dived into a nearby pond. They were spotted by an SS soldier who trained his machine gun on them.

Captain Lynn-Allen was hit in the forehead at point-blank range and died instantly. Evans was also hit – in the neck – but he was not killed. He feigned death until the soldier departed. Then he crawled to a nearby farmhouse and begged for help.

He was seriously injured from the grenade explosion, with his arm hanging limply from its tendons. His life was to be saved, ironically, by a German soldier who was appalled by the actions of the SS. He performed first aid on Evans and then drove him to a local hospital where his arm was amputated. He spent the rest of the war as a prisoner.

The men at Dunkirk had got off the beaches and back to England during the massacre at Esquelbecq. They had no idea that they owed their lives to the heroic last stand of the men from the Royal Warwickshires – a last stand from which only one man, Private Bert Evans, emerged with his life.

Slave Girl in the Harem

Twenty-four-year-old Maria ter Meetelen had already lived through more adventures than most people experience in a lifetime. She had left her native Amsterdam in 1721 disguised as a man and travelled around France and Spain.

Next, she had enlisted as a dragoon in the Spanish town of Vitoria, but her career was short-lived 'because it came out that I was not the person I was registered as'. In 1728, she abandoned her various disguises and married a Dutch sailor named Claes van der Meer.

The two of them eventually resolved to return to the Netherlands, securing a passage from Cadiz in the summer of 1731. They hoped to be home within a month. In the event, it was to take Maria rather longer. As the ship sailed along the coast of Portugal it came under attack from Barbary corsairs. Resistance was useless, for there were just seven crew and four passengers aboard the Dutch ship. They were hopelessly outgunned by the 150 corsairs.

Maria was seized, bound and taken prisoner; her life and fortunes were about to change for ever. Along with her husband and shipmates, she was put ashore at Salé on the last day of July 1731. She was then marched directly to Meknes, the imperial capital of Morocco.

Maria's husband died within a few days of their arrival in North Africa, leaving her in a precarious situation. She was in danger of being forced into the sultan's harem, 'for I was young and beautiful, according to the people of that country'.

It was not long before she was escorted to the palace of the no-toriously debauched sultan Moulay Abdullah. 'I found myself in front of the sultan,' she wrote, 'in his room, where he was lying with fifty of his women, each more beautiful than the last. They were dressed like goddesses and extraordinarily stunning. Each had an instrument and they were playing and singing.'

The women of the harem were segregated into a strict hierarchy: four of the sultan's principal wives were seated opposite him; 'they shone with gold and silver and fine pearls'. They also wore crowns of gold adorned with precious stones and their fingers were decked with golden rings.

Maria's gaze switched from the women of the harem to the sultan himself. He was the very picture of decadence. 'He had his head resting on the knees of one of his wives, his feet on the knees of another; a third was behind him and the fourth in front, and they were caressing him.'

As the sultan watched Maria approach, he ordered the women playing music to stop. 'He told me to come nearer, sit down and play the zither.'

The sultan was entranced by Maria and ordered her to 'turn Turk' and join his harem. Maria refused to convert to Islam and was promptly led away by one of his wives.

'This wife', wrote Maria, 'had one sole occupation, which was to prepare young virgins for the sultan, because he required a virgin each Friday.'

Maria was warned that if she did not obey the sultan's wishes, she would have her skin torn off and suffer many other brutal tortures before being burned alive.

Now resorting to cunning, Maria told the sultan's wives that she couldn't join them in the harem because she was pregnant. This earned her their immediate sympathy. At considerable risk to themselves, they argued her case with the sultan, who eventually granted permission for her to marry the father of her child.

Maria had to think on her feet. She already had her eye on one of the Dutch slaves, a man named Pieter Janszoon. Now, after explaining her predicament, she begged him to marry her.

Janszoon was initially reluctant, for his friends and family had raised a ransom and he was due to be set free. But Maria was so persistent that he eventually consented and the two of them were married by a local Catholic priest.

Maria left a vivid description of the conditions that her fellow European slaves had to endure. 'They were obliged to work extremely hard, in blistering sunshine, digging, working the quarries, and receiving in recompense a tiny roll of bread, and sometimes nothing at all.'

Pieter himself was no longer a slave, for his ransom money had at long last arrived in Morocco. Maria's status was rather more doubtful: she inhabited a dangerous world of semi-freedom.

In spite of the restrictions on their movements, the two of them proved unusually enterprising. The Islamic prohibition of alcohol did not apply to Christian slaves, so Pieter and Maria now opened a bar inside the slaves' quarters. This bar provided them with an income of sorts, although their existence was to remain insecure for years.

Maria seized every opportunity to ingratiate herself with the sultan's wives and her success at court was viewed with envy by her enslaved compatriots.

In 1743, after twelve years in captivity, Maria was finally freed under the terms of a ransom agreement negotiated by the Dutch state. By the time she and her husband returned to the Netherlands, she had spent twelve years in slavery. She, Pieter and her eight children settled in the town of Medemblik, but after two years of domesticity Pieter signed up for a voyage to the East Indies from which he never returned.

In 1748, Maria published her memoirs of life in captivity: it remains one of the most extraordinary (and least known) accounts of life as a European slave.

The rest of her life was marked by further vicissitudes. Her husband's death in the East Indies was followed by the deaths of all eight of her children. Maria decided to leave Holland for good and start a new life in South Africa.

This was presumably where she died, for she is never heard of again.

The Man Who Broke into Auschwitz

Witold Pilecki had already proved that he was immune to fear. One of the founder members of the Secret Polish Army, he had undertaken daring guerrilla attacks on Hitler's occupying army.

Now, he was about to volunteer for one of the most extraordinary adventures of the Second World War, one that required him to place his life in the gravest possible danger. His self-imposed mission was to find out what was taking place inside Auschwitz, the Nazis' most notorious extermination camp.

Pilecki's first task was to acquire forged identity papers. He then got himself deliberately arrested during a Gestapo round-up in Warsaw.

Two days later, after being tortured, he was sent to Auschwitz as prisoner number 4859.

He began gathering information about the camp as soon as he arrived. He did not have to wait long to witness the SS guards' violence towards prisoners.

'By beating their heads, kicking those lying on the ground in their kidneys and other sensitive places, jumping with boots upon their chests and bellies, they were inflicting death with some kind of nightmarish enthusiasm.'

He was taken to the bathhouse where he was stripped of all his possessions. His hair was cut off and then the bathroom chief, who took a dislike to him, punched him in the face, causing two teeth to come out.

Pilecki was given a striped uniform and then assigned to blockhouse 17a.

The blockhouse leader, known as 'Bloody Alois', was a psychopath. 'He used to beat, torture, torment and kill several persons a day.'

Pilecki and his fellow inmates slept on the floor: the day began at 4.20 a.m. in summer, an hour earlier in winter. They then had twelve hours of torment at the hands of their prison guards.

Pilecki recorded all of the inhumane treatment they suffered. One of his jobs was to build the camp crematorium: 'We were', he noted wryly, 'building the crematorium for ourselves.'

After a day's hard labour, the men often had to perform exercises. A favourite among the camp guards was getting the inmates to perform a swimming-style breaststroke, albeit without the benefit of a swimming pool or water. They had to 'swim' around the camp's gravel parade ground until their chests were bleeding and raw.

Pilecki's principal reason for getting himself into Auschwitz was to report to the outside world on what was taking place in the camp. To this end, he built a radio transmitter using smuggled parts and began to transmit information to the Polish underground. His reports provided first-hand information about conditions in Auschwitz; the gas chambers, enforced sterilizations and frightening human experiments were all transmitted in the reports.

His stories make for terrible reading: violent and unpredictable guards, inmates torn to pieces by dogs and men forced to stand for hours in the driving snow.

Pilecki kept his transmitter in use until the autumn of 1942, when he realized there was a danger of the camp guards discovering it. He dismantled it and didn't use it again.

Within a few months of arriving at Auschwitz, Pilecki had also begun to lay the foundations of a highly secret resistance organization. Called the Związek Organizacji Wojskowej (Union of Military Organization), or ZOW for short, it was charged with distributing illicit food and clothing. It also helped train inmates for a camp take-over in the event of an Allied attack.

The Gestapo did everything they could to root out members of ZOW and eventually succeeded in killing many of them. Pilecki knew it would only be a matter of time before they came for him. By 1943, he realized he had to escape.

One day, he was assigned a shift in a bakery that lay outside the perimeter fence. He knew that this was probably his last chance of getting away. On the night of 26 April 1943 – after two and a half years in Auschwitz – he and two fellow members overpowered their guard and cut the phone line. They then made a dash for freedom.

They crossed the River Soła and headed on foot towards Oświęcim. After a journey of high drama, they eventually made contact with the Polish Home Army. Almost four months later, Pilecki got back to Warsaw where he wrote up his detailed report.

His description of life in Auschwitz included much information about the scale of the killing. 'During the first three years, at Auschwitz there perished two million people; in the next two years, three million.'

Pilecki hoped his account would prompt an Allied air attack on the camp: this, he reasoned, was the best means of helping the inmates to escape. But the British government considered the report to be grossly exaggerated and did nothing. His work was to languish on a pile of unpublished documents, a neglected record of man's inhumanity to man.

Astonishingly, it was not published until the year 2000, more than half a century after Auschwitz was finally liberated. Pilecki was by then long dead. He was executed by Stalin's secret police in 1948 for allegedly working as a British spy. He was buried in an unmarked grave.

All the President's Slaves

When Thomas Jefferson wrote the first draft of the Declaration of Independence, he was anxious to include a passage condemning slavery. He described the slave trade as 'this execrable commerce' and lambasted the British monarch for promoting the lucrative market in slaves, 'captivating and carrying them into slavery in another hemisphere or to incur miserable death in their transportation thither'.

These were noble sentiments that came from the pen of a noble-minded individual. Yet Jefferson, the third president of the United States, owned more than two hundred slaves of his own, most of them working on his magnificent Monticello estate. He even bequeathed them to his children.

In 1996, DNA tests on a descendant of Sally Hemmings, one of those slaves, revealed that Jefferson had fathered children with Sally. Since then, the story of their relationship has received widespread coverage.

Rather less well known, but equally fascinating, is the story of Isaac Jefferson Granger, another of the president's slaves. Isaac's story might have been lost to the world, had it not been for a clergyman, Reverend Charles Campbell, who interviewed him in 1847. His memoir sheds much light on how Jefferson treated his slaves, as well as providing a snapshot of daily life at Monticello.

There is a single surviving photograph of Isaac. It depicts a thickset black man with broad arms and huge hands. He stares at the camera without the trace of a smile.

He was born into slavery in 1775, the third son of a married slave couple, Ursula and George. They also worked at Jefferson's Monticello estate: George would eventually rise to become overseer of the entire estate, earning himself the nickname 'King George' in the process. His wife ('Queen Ursula') was laundress and pastry cook.

Isaac turned twenty-six in the year that Jefferson became president and he accompanied his master to Philadelphia. He travelled on horseback, a rare honour for a slave, and was apparently well treated. It was in Philadelphia that Jefferson set Isaac to work on an apprenticeship, learning metalworking skills. Slaves were far more useful and valuable if they had a craft.

'He went to learn the tinner's trade,' reads Campbell's account. 'First week [he] learned to cut out and solder.' He was soon competent enough to produce little pepper boxes and graters.

Isaac warmed to his slave master, who was kind, jovial and treated his slaves well. 'The old master used to talk to me mighty free,' Isaac recalled, 'and ask me: "How you come on Isaac, larnin de tin business?"'

Then Isaac was put to work making nails and soon became Monticello's most productive nail-maker. According to Jefferson's meticulous account books, in one forty-seven-day period he made 507 pounds of nails. In doing so, he earned the highest daily return for his master: the equivalent of eighty-five cents a day.

Isaac proved so loyal that he was eventually made a gatekeeper of Monticello, opening the several sets of gates to Jefferson's friends. Among the regular visitors was Colonel Gary, whom Isaac disliked intensely. He was 'as dry looking [a] man as ever you see in your life'.

Gary treated Isaac in a very different fashion from Jefferson. He frequently beat him on arriving at Monticello and would then beat him again later in the day. 'The colonel would look about for him and whip him with his horsewhip,' wrote Campbell, who added that the colonel had 'given Isaac more whippings than he has fingers and toes'.

Colonel Gary would often stay several weeks at Jefferson's house: during that time, most of the slaves would be abused by him. It is not known if Jefferson objected to his behaviour.

When Jefferson grew infirm, Isaac became his carer and nurse. 'He was took with a swelling in his legs,' said Isaac. '[I] used to bathe 'em and bandage 'em.' He would then wheel the ex-president around the grounds of Monticello in a ham-barrow.

Isaac's memories of his slave master were unusually fond and his account suggests that Jefferson was kind to his slaves. When the Reverend Campbell asked Isaac what he thought of Jefferson, he described him as 'a mighty good master'.

In October 1797, Thomas Jefferson made a gift of Isaac, his wife, Iris, and their two sons to his daughter. Isaac eventually won his freedom, although it is not known how this came about. Nor is anything known about the fate of his wife and children. Reverend Campbell only noted that Isaac died 'a few years after these recollections were taken down'.

Although he died a free man, he almost certainly never lived to see the abolition of slavery. That did not come about until 1865, more than a century after Thomas Jefferson, with no apparent irony, had described it as 'an abominable crime'.

Part XXXII
The Bubble that Burst

I can calculate the movement of stars,
but not the madness of men.

Isaac Newton, after losing a fortune from his investment in
the South Sea Bubble scam

The Worst Banker in History

John Blunt seemed to have it all. He was a smart financier with an uncanny knack of turning everything he touched into gold. He was also blessed with a gilded tongue that he used to charm and manipulate those in power.

By 1720, Blunt was at the height of his fame: he was a director of the highly profitable South Sea Company and also a director of the Hollow Sword Blade Company. The latter, despite its name, was a successful merchant bank.

In January 1720, Blunt turned his attentions to the woeful state of Britain's economy. The national debt stood at £31 million, far higher than in previous years, and the government was struggling to meet the £1.5 million annual interest payments.

The economic mismanagement was being presided over by two of the key figures in the government, Earl Sunderland and Earl Stanhope, neither of whom had any experience of high finance. They had deferred financial policy to John Aislabie, the Chancellor of the Exchequer, who was not only inept but also extremely gullible. He was intrigued when Blunt came to him with a scheme designed to save the British economy.

Blunt's idea was for the South Sea Company to take over Britain's entire national debt. This would be done on one condition: for every £100 of government debt that the company assumed, Blunt demanded the right to issue £100 of new stock for the South Sea Company. This new stock was intended to pay for the old.

On paper, it sounded like a simple case of exchanging good for bad. If an individual held £1,200 of bad government securities and wished to convert them into South Sea Company stock, the company would exchange the worthless securities for twelve new shares valued at £100 each.

But Blunt's scheme was not born of altruism. He was a businessman and he sniffed at the opportunity to make money. Lots of it. He realized that if the market value of each South Sea Company share could be manipulated upwards to, say, £300, then the company would only have to hand over four shares to the individual, since these would equal £1,200.

Blunt himself would continue to hold the eight remaining shares, which he could then sell at £300 each, netting the tidy sum of £2,400. In one simple transaction, he would make a huge profit.

Chancellor Aislabie was impressed with the simplicity of the proposed financial package. Although Blunt himself stood to make a fortune, he would also have eradicated the country's crippling national debt.

Aislabie presented the idea to Members of Parliament, who were only too aware that Blunt had a proven track record at manipulating the markets. Few doubted he would be able to artificially inflate the value of the South Sea Company shares.

After a short debate on the floor of the House, ministers voted to back his scheme. It was a momentous decision for both Parliament and the country. Henceforth, Britain's economy would be in the hands of a wily financier with a dubious past.

There was one drawback to Blunt's policy: it was predicated on him being able to inflate the market value of the South Sea Company shares and keep them artificially high. Unlike a similar scheme in France, which was backed by land in Louisiana, Blunt's was based on nothing more than the prestige of the South Sea Company and the fact that the king was its governor.

Blunt was shrewd enough to realize that the success of his package required the oxygen of publicity, and publicity was one thing at which he excelled. He bribed ministers to set the ball rolling by investing their own money in his enterprise. It was not long before financiers and merchants followed suit, spending huge sums of money on the newly issued shares.

The king himself bought heavily into the scheme and, in a matter of weeks, had made £86,000 profit on his investment. He promptly knighted John Blunt in recognition of his financial wizardry. Blunt became the most celebrated man in the country, as Aislabie was quick to recognize. 'The eyes of the world were turned from the chief ministers of state to this great oracle,' he wrote.

The speculating frenzy lasted for eight months and soon involved people from up and down the country. Even the impoverished under-class invested in Blunt's scheme as the value of shares continued to exceed all expectations, rising ten-fold to £1,000 in the summer of 1720.

And then, overnight, the bubble burst. The share value crashed through the floor as there was a sudden crisis of confidence. People awoke to the fact that Blunt's investments were completely hollow. There was no money to support his shares: indeed they were nothing more than worthless sheets of paper.

In the space of a few days, the South Sea Company imploded and thousands of families lost their life savings. Rich and poor were affected. Isaac Newton had invested particularly heavily. He lost a staggering £20,000. The poet John Gay lost a similar amount. Many more people were left completely bankrupt by Blunt's empty scheme. 'They have lived their dream,' wrote Alexander Pope, 'and on awakening found nothing in their hands.'

John Blunt ran away from the crisis he had caused. He went into hiding in Kent until his whereabouts were discovered and he was ordered back to London. He was stripped of his remaining assets and then forced to leave the capital in disgrace.

But ultimately he had the last laugh. He was given a house and huge allowance by his son, one of the few people to have retained the fortune he made out of the artificially created boom.

Bone Wars

His skull is kept under lock and key at the University of Pennsylvania, testament to one of the most bizarre feuds of the nineteenth century. Edward Drinker Cope donated his skull to medical science on his death in 1897, but there was nothing benevolent about his donation. He wanted it to be studied and measured in the belief that it would prove one thing: that his brain was larger than that of his great scientific rival, Othniel Marsh.

It was a final, posthumous throw of the dice for Edward Cope, one that was predicated on his belief that brain size was a measure of intelligence. It was also the parting shot in a bitter feud that had lasted more than three decades. For Cope and Marsh were the protagonists in what has become known as the Bone Wars, a desperate struggle to be recognized as the most brilliant palaeontologist of the Victorian age.

The relationship between the two men had not always been hostile. Indeed, they had once been firm friends. They first met in Berlin in the winter of 1863 and discovered that they shared a common passion: palaeontology. Both men were obsessed with dinosaurs and fossilized bones.

The two of them returned to America from Berlin and embarked on their joint quest to discover and classify as many bones as possible.

Theirs was an unusual friendship, for the two men came from very different backgrounds. Othniel Marsh was a distinguished scientist who taught at the University of Yale. With his thick waistcoat and lengthy beard, he looked the very picture of a nineteenth-century scientist. He was wealthy, too. His uncle, the millionaire George Peabody, provided him with a steady flow of funds.

Edward Cope was altogether more idiosyncratic, a child genius with little formal education: his first academic paper was published when he was still in his teens. Hot-headed and sharp, he was nevertheless a shrewd observer of men.

Their brief friendship had flourished while they remained in Berlin, but it did not long survive their return to America. The difficulties first surfaced when Marsh was invited to view the fossil of a plesiosaur, a marine creature that became extinct 66 million years ago, which Cope had discovered and reassembled. Marsh declared (with undisguised relish) that Cope had mistakenly placed the skull at the end of the tail.

Cope was outraged by the comments of his erstwhile friend. He refused to accept Marsh's judgement and the two men decided to settle the score by inviting an adjudicating expert. The adjudicator's declaration in favour of Marsh marked the end of their friendship. From that point onwards, there was a frosty hostility between them.

The hostility soon turned to hatred. Both men had been informed of a haul of spectacular fossils discovered in Colorado. Marsh used his vast fortune to buy the exclusive rights to the bones, thereby infuriating Cope.

But Cope soon got his revenge. He learned of an even more significant find in Cañon City, Colorado. He reached the site long before his rival and made a detailed study of the bones, publishing his findings and greatly enhancing his reputation.

The feud between the two men became increasingly bitter. Othniel

Marsh was brought news that two Union Pacific Railroad workers had found a quarry of dinosaur bones at Como Bluff, Wyoming: he once again used his wealth to hire the workers as his exclusive diggers.

Cope was short of funds but he nevertheless sent his own men to dig in the same area. The rivalry between the two men was by now so intense that their teams of workmen often came to blows, hurling rocks at each other while they worked.

Marsh looked certain to be the eventual winner in the Bone Wars: Cope simply did not have the resources to hire scores of diggers. Marsh also retained his academic post at the University of Yale, which gave him the intellectual credibility that Cope so desired.

But Cope had made some extraordinary finds and he had also classified them with great skill. Marsh deliberately gave his dinosaurs different names and classifications, in an attempt to outdo his rival. It would take palaeontologists years to decide who was correct about each individual dinosaur. The winner was invariably the self-taught Edward Cope.

Cope's limited resources eventually dried up. He was rejected for a job at the Smithsonian Institution and scraped a living by giving lectures about his discoveries.

Just when it seemed as if he was about to be overshadowed by Marsh, he was offered a job at the University of Pennsylvania. It marked a turning point in his life, for at last he saw his opportunity to strike back. Over the previous decades, he had kept a logbook of all the most notable scientific mistakes made by Marsh. Now, he went to the *New York Herald* and gave them a story that was to send shock-waves across America.

Under the headline 'Scientists Wage Bitter Warfare', the public learned how the two greatest palaeontologists of the age, both famous for their discoveries, were engaged in a deeply personal battle.

'Most scientists of the day recoiled in horror, and read on with interest, to find that Cope's feud with Marsh had at last become front-page news.' So wrote Elizabeth Shor, a recent historian of their rivalry.

The feud lingered on until 1897, when Edward Cope died of a gastro-intestinal illness. Othniel Marsh died two years later, having previously declined Cope's challenge to bequeath his skull to medical science.

It was left for history to judge who won the Bone Wars. In purely numerical terms, Marsh was the winner. He discovered eighty hitherto unknown species of dinosaur, whereas Cope uncovered just fifty-six. But Cope produced a number of brilliant scientific papers on the subject, as well as accurately classifying many of his finds.

Ultimately, the two men were both winners and losers. They discovered scores of new species and sparked an enduring interest in the early history of our planet. But the price of success was high: a ruptured friendship that was allowed to descend into a bitter and deeply personal feud.

The Hidden Life of Jonathan Wild

Jonathan Wild could scarcely believe his good fortune. He had risen from the gutter to become the greatest crime-buster of the eighteenth century. He had sent more than sixty thieves to the gallows and destroyed numerous criminal gangs. More importantly, to the citizens of London, he had demonstrated an uncanny ability to return stolen goods to their owners.

The Privy Council was so grateful for his work that they rewarded him with an office in the Old Bailey. Wild responded by giving himself the title of 'Thief-Taker General of Great Britain'.

What nobody knew was that Jonathan Wild was the greatest criminal of all. For years he had duped everyone into believing he was on the side of the law, a self-appointed policeman working hard to apprehend criminals. By the mid-1720s, he had amassed a fortune.

His method was as ingenious as it was simple. He ran a large gang of thieves who stole on his behalf. He would then take possession of the stolen goods and wait for the various thefts to be announced in the local news-sheets.

When this happened, he would announce that his 'thief takers' had recovered the stolen items. These were duly returned to their rightful owners, but only on the payment of a substantial reward. Wild used this money to recompense his 'thief takers' for their criminal activity, while retaining a substantial share for himself.

His system was ingenious because it put a gap between him and the law. He was always quick to point out that he was not selling stolen goods, which carried severe penalties, but merely returning them to their rightful owners.

Before long, Wild had a virtual monopoly on organized crime in the capital. Yet no one (apart from his thieves) was aware of his role as master criminal. Rather, he was celebrated in news-sheets and ballads as an honest thief-taker who stood on the side of justice.

Wild did much to promote this view of himself. Whenever his thieves became troublesome, he simply 'shopped' them to the authorities. They protested and tried to implicate him, but his word was always believed over theirs.

No one ever thought to question Wild's activities. Indeed, the Privy Council was so impressed with his work that they began to consult him about methods of controlling crime. Wild's recommendation, not surprisingly, was to raise the rewards for those who caught thieves. The council acted on his advice, increasing the reward from £40 to £140 in a single year.

For almost a decade Wild retained his position as master-criminal. But by 1724 he had started to overreach himself and the first cracks appeared in his criminal empire. He was implicated in an abortive jailbreak and found himself under arrest. He was temporarily locked up in Newgate Prison.

In the ensuing investigation, his nefarious activities slowly came to light. He might yet have saved himself, for he had a wealth of powerful connections. He might even have retained his criminal crown, had it not been for the capriciousness of the thieves he had controlled for so long. They realized that his luck was on the wane and dramatically turned against him.

Wild was exposed as a common criminal, one who had duped Londoners for more than a decade. The mood of the public changed overnight. He was no longer celebrated as the greatest thief-taker of them all. Now, everyone was baying for his blood.

He was sent for trial at the Old Bailey, where he was expected to be tried for the hundreds of crimes he had orchestrated. But the evidence for many of the robberies was dependent on witnesses who were, at best, unreliable. Instead, he was indicted for two specific crimes of stealing lace. He was acquitted of the first charge – amazingly – but found guilty of the second. It was enough to send him to the gallows.

Wild was terrified when he learned he was a condemned man. On the morning of his execution, 24 May 1725, he tried to take his own life by drinking laudanum. But it merely made him vomit and induced a temporary coma.

When he recovered consciousness he was taken to the gallows at Tyburn. So great was the crowd that the event had to be ticketed. Ominously, many of those making their way to the execution site were carrying rocks and stones.

As Wild approached the gallows, someone threw a rock at his head, causing a large gash. Others began hurling faeces, dead rats and large stones, until blood was streaming down his face. 'There was nothing but hollowing and huzzas, as if it had been upon a triumph,' wrote Daniel Defoe, who was among the crowd.

Wild died calmly, probably because he was still suffering the effects of the laudanum, and was interred next to his third wife. But his corpse was later exhumed in order that it could be used for surgical experiments.

His skeleton was eventually sold to the Royal College of Surgeons and put on display at the Royal College's Hunterian Museum. It remains there to this day as a warning that crime can pay, but only for a while.

Part XXXIII
All About Sex

I had the broad hips and pelvis built for child-bearing.

Hildegard Trutz explains why the Nazis considered
her the perfect Aryan mother

The Last Eunuch of China

He was just nine years of age when he took the decision that was to transform his life. Sun Yaoting had been chatting with an elderly eunuch who had become rich from serving the Chinese emperor. Soon afterwards, in the autumn of 1911, Sun decided to follow the same path. He asked his father to castrate him in order that he could serve Emperor Puyi, known to history as the 'Last Emperor'.

It was a momentous decision. Unlike eunuchs in the Ottoman Empire, Chinese eunuchs had every bit of their genitals removed. It was an operation that caused not only excruciating pain, but led to a lifetime of sexual frustration, impotence and incontinence.

Sun remained undaunted. On the appointed day, he removed his clothes and lay completely still while his father bound up his hands and feet with rope. Then, with a single violent swoop of a razor, he performed the operation. In a matter of seconds – and a torrent of blood – Sun had become a eunuch.

He was bandaged with oiled cloth to staunch the bleeding, but the pain was so agonizing that the young lad lay in a coma for three days. For eight weeks he was virtually paralysed and for months afterwards he was unable to walk because of the excruciating pain. But he eventually recovered from the loss of blood and looked forward to joining the emperor's royal household in the Forbidden City.

Emperor Puyi had more than a thousand eunuchs, many of whom wielded positions of great influence. The emperor rarely left the inner recesses of the palace, meaning that the eunuchs became crucial intermediaries between the outer bureaucratic world and the inner imperial one.

Puyi himself would later write of these 'slaves', who attended him day and night. 'They waited on me when I ate, dressed and slept. They accompanied me on my walks and to my lessons; they told me stories and had rewards and beatings from me, but they never left my presence. They were my slaves and they were my earliest teachers.'

This was the role to which Sun now aspired. He wanted to get the ear of the emperor in order that he might acquire power and influence.

But then came the news that was to leave him in a deep state of shock. The emperor had abdicated, the imperial court was being dismantled and Sun's castration had been in vain.

The dynasty did not die immediately and Sun was not left entirely without hope. He initially found employment with one of the emperor's uncles; later, he worked for Puyi's wife.

In the decades that followed, he was to serve the former imperial family with devotion. He accompanied them to Manchuria, where Puyi was installed as the puppet emperor of the Japanese colonial state of Manchukuo in 1932.

He was also witness to all the innermost secrets of the imperial household, such as the emperor's refusal to sleep with his wife on their wedding night and his obsession with a fellow eunuch, 'who looked like a pretty girl with his tall, slim figure, handsome face and creamy white skin'.

Sun was luckier than the majority of the emperor's eunuchs, who had been abandoned by the court and left penniless. Some became outcasts in society. Many more committed suicide. Others sought sanctuary in the temples of Beijing.

Sun's own life took a downward turn in 1949, when the Communists came to power. Gone were the days when eunuchs were viewed with fear and admiration. Now they were despised as outmoded relics of China's feudal past.

During the Cultural Revolution, Sun lost his most treasured possession, his severed, pickled genitals. Eunuchs always kept them in a jar, in order that they could be buried together. It was believed that such a practice would guarantee their reincarnation as 'whole' men. But Sun's genitals were thrown away like common garbage, causing him to weep openly.

Sun was to live another three decades, dying in 1996 at the age of ninety-four. He never recovered from the loss of his pickled 'treasure'.

'When I die,' he said sadly, 'I will come back as a cat or a dog.'

Never Go to Bed with a Knife

It was the most sensational trial in years – one so sexually charged that even the judge confessed to being aroused by the evidence.

In the dock stood Sada Abe, one-time geisha, prostitute and waitress who was accused of strangling her lover in an elaborate sex game. That was not all. Once he was dead she had cut off his penis and testicles with a large kitchen knife and kept them as a sex toy.

There was never any doubt as to her guilt: Abe freely admitted to what she had done. What made the case so compelling was her graphic testimony. The sexual practices in which she indulged were so dark and dangerous that they sent shockwaves through the conservative Japanese society of the 1930s. Yet they were also to turn Sada Abe into a national celebrity, with her exploits feted in scores of books and half a dozen films. Even today, Sada Abe has the status of a bizarre icon.

Abe's sexual life had begun brutally at the age of fifteen when she was raped by a family acquaintance. Her father subsequently sold her to a geisha house, justifying his actions by saying it would bring structure to her life. But Abe proved an unwilling student. Before long she had turned to street prostitution, working in Osaka's brothel district.

In 1936, she had a dramatic change of lifestyle, getting herself a job in a Tokyo restaurant owned by a gregarious individual named Kichizo Ishida. The forty-two-year-old Ishida was married, but this had not stopped him from having a string of extramarital affairs. In Sada Abe, he found a partner who was willing to experiment with dangerous sexual practices.

Abe grew increasingly fixated with Ishida, but she also became obsessively jealous of his wife. She wanted to have Ishida all to herself and possess him, but he refused to leave the family home.

One evening, Abe went to the theatre and watched a play in which a geisha threatened her lover with a knife. Enthralled by what she saw, she bought herself a large kitchen knife and suggested to Ishida that it could be an instrument for sexual pleasure.

Most men would have made their excuses and left, but not Ishida. He was aroused by her threats and agreed that the knife could add an interesting twist to their extreme lovemaking. The two of them headed to the red-light district in the Ogu neighbourhood where they rented a room.

Every last detail of that fateful night was recounted by Sada Abe at her trial. She told the judge how she had put the kitchen knife to the base of Ishida's penis and said she would make sure he would never play around with another woman. Ishida assumed she was joking and got a perverse kick out of the threat.

After forty-eight hours of sustained lovemaking, Sada Abe began a whole new sex game. She removed the sash from her kimono and wound it tightly around Ishida's neck. It was the first time he had experienced erotic asphyxiation and he found that it heightened his sexual pleasure.

Sada asked him to do the same to her. She, too, found it exhilarating. They repeated the process for more than two hours, until Ishida's face became so distorted that it would not return to its normal appearance. He took thirty tablets of the sedative Calmotin to soothe the pain.

At around 2 a.m. on the morning of 18 May, as Ishida slept, Abe wrapped her sash twice around his neck and strangled him to death. She later told police: 'After I had killed Ishida I felt totally at ease, as though a heavy burden had been lifted from my shoulders, and I felt a sense of clarity.'

After lying with his corpse for several hours, she severed his genitalia with the kitchen knife and wrapped them in a magazine cover. She used his blood to write *Sada, Kichi Futari-kiri* ('Sada, Kichi together') on his left thigh and also on the bed sheet. She then put on his underwear and left the inn at about 8 a.m.

Ishida's mutilated corpse caused a sensation when it was found. Sada Abe was the obvious culprit, but she had disappeared without trace. A nationwide hunt failed to find her, even though she did nothing to hide her whereabouts. She stayed in a Tokyo inn, had a massage and went to various bars.

Her behaviour, already disturbingly bizarre, now took an even darker turn. In the privacy of her hotel room, she started to engage in necrophilia. 'I felt attached to Ishida's penis and thought that only after taking leave from it quietly could I then die. I unwrapped the paper holding them and gazed at his penis and scrotum. I put his penis in my mouth and even tried to insert it inside me. It didn't work however, though I kept trying and trying.'

Two days after the murder, the police eventually tracked Abe down to her hotel room. She gave herself up immediately. 'Don't be so formal,' she said to the police. 'You're looking for Sada Abe, right? Well, that's me. I am Sada Abe.' The police were still not convinced, so she showed them Ishida's genitalia.

The interrogating officer was struck by Abe's demeanour when asked why she had killed Ishida. 'Immediately she became excited and her eyes sparkled in a strange way.'

Her answer was: 'I loved him so much. I wanted him all to myself. But since we were not husband and wife, as long as he lived he could be embraced by other women. I knew that if I killed him no other woman could ever touch him again, so I killed him.'

On 21 December 1936, Sada Abe was convicted of the murder and mutilation of a corpse. She was sentenced to just six years in prison – an extremely lenient sentence for murder – yet she didn't even serve the full term. On 10 November 1940, her sentence was commuted and she was released. Despite her horrific crime, she was allowed to walk free.

In the years that followed she was often asked why she had severed Ishida's penis. Her answer was logical if bizarre. 'I wanted to take the part of him that brought back to me the most vivid memories,' she said.

For a while she cashed in on her notoriety, but eventually she tired of the publicity and disappeared from the public eye. Her last years are believed to have been spent in a Kansai nunnery.

As for Ishida, his penis and testicles were moved to the pathology museum at Tokyo University's Medical School. They remained on public display for some years until they mysteriously disappeared. No one has subsequently been able to trace their whereabouts.

The Woman Who Gave Birth for Hitler

Hildegard Trutz had been a loyal supporter of the Nazis ever since Hitler came to power. She had joined the Bund Deutscher Mädel (the female equivalent of the Hitler Youth) in 1933 and loved attending its weekly meetings. 'I was mad about Adolf Hitler and our new better Germany,' she later admitted. 'I learned how tremendously valuable we young people were to Germany.'

Trutz quickly became a figurehead of her local organization, in part because of her Germanic blonde hair and blue eyes. 'I was pointed out as the perfect example of the Nordic woman,' she said, 'for besides my long legs and my long trunk, I had the broad hips and pelvis built for child-bearing.'

In 1936, when she was eighteen, Trutz finished her schooling and was at a loss as to what to do next. She chatted with a BDM leader who made a suggestion that was to change Trutz's life for ever. 'If you don't know what to do,' said the leader, 'why not give the Führer a child? What Germany needs more than anything is racially valuable stock.'

Trutz was unaware of the state-sponsored programme known as Lebensborn. Its aim was to raise the birth rate of blond-haired, blue-eyed 'Aryan' children through interbreeding. Racially 'pure' women were chosen to sleep with SS officers in the hope that they would fall pregnant.

The BDM leader explained to her exactly how Lebensborn worked. She would be given a series of medical tests, along with a thorough investigation of her background. It was essential that she had no Jewish blood. Once given the all-clear, she would be able to select a breeding partner from a group of SS officers.

Trutz listened with growing enthusiasm. 'It sounded wonderful,' she later admitted, and she signed up immediately. Aware that her parents would disapprove, she told them she was undertaking a residential course in National Socialism.

She was escorted to an old castle in Bavaria, near the Tegernsee. There were forty other girls in residence and all were living under assumed names. 'All you needed to be accepted there was a certificate of Aryan ancestry as far back at least as your great-grandparents.'

The castle itself was the height of luxury. There were common rooms for sports and games, a library, music room and even a cinema. According to Trutz: 'The food was the best I have ever tasted; we didn't have to work and there were masses of servants.' She was by her own admission self-indulgent and lazy and she quickly learned to enjoy life in the castle.

'The whole place was in the charge of a professor, a high-up SS doctor, who examined each of us very thoroughly as soon as we arrived,' Trutz said. 'We had to make a statutory declaration that there had never been any cases of hereditary diseases, dipsomania or imbecility in our family.'

The professor also warned the girls that they would have to sign a document renouncing all claims to any children they produced, as they were to be the property of the state. They would be brought up in special institutions that would instil an absolute loyalty to the Nazi ideal.

After their initiation, Trutz and the other girls were introduced to the SS men who were to be their breeding partners. Trutz liked what she saw. 'They were all very tall and strong with blue eyes and blond hair.' There was a getting-to-know-you session, with the group playing games together, watching films and enjoying social evenings in the castle.

'We were given about a week to pick the man we liked and we were told to see to it that his hair and eyes corresponded exactly to ours,' said Trutz. The girls were not told the names of any of the men: anonymity was a key principle of the Lebensborn programme.

'When we had made our choice, we had to wait until the tenth day after the beginning of the last period.' Each girl was given another medical examination and told to receive her chosen SS man in her room that very night. Trutz was unbelievably excited, not just about the sexual activity, but the fact that she was doing it all for her beloved Führer.

'As both the father of my child and I believed completely in the importance of what we were doing, we had no shame or inhibitions of any kind.' She was particularly impressed with the 'smashing looks' of her chosen partner, although she thought he was probably a little stupid.

The officer slept with Trutz for three evenings in that first week. On the other evenings, he had to sleep with other girls at the castle.

Trutz fell pregnant almost immediately and was moved into a maternity home for the next nine months. 'My confinement came neither too soon nor too late,' she said. 'It was not an easy birth, for no good German woman would think of having any artificial aids, such as injections to deaden the pain, like they had in the degenerate Western democracies.'

She weaned her baby son for two weeks and then he was removed from her side and taken to a special SS home where he was to be brought up as a loyal servant of the Nazi state. Trutz never saw him again. Nor, for that matter, did she see the father.

In the years that followed she was tempted to breed more children, but she eventually fell in love with a young officer and they got married. When she told her new husband about her involvement in the Lebensborn programme, she was 'rather surprised to find that he was not as pleased about it as he might have been'. But he could not openly criticize her, 'seeing that I had been doing my duty to the Führer'.

Trutz never discovered what became of her child and his eventual fate remains a mystery. Like so many Lebensborn babies, he almost certainly found himself ostracized in post-war Germany, his birth and upbringing a stigma that could never be completely expunged.

It is estimated that some 20,000 babies were bred during the twelve years of the Third Reich, principally in Germany and Norway. Many were adopted after the war, by which time the records of their birth had been destroyed. To this day the majority have never been able to discover the terrible truth about their conception and birth.

Further Reading

Hitler's English Girlfriend

Litchfield, David R., *Hitler's Valkyrie: The Uncensored Biography of Unity Mitford* (History Press, 2013)

Lovell, Mary, *The Sisters: The Saga of the Mitford Family* (Norton, 2003)

Pryce-Jones, David, *Unity Mitford: A Quest* (Weidenfeld & Nicolson, 1995)

Hitler's American Nephew

Brown, Jonathan, and Duff, Oliver, 'The Black Sheep of the Family? The Rise and Fall of Hitler's Scouse Nephew', *Independent*, 17 August 2006, http://www.independent.co.uk/news/uk/this-britain/the-black-sheep-of-the-family-the-rise-and-fall-of-hitlers-scouse-nephew-412206.html

Gardner, David, *The Last of the Hitlers* (BMM, 2001)

Kilgannon, Corey, 'Three Quiet Brothers on Long Island, All of Them Related to Hitler', *New York Times*, 24 April 2006

When Hitler Took Cocaine

Doyle, D., 'Hitler's Medical Care', Royal College of Physicians of Edinburgh, 2005, http://www.ncbi.nlm.nih.gov/pubmed/15825245

Heston, Leonard H., *The Medical Casebook of Adolf Hitler: His Illnesses, Doctors and Drugs* (Cooper Square Publishers, New York, 2000)

Irving, David, *Adolf Hitler: The Secret Diaries of Hitler's Doctor* (Scribner, 1983)

Waite, Robert G. L., *The Psychopathic God: Adolf Hitler* (Da Capo Press, New York, 1993)

A Corpse on Everest

Anker, Conrad, and Roberts, David, *The Lost Explorer: Finding Mallory on Mount Everest* (Simon & Schuster, 1999)

Davis, Wade, *Into the Silence: The Great War, Mallory and the Conquest of Everest* (Vintage, 2012)

Hemmleb, Jochen, Johnson, Larry A., Simonson, Eric R. and Nothdurft, William E., *Ghosts of Everest: The Search for Mallory & Irvine* (Mountaineers Books, Seattle, 1999)

Hemmleb, Jochen, and Simonson, Eric R., *Detectives on Everest: The Story of the 2001 Mallory & Irvine Research Expedition* (Mountaineers Books, Seattle, 1999)

Drunk on the *Titanic*

Encyclopedia Titanica: http://www.encyclopedia-titanica.org/titanic-survivor/charles-john-joughin.html

Lord, Walter, *A Night to Remember* (Transworld, 1955)

Titanic Enquiry Project: http://www.titanicinquiry.org/BOTInq/BOTInq06Joughin01.php

The Man Who Was Buried Alive

Bond, Michael, *The Power of Others* (Oneworld Publications, 2014)

Ice Cap Station, http://www.icecapstation.com/august.html

Scott, Jeremy, *Dancing on Ice: A Stirring Tale of Adventure, Risk and Reckless Folly* (Old Street Publishing Ltd, 2008)

The Long War of Hiroo Onoda

Kawaguchi, Judith, 'Words to Live By', interview with Hiroo Onoda in *Japan Times*, January 2007

McFadden, Robert D., 'Hiroo Onoda, Soldier Who Hid in Jungle for Decades, Dies at 91', *New York Times*, 17 January 2014

Onoda, Hiroo, article and video of interview with 88-year-old Onoda and his wife, filmed in 2010: http://www.abc.net.au/lateline/content/2010/s3065416.htm

Terry, Charles S., *No Surrender: My Thirty-Year War* (Kodansha International, 1974)

The Kamikaze Pilot Who Survived

Allred, Gordon T., and Kuwahara, Yasuo, *Kamikaze: A Japanese Pilot's Own Spectacular Story of the Famous Suicide Squadrons* (Ballantine, 1956)

Hamazono, Shigeyoshi, entry on World War II Database: http://ww2db.com/person_bio.php?person_id=310

McCurry, Justin, 'We were ready to die for Japan', *Guardian*, 28 February 2006, http://www.theguardian.com/world/2006/feb/28/worlddispatch.secondworldwar

Surviving Hiroshima and Nagasaki

McCurry, Justin, 'A Little Deaf in One Ear: Meet the Japanese Man who Survived Hiroshima and Nagasaki', *Guardian*, 25 March 2009, http://www.theguardian.com/world/2009/mar/25/hiroshima-nagasaki-survivor-japan

McNeill, David, 'How I Survived Hiroshima and then Nagasaki', *Independent*, 26 March 2009, http://www.independent.co.uk/news/world/asia/how-i-survived-hiroshima-ndash-and-then-nagasaki-1654294.html

Yamaguchi, Tsutomu, Matsuo, Mari, Sakaoka, Naomi, and Brown, Anthony, 'Double A-Bomb Victim: My Life beneath the Atomic Clouds, 2013', http://hdl.handle.net/10069/33740

Agatha Christie's Greatest Mystery

Christie, Agatha, Official Site, http://www.agathachristie.com

Morgan, Janet P., *Agatha Christie: A Biography* (Collins, 1984)

Norman, Andrew, *Agatha Christie: The Unfinished Portrait* (History Press, 2007)

Thompson, Laura, *Agatha Christie: An English Mystery* (Headline, 1997)

Dressed to Kill

Lawrence, Dorothy, *Sapper Dorothy Lawrence: The Only English Woman Soldier, Late Royal Engineers 51st Division 179th Tunnelling Company BEF* (Bodley Head, 1919)

Mission into Danger

Halberstam, Yitta, and Leventhal, Judith, *Small Miracles of the Holocaust* (Lyons Press, 2008)

Lukas, Richard, *Forgotten Survivors: Polish Christians Remember the Nazi Occupation* (University Press of Kansas, 2004)

Mieszkowska, Anna, *Irena Sendler, Mother of the Children of the Holocaust* (Praeger, 2010)

PBS documentary about Irena Sendler: http://www.pbs.org/program/irena-sendler/

The Real War Horse

Seeley, Jack, *My Horse Warrior* (Hodder & Stoughton, 1934)

——, *Warrior: The Amazing Story of a Real War Horse* (with an introduction by Jack Seeley's grandson) (Racing Post Books, 2013)

Warrior: A Real War Horse: http://www.warriorwarhorse.com/

Pigeon to the Rescue

Cothren, Marion, *Cher Ami: The Story of a Carrier Pigeon* (Little, Brown & Co., 1934)

Laplander, Robert J., *Finding the Lost Battalion: Beyond the Rumors, Myths and Legends of America's Famous WWI Epic* (Lulu, 2007)

Smithsonian website: http://www.si.edu/Encyclopedia_SI/nmah/cherami.htm

Barking for Victory

Bausum, Anne, and Sharpe, David E., 'Sergeant Stubby: How a Stray Dog and His Best Friend Helped Win World War I and Stole the Heart of a Nation', *National Geographic*, May 2014

Connecticut Military Department, *Stubby the Military Dog,* http://www.ct.gov/mil/cwp/view.asp?a=1351&q=257892

Smithsonian website: http://historywired.si.edu/detail.cfm?ID=519

Angel of Death

Rose, Lionel, *The Massacre of the Innocents* (Routledge, 1986)

Vale, Allison, and Rattle, Alison, *Amelia Dyer: Angel Maker* (André Deutsch, 2007)

Who Killed Rasputin?

Cook, Andrew, *To Kill Rasputin: The Life and Death of Grigori Rasputin* (History Press, 2007)

Milton, Giles, *Russian Roulette* (Sceptre, 2013)

Nelipa, Margarita, *The Murder of Grigorii Rasputin: A Conspiracy That Brought Down the Russian Empire* (Gilbert Books, 2010)

Smith, Michael, *Six* (Biteback, 2010)

Yusupov, Felix, *Lost Splendour: The Amazing Memoirs of the Man Who Killed Rasputin* (Jonathan Cape, 1953)

Till Death Us Do Part

Walsh, Cecil, *The Agra Double Murder* (Ernest Benn, 1929)

Whittington-Egan, Molly, *Khaki Mischief: The Agra Murder Case* (Souvenir Press, 1990)

By Balloon to the North Pole

PRISM (Polar Radar for Ice Sheet Measurements), 'The Mystery of Andrée', an archive of American newspaper articles 1896–9, with reports about the preparation of the expedition and theories about the explorers' fate, http://kuprism.org/polarscientist/andreemystery/andreeindex.html

Sollinger, Guenther, *S. A. Andrée: The Beginning of Polar Aviation 1895–1897* (Moscow, 2005)

Wilkinson, Alex, *The Ice Balloon: S. A. Andrée and the Heroic Age of Arctic Exploration* (Fourth Estate, 2012)

Escape from Alcatraz

Babyak, Jolene, *Breaking the Rock: The Great Escape from Alcatraz* (Ariel Vamp Press, 2001)

Bruce, Campbell J., *Escape from Alcatraz* (Hammond, 1964)

FBI file on the Alcatraz case, http://vault.fbi.gov/Alcatraz%20Escape

A Lonely Trek Through the Andes

Andes Survivors Website, http://www.alpineexpeditions.net/andes-survivors.html

Interviews with Andes Survivors: http://www.viven.com.uy/571/eng/Entrevistas.asp

Parrado, Nando (with Vince Rause), *Miracle in the Andes: 72 Days on the Mountain and My Long Trek Home* (Orion, 2006)

Read, Piers Paul, *Alive: The Story of the Andes Survivors* (Lippincott, Williams & Wilkins, 1974)

The First Celebrity Kidnap

Ahlgren, Gregory, and Monier, Stephen, *Crime of the Century: The Lindbergh Kidnapping Hoax* (Branden Books, 1993)

Cahill Jr., Richard T., *Hauptmann's Ladder: A Step-by-Step Analysis of the Lindbergh Kidnapping* (Kent State University Press, 2014)

Fisher, Jim, *The Lindbergh Case* (Rutgers University Press, 1994)

FBI case notes on the Lindbergh kidnapping, http://www.fbi.gov/about-us/history/famous-cases/the-lindbergh-kidnapping/the-lindbergh-kidnapping

Sir Osman of Hyderabad

Bawa, V. K., *The Last Nizam: The Life and Times of Mir Osman Ali Khan* (Viking, 1991)

Jaisi, Sidq, *The Nocturnal Court: The Life of a Prince of Hyderabad* (Oxford University Press, India, 2004)

Time Magazine, 'His Exalted Highness, The Nizam of Hyderabad', 1937

The Very Strange Death of Alfred Loewenstein

Anon., 'Suicide Hinted in Strange Death of Europe's Croesus', *Evening Independent* (St Petersburg, Florida, 1928)

Norris, William, *The Man Who Fell from the Sky* (Viking, 1987)

Privat, Maurice, *La Vie et la Mort d'Alfred Loewenstein* (La Nouvelle Société d'Edition, 1929)

The Mysterious Death of Joseph Stalin

Brent, Jonathan, and Naumov, Vladimir, *Stalin's Last Crime: The Doctors' Plot* (John Murray, 2003)

Faria, Miguel A., 'Stalin's Mysterious Death', *Surgical Neurology International*, vol. 2, 2011

Radzinsky, Edward, 'The Last Mystery of Stalin' (Sputnik, 1997), and available online, http://revolutionarydemocracy.org/rdv4n2/staldeth.htm

Red Frankenstein

Fridman, E. P., and Bowden, D. M., 'The Russian Primate Research Center', *Laboratory Primate Newsletter*, January 2009; also online at: http://www.brown.edu/Research/Primate/LPN48-1.html#center)

Johnson, Eric, 'Scientific Ethics and Stalin's Ape-Man Superwarriors', *Scientific American*, November 2011

Pain, Stephanie (ed.), 'The Soviet Ape-Man Scandal', *New Scientist*, August 2008

Rossiianov, K., 'Beyond Species: Il'ya Ivanov and His Experiments on Cross-Breeding Humans and Anthropoid Apes', *Science in Context*, vol. 15, issue 2, pp. 77–316

When Stalin Robbed a Bank

Brackman, Roman, *The Secret File of Joseph Stalin: A Hidden Life* (Routledge, 2000)

Kun, Miklós, *Stalin: An Unknown Portrait* (Central European University Press, 2003)

Sebag Montefiore, Simon, *Young Stalin* (London, 2008)

Cabin Boy on the *Hindenburg*

Franz, Werner, 'A Survivor's Story' (YouTube interview, http://www.youtube.com/watch?v=dsWAGg7j1lE)

Freiherr von Medem, W. E., *Kabinenjunge Werner Franz vom Luftschiff Hindenburg* (Franz Schneider, 1938)

Russell, Patrick, 'Faces of the Hindenburg: Werner Franz', http://facesofthe-hindenburg.blogspot.fr/2009/09/werner-franz.html

Attack by Killer Whale

Robertson, Dougal, *Survive the Savage Sea* (Praeger, 1973)

——, *Last Voyage of the Lucette* (Seafarer Books, 2004)

Williams, Sally, 'Shipwrecked: Nightmare in the Pacific', *Guardian*, 22 August 2009, http://www.theguardian.com/lifeandstyle/2009/aug/22/shipwreck-lucette-sailing

Template for 9/11

Kakachi, Zahida, and Morin, Christophe, *Le Vol Alger-Marseille: Journal d'otages* (Plon, 2006)

Nundy, Julian, 'Jet hijackers die as 170 are freed', *Independent*, 27 December 1994, http://www.independent.co.uk/news/uk/jet-hijackers-die-as-170-are-freed-1390663.html

Taylor, Peter, *Age of Terror: The Paris Plot*, BBC Two documentary, February 2009

Escape from Auschwitz

Vrba, Rudolf, *I Escaped from Auschwitz* (Robson, 2006)

—— and Bestic, Alan, *I Cannot Forgive* (Regent College, 1997)

—— and Wetzler, Alfred, 'The Auschwitz Protocol: The Vrba-Wetzler Report', http://www.holocaustresearchproject.net/othercamps/auschproto.html

Trapped in a Firestorm

Milton, Giles, *Wolfram: The Boy Who Went to War* (Sceptre, 2011)

Schottgen, Hannelore, *Wie Dunkler Samt Um Mein Herz: Eine Jugend in Der Nazizeit* (Wartberg, 2003)

Captured by North Korea

Official Website, 'The Lonely Bull: USS Pueblo', http://www.usspueblo.org/

Wilson Center, Digital Archive, USS Pueblo Crisis, http://digitalarchive.wilsoncenter.org/collection/85/uss-pueblo-crisis

Rehearsal for D-Day

Garn, Kenneth, *The Secret D-Day* (Heritage, 2004)

Lewis, Nigel, *Exercise Tiger: The Dramatic True Story of a Hidden Tragedy of World War II* (Prentice Hall, 1990)

Small, Ken, *The Forgotten Dead* (Bloomsbury, 2004)

Ice Man

Fowler, Brenda, *Iceman: Uncovering the Life and Times of a Prehistoric Man Found in an Alpine Glacier* (Pan, 2002)

Sindler, Konrad, *The Man in the Ice* (Doubleday, 1995)

South Tyrol Museum of Archaology, *Otzi* (official website: http://www.iceman.it/)

Stealing Charlie Chaplin

'Charlie Chaplin's Stolen Body Found', BBC, 1978

Robinson, David, *Charlie Chaplin: His Life and Art* (Paladin, 1986)

The Man Who Never Died

Darwin, Mike, 'Dear Dr Bedford', *Cryonics*, July 1991

——, 'Evaluation of the Condition of Dr James H. Bedford After 24 Years of Cryonic Suspension', *Cryonics*, August 1991

Perry, Mike, 'The First Suspension', *Cryonics*, 1991

——, 'Suspension Failures: Lessons from the Early Years', *Cryonics*, 1992

How to Survive an SS Massacre

Cooper, D., *Le Paradis*, BBC People's War, http://www.bbc.co.uk/history/ww2peopleswar/stories/83/a2328383.shtml

Jolly, Cyril, *The Vengeance of Private Pooley* (Heinemann, 1956)

Mikaberidze, Alexander, *Atrocities, Massacres and War Crimes* (ABC, 2013)

Plowright, Molly, 'The Story of Albert Pooley', *Glasgow Herald*, August 1962

Target America

Abella, Alex, *Shadow Enemies: Hitler's Secret Terrorist Plot Against the United States* (Lyons Press, 2003)

Dobbs, Michael, *Saboteurs: The Nazi Raid on America* (Random House, 2005)

FBI, *George Dasch and the Nazi Saboteurs* official website, http://www.fbi.gov/about-us/history/famous-cases/nazi-saboteurs/george-john-dasch-and-the-nazi-saboteurs

The Double Life of Dr Aribert Heim

Al-Altrush, Samir, and Spencer, Richard, 'Nazi fugitive "Dr Death" Aribert Heim identified in Egypt by briefcase contents', *Daily Telegraph*, 14 August 2009

'The Briefcase of Aribert Heim', *New York Times*, 19 July 2013

Zuroff, Efraim, *Operation Last Chance* (Palgrave Macmillan, 2011)

The African Cannibal

Knappman, Edward, *Great World Trials* (Cengage Gale, 1997)

Titley, Brian, *Dark Age: The Political Odyssey of Emperor Bokassa* (McGill-Queen's University Press, 2002)

'Trying the Butcher of Bangui', *Newsweek*, December 1986

The Mad Baron of Mongolia

Hopkirk, Peter, *Setting the East Ablaze* (John Murray, 2006)

Middleton, Nicholas, *The Bloody Baron* (Short Books, 2004)

Palmer, James, *The Bloody White Baron* (Faber, 2009)

How to Kill a Dictator

McGuinness, Patrick, *The Last Hundred Days* (Seren, 2011)

Sebestyn, Victor, *Revolution 1989: The Fall of the Soviet Empire* (Phoenix, 2010)

Sweeney, John, *The Life and Evil Times of Nicolae Ceauşescu* (Hutchinson, 1991)

Taking Hitler to Court

Carter Hett, Benjamin, *Crossing Hitler: The Man Who Put the Nazis on the Witness Stand* (Oxford, 2008)

——, 'Hans Litten and the Politics of Criminal Law in the Weimar Republic', in Dubber, Markus, and Farmer, Lindsay, *Modern Histories of Crime and Punishment* (Stanford University Press, 2007)

Kelly, Jon, 'Hans Litten: The Man Who Annoyed Adolf Hitler', BBC News Magazine, August 2011

Lone Wolf

Gabaldon, Guy, *Saipan: Suicide Island* (publisher and date unknown)

——, 'An Interview and Discussion', *War Times Journal*, 1988

Official website of Guy Gabaldon, http://www.guygabaldon.com/

Fight of the Century

Orbach, Barak, *The Johnson-Jeffries Fight and Censorship of Black Supremacy* (University of Arizona, 2010), http://papers.ssrn.com/sol3/papers.cfm?abstract_id=1563863)

Runstedtler, Theresa, *Jack Johnson, Rebel Sojourner: Boxing in the Shadow of the Global Color Line* (University of California Press, Berkeley, 2012)

Ward, Geoffrey, *Unforgivable Blackness: The Rise and Fall of Jack Johnson* (Pimlico, 2006)

The Unbelievable Missing Link

Russell, Miles, *Piltdown Man: The Secret Life of Charles Dawson* (History Press, 2003)

———, *The Piltdown Man Hoax: Case Closed* (History Press, 2012)

Walsh, John Evangelist, *Unraveling Piltdown* (TSP, 1997)

The World's Most Secret Address

Albrecht, Brian, 'Long Hidden: A Nazi Interrogation Unit Gets Its Due', The Plain Dealer (website), 2008

Dvorak, Petula, 'World War II Secret Interrogators Break their Silence', *Washington Post*, 20 August 2006

Jacobson, Annie, *Operation Paperclip: The Secret Intelligence Program that Brought Nazi Scientists to America* (Little, Brown, 2014)

The Man Who Stole the *Mona Lisa*

Hoobler, Dorothy, and Thomas, *The Crimes of Paris* (Little, Brown, 2009)

Kuper, Simon, 'Who Stole the Mona Lisa: The World's Most Famous Art Heist', *Slate*, August 2011

Nilsson, Jeff, '100 Years Ago: The Mastermind Behind the *Mona Lisa* Heist', *Saturday Evening Post*, 7 December 2013

When Lenin Lost His Brain

Gregory, Paul R., *Lenin's Brain and Other Tales from the Secret Soviet Archives* (Hoover Institution Press Publication, 2008)

Kreutzberg, G.W., Klatzo, I., Kleihues, P., Oskar and Cécile Vogt, 'Lenin's Brain and the Bumble-bees of the Black Forest', *Brain Pathology*, vol. 4, October 1992

Zbarski, I. B., Samuel Hutchinson, *Lenin's Embalmers* (Harvill Press, 1998)

Into the Monkey House

Adams, Rachel, *Sideshow USA: Freaks and the American Cultural Imagination* (University of Chicago Press, 2001)

Verner Bradford, Phillips, and Blume, Harvey, *Ota Benga: The Pygmy in the Zoo: One Man's Degradation in Turn of the Century America* (Schwartz Publishing, 1993)

The Human Freak Show

Crais, Clifton, and Scully, Pamela, *Sara Baartman and the Hottentot Venus: A Ghost Story and a Biography* (Princetown University Press, 2010)

Holmes, Rachel, *The Hottentot Venus: The Life and Death of Saartjie Baartman: Born 1789 – Buried 2002* (Bloomsbury, 2008)

Qureshi, Sadiah, 'Displaying Sara Baartman, the Hottentot Venus', *History of Science*, issue 42, 2004

Freak Wave

Dash, Mike, *The Vanishing Lighthousemen of Eilean Mór* (Fortean Studies, 1998)

McCloskey, Keith, *The Lighthouse: The Mystery of the Eilean Mór Lighthouse Keepers* (History Press, 2014)

Northern Lighthouse Board, 'The Mystery of Flannan Isle', http://www.nlb.org.uk/historical/flannans.htm

Japan's Deadly Balloon Bomb

Anon., 'Saw Wife and Five Children Killed by Jap Balloon Bomb', *Seattle Times*, 1 June 1945, http://web.archive.org/web/20140417180525/http://www.stelzriede.com/ms/html/sub/mshwfug2.htm

Mikesh, Robert C., *Japan's World War II Balloon Bomb Attacks on North America* (Smithsonian Institution Scholarly Press, 1990)

Powles, James M., 'Silent Destructions: Japanese Balloon Bombs', *World War II*, vol. 17, 2003

Never Go to Sea

Miskolcze, Robin, *Women and Children First* (University of Nebraska Press, 2008)

Saunders, Ann, *A Narrative of the Shipwreck and Sufferings of Miss Ann Saunders* (1827)

Eiffel's Rival

Barker, Felix, and Hyde, Ralph, *London as it Might Have Been* (John Murray, 1995)

Hodgkins, David, *The Second Railway King: The Life and Times of Sir Edward Watkin, 1819–1901* (Merton Priory Press, 2002)

Lynde, Fred. C., *Descriptive Illustrated Catalogue of the Sixty-Eight Competitive Designs for the Great Tower for London* (Tower Company, 1890)

Emperor of the United States

Cowen, Robert Ernest, 'Norton I, Emperor of the United States and Protector of Mexico', San Francisco California Historical Society, 1923, http://www.emperornorton.net/NortonI-Cowan.html

Drury, William, *Norton I, Emperor of the United States* (Dodd, Mead, 1986)

Lane, Stanley Allen, *Emperor Norton: Mad Monarch of America* (Cadwell Caxton, 1939)

The Man Who Bought his Wife

Brander, Michael, *The Perfect Victorian Hero: The Life and Times of Sir Samuel White Baker* (Mainstream, 1982)

Shipman, Pat, *To the Heart of the Nile: Lady Florence Baker and the Exploration of Central Africa* (HarperCollins, 2004)

Hitler's Final Hours

Fest, Joachim, *Inside Hitler's Bunker: The Last Days of the Third Reich* (Farrar, Straus & Giroux, 2004)

Junge, Traudl, and Muller, Melissa, *Until the Final Hour: Hitler's Last Secretary* (Weidenfeld & Nicolson, 2003)

Trevor-Roper, Hugh, *Last Days of Hitler* (Macmillan, 1995)

Seizing Eichmann

Aharoni, Zvi, and Dietl, Wilhelm, *Operation Eichmann: The Truth About the Pursuit, Capture and Trial* (Wiley, 1997)

Harel, Isser, *The House on Garibaldi Street: The First Full Account of the Capture of Adolf Eichmann* (Viking, 1995)

Pearlman, Moshe, *The Capture of Adolf Eichmann* (Weidenfeld & Nicolson, 1961)

The Celebrity Executioner

Klein, Leonora, *A Very English Hangman: The Life and Times of Albert Pierrepoint* (Corvo Books, 2006)

Pierrepoint, Albert, *Executioner: Pierrepoint* (Harrap, 1974)

Trapped on an Iceberg

Grenfell, Wilfred, *Adrift on an Ice-Pan* (Houghton Mifflin, 1909)

Reason, J., *Deep Sea Doctor* (Edinburgh House Press, 1941)

Volcano of Death

San Diego State University Department of Geological Science, 'How Volcanoes Work: Mt Pelée Eruption (1902)', http://www.geology.sdsu.edu/how_volcanoes_work/Pelee.html

Scarth, Alwyn, *La Catastrophe: The Eruption of Mount Pelée, the Worst Volcanic Disaster of the 20th Century* (Oxford University Press, 2002)

Zebrowski, Ernest, *The Last Days of St. Pierre: The Volcanic Disaster that Claimed 30,000 Lives* (Rutgers University Press, 2002)

The Female Robinson Crusoe

McClanahan, Alexandra, 'The Heroine of Wrangel Island', http://www.litsite. org/index.cfm?section=History%20and%20Culture&page=Life%20in%20 Alaska&ContentId=850&viewpost=2

Niven, Jennifer, *Ada Blackjack: A True Story of Survival in the Arctic* (Hyperion, 2003)

The Last Post

Perisco, Joseph, *Eleventh Month, Eleventh Day, Eleventh Hour* (Arrow Books, 2005)

Rodricks, Dan, 'The Sad, Senseless End of Henry Gunther', *Baltimore Sun*, 11 November 2008

To Hell and Back

Graham, Don, *No Name on the Bullet* (Viking Press, 1989)

Murphy, Audie, *To Hell and Back* (St Martin's Press, 2002)

Official website: 'Audie L. Murphy Memorial Website', http://www.audie-murphy.com

Let's Talk Gibberish

McClain, Sally, *Navajo Weapon: The Navajo Code Talkers* (Rio Nuevo Publishers, 2002)

Tso, Samuel, 'Code Talker Samuel Tso: Navajo Oral History Project', Navajo People, Culture and History: http://navajopeople.org/blog/code-talker-samuel-tso-navajo-oral-history-project/

Good Ship *Zong*

Krikler, Jeremy, 'The *Zong* and the Lord Chief Justice', *History Workshop Journal*, vol. 64, 2007

Walvin, James, *The Zong: A Massacre, the Law and the End of Slavery* (Yale, 2011)

Weisbord, Robert, 'The Case of the Slave-ship *Zong*, 1783', *History Today*, vol. 19, 1969

The Suspicions of Inspector Dew

Connell, Nicholas, *Walter Dew: The Man Who Caught Crippen* (History Press, 2012)

Goodman, Jonathan, *The Crippen File* (Allison & Busby, 1985)

Saward, Joe, *The Man Who Caught Crippen* (Morienval Press, 2010)

Dead as a Dodo

Hume, Julian, Martill, David, and Dewdney, Christopher, 'Palaeobiology: Dutch Diaries and the Demise of the Dodo', *Nature*, vol. 429, 2004

Roberts, David L., and Solow, Andrew R., 'Flightless Birds: When did the Dodo become Extinct?', *Nature*, vol. 426, 2003

A Sting in the Tale

Forbes, Rosita, *The Sultan of the Mountains: The Life Story of Raisuli* (Henry Holt & Company, 1924)

Harris, Walter, *The Land of the African Sultan: Travels in Morocco* (Sampson Low, Marston, 1889)

——, *Morocco That Was* (William Blackwood & Sons, 1921)

And Then There Were None

Collins, Paul, *Hell's Gates: The Terrible Journey of Alexander Pearce, Van Diemen's Land Cannibal* (South Yarra, 2002)

Sprod, Dan, *Alexander Pearce of Macquarie Harbour* (Cat & Fiddle Press, 1977)

Edwin Darling's Nightmare

Island Farm Websites: 'Island Farm Prisoner of War Camp: 198', http://www.islandfarm.fsnet.co.uk and 'Welcome to Island Farm', http://www.bracklaordnance.co.uk/island%20farm.htm

Philips, Peter, *The Great German Escape* (Seren, 2005)

Williams, Herbert, *Come Out, Wherever You Are: The Great Escape in Wales* (Gomert Press, 2004)

When Churchill Slaughtered Sheep

Imperial War Museum, *X-Base Gruinard Trials, 1941–42*, film, catalogue no: DED 252

Lewis, Jeremy, *Changing Direction: British Military Planning for Postwar Strategic Defence, 1942–47* (Routledge, 2008)

Pearson, Graham S., 'Gruinard Island Returns to Civilian Use', *Applied Science and Analysis Newsletter*, issue 86, October 1990

The Black Sheep

Service, Robert, *Trotsky: A Biography* (Macmillan, 2009)

Sheridan, Clare, *Mayfair to Moscow: Clare Sheridan's Diary* (Boney & Liveright, 1921)

——, *Russian Portraits* (Jonathan Cape, 1921)

Tweedie, Neil, and Day, Peter, 'MI5 Suspected Churchill's Cousin was a Red Spy', *Daily Telegraph*, 28 November 2002

Winston's Bombshell

Capet, Antoine, 'The Creeds of the Devil: Churchill between the Two Totalitarianisms, 1917–1945' (http://www.winstonchurchill.org/support/

the-churchill-centre/publications/finest-hour-online/725-the-creeds-of-
the-devil-churchill-between-the-two-totalitarianisms-1917-1945#sdfoot-
note34sym)

Jones, Simon, 'The Right Medicine for the Bolshevist: British Air-Dropped
Chemical Weapons in North Russia, 1919', *Imperial War Museum Review*,
12, 1999

National Archives, WO 32/5749, 'The Use of Gas in North Russia; WO
33/966 European War Secret Telegrams', Series H, Vol. 2, Feb–May 1919;
WO 32/5184; WO 32 5185; WO 158/735; WO 142/116; WO 95/5424;
AIR/462/15/312/125; WO 106/1170; T 173/830

The Double Life of Chevalier d'Eon

D'Éon de Beaumont, Charles, *The Maiden of Tonnerre: The Vicissitudes of
the Chevalier and the Chevalière d'Éon* (Johns Hopkins University Press,
2001)

Kates, Gary, *Monsieur d'Éon is a Woman: A Tale of Political Intrigue and Sexual
Masquerade* (Johns Hopkins University Press, 2001)

Telfer, John Buchan, *The Strange Career of the Chevalier d'Eon de Beaumont,
Minister Plenipotentiary from France to Great Britain in 1763* (Longmans, Green
& Co., 1885)

How to Catch a Spy

Howe, Russell Warren, *Mata Hari: The True Story* (Dodd Mead, 1986)

Shipman, Pat, *Femme Fatale: Love, Lies, and the Unknown Life of Mata Hari*
(Weidenfeld & Nicolson, 2007)

Wheelwright, Julie, *The Fatal Lover: Mata Hari and the Myth of Women in Espionage*
(Collins & Brown, 1992)

The Last Secret of the Cold War

Binding, Tim, 'Buster Crabb was murdered by MI5', *Mail on Sunday*, 26 March
2006

Hale, Don, *The Final Dive: The Life and Death of Buster Crabb* (NPI Media, 2 November 2007)

Hutton, J. Bernard, *The Fake Defector: The Truth about Commander Crabb* (Howard Baker, 1970)

Getting Clinical: The Madness of King George

Johnson, Carolyn, 'Madness of King George III May Have Been his Doctors' Fault', *Boston Globe*, 1 August 2005

Macalpine, Ida, and Hunter, Richard, 'The "Insanity" of King George III: A Classic Case of Porphyria', *British Medical Journal*, 1966

Worsley, Lucy, *Fit to Rule*, BBC 2, 15 April 2013

How to Meet the Queen in Bed

Dugan, Emily, 'Michael Fagan: "Her Nightie Was One of Those Liberty Prints, Down to her Knees" ', *Independent on Sunday*, 19 February 2012

Linton, Martin, and Wainwright, Martin, 'Whitelaw Launches Palace Inquiry', *Guardian*, 13 July 1982

Scotland Yard, 'Text of Scotland Yard's Report on July 9 Intrusion into Buckingham Palace', *New York Times*, 22 July 1982

The Man with a Deadly Secret

Barrie, Charles, *Kill the Queen! The Eight Assassination Attempts on Queen Victoria* (Amberley Publishing, 2012)

Berkshire Records Office, 'Edward Oxford, Biography', http://www.berkshirerecordoffice.org.uk/albums/broadmoor/edward-oxford

Murphy, Paul, *Shooting Victoria* (Pegasus Books, 2012)

Accident by Design

Mitchell, Irene Musillo, *Beatrice Cenci* (*History*, American University Studies, Series 9, 1991)

Nicholl, Charles, 'Screaming in the Castle: The Case of Beatrice Cenci', *London Review of Books*, July 1998

Shelley, Percy, *The Selected Poetry and Prose of Shelley*, including *The Cenci* (Wordsworth Editions, 1994)

The Banquet of Chestnuts

Burchard, John, *Pope Alexander VI and his Court: Extracts from the Latin Diary of the Papal Master of Ceremonies, 1484–1506* (F. L. Glaser, (ed.), New York, 1921)

Manchester, William, *A World Lit Only by Fire* (Little, Brown & Company, 1992)

Paulist Fathers, *The Borgia Myth*, *Catholic World*, 1886 (Catholic Publication Society, New York, vol. 44)

Into Thin Air

Kusche, Larry, *The Disappearance of Flight 19* (Harper & Row, 1980)

Myhre, Jon F., *Discovery of Flight 19* (Paragon, 2012)

Quasar, Gian, *They Flew into Oblivion* (Brodwyn, Moor & Doane, 2013)

Mountain of Death

Fleming, Fergus, *Killing Dragons: The Conquest of the Alps* (Granta, 2011)

Lyall, Alan, *The First Descent of the Matterhorn* (Gomer Press, 1997)

Whymper, Edward, *Scrambles Amongst the Alps* (Kessinger Publishing, 2010; originally published 1872)

The Man Who Fell to Earth

Kittinger, Joseph, *The Long, Lonely Leap* (New York, 1961)

——, *Come and Get Me: An Autobiography of Colonel Joe Kittinger* (University of New Mexico Press, 2011)

Schroeder, Scott, *The Highest Step in the World: Joe Kittinger and the Excelsior Missions*, Interview with Joe Kittinger, 2010

Wild Child

Itard, E.M., *An Historical Account of the Discovery and Education of a Savage Man: Or, the First Developments, Physical and Moral, of the Young Savage Caught in the Woods Near Aveyron in the Year 1798* (London, 1802)

Lane, Harlan, *The Wild Boy of Aveyron* (Harvard University Press, 1975)

Shattuck, Roger, *Forbidden Experiment: Story of the Wild Boy of Aveyron* (Secker & Warburg, 1980)

A Question of Sex

De Bougainville, Louis Antoine, *Voyage around the world 1766–1769*, a transcription of John Reinhold Forster's translation of *Le voyage autour du monde, par la frégate La Boudeuse, et la flûte L'Étoile* (London, 1772)

Dunmore, John, *Monsieur Baret: First Woman Around the World* (Heritage Press, 2002)

Ridley, Glynis, *The Discovery of Jeanne Baret* (Crown Publishing, 2010)

The Beast that Came from Nowhere

Pourcher, Pierre, *The Beast of Gevaudan* (Author House, 2006; originally published in French in 1889)

Thompson, Richard H., *Wolf-Hunting in France in the Reign of Louis XV: The Beast of the Gévaudan* (Edwin Mellen Press, 1992)

The Last Stand

Hurst, Ben, 'War Hero Bert Evans – the Last Wormhoudt Massacre Survivor Dies aged 92', *Birmingham Mail*, 11 October 2013

Craig, Olga, 'Wormhoudt: "Every Day I thank God We Did our Duty"', *Daily Telegraph*, 23 May 2010

Slave Girl in the Harem

Meetelen, Maria ter, *Wonderbaarlyke en merkwaardige gevallen van een twaalf jarige slaverny, van een vrouspersoon, genaemt Maria ter Meetelen, woonagtig tot Medenblik* (Hoorn, 1748, also available in French)

Van der Veen, Sytze, 'Online Dictionary of Dutch Women', http://resources. huygens.knaw.nl/vrouwenlexicon/lemmata/data/Meetelen/en

The Man Who Broke into Auschwitz

Foot, M. R. D., *Six Faces of Courage* (Pen & Sword, 2003)

Pilecki, W., and Garlinski, J., *The Auschwitz Volunteer: Beyond Bravery* (Aquila Polonica, 2012)

All the President's Slaves

Jefferson, Isaac, *Memoirs of a Monticello Slave as Dictated to Charles Campbell in the 1840's by Isaac, One of Thomas Jefferson's Slaves* (Windham Press, 2013)

Seagrave, Ronald, *Jefferson's Isaac: From Monticello to Petersburg* (Outskirts Press, 2011)

The Worst Banker in History

Balen, Malcolm, *A Very English Deceit: The Secret History of the South Sea Bubble and the First Great Financial Scandal* (Fourth Estate, 2009)

Carswell, John, *The South Sea Bubble* (Sutton Publishing, 2001)

Fitzwilliam Museum, 'John Gay', http://www.fitzmuseum.cam.ac.uk/dept/ pdp/prints/resources/portraitofthemonth/JohnGay.html

Bone Wars

Shor, Elizabeth, *The Fossil Feud Between E. D. Cope and O. C. Marsh* (Exposition Press, 1974)

Wallace, David Rains, *The Bonehunters' Revenge* (Houghton Mifflin, 2000)

The Hidden Life of Jonathan Wild

Fielding, Henry, *Life of Jonathan Wild the Great* (Wildside Press, 2003)

Howson, Gerald, *Thief-Taker General: Jonathan Wild and the Emergence of Crime and Corruption as a Way of Life in Eighteenth-Century England* (Oxford, 1970)

The Last Eunuch of China

Faison, Seth, 'The Death of the Last Emperor's Last Eunuch', *New York Times*, 20 December 1996

Yinghua, Jia, and Sun, Haichen (translator), *The Last Eunuch of China: The Life of Sun Yaoting by Jia Yinghua* (China Intercontinental Press, 2008)

Never Go to Bed with a Knife

Johnston, William, *Geisha, Harlot, Strangler, Star: A Woman, Sex, and Morality in Modern Japan* (Columbia University Press, 2005)

Schreiber, Mark, *The Dark Side: Infamous Japanese Crimes and Criminals* (Kodansha, 2001)

The Woman Who Gave Birth for Hitler

Hagen, Louis, *Ein Volk, Ein Reich: Nine Lives under the Nazis* (History Press, 2011; first published in 1951 as *Follow My Leader*)

Clay, Catrine, and Leapman, Michael, *Master Race: The Lebensborn Experiment in Nazi Germany* (Hodder & Stoughton, 1995)

Index

Index